New Money, Nice Town

New Money, Nice Town

HOW CAPITAL WORKS IN THE NEW URBAN ECONOMY

LEONARD NEVAREZ

Routledge
New York • London

Published in 2003 by
Routledge
29 West 35th Street
New York, NY 10001
www.routledge-ny.com

Published in Great Britain by
Routledge
11 New Fetter Lane
London EC4P 4EE
www.routledge.co.uk

10 9 8 7 6 5 4 3 2 1

Library of Congress Cataloging-in-Publication Data

Nevarez, Leonard
   New money, nice town : how capital works in the new urban economy / Leonard Nevarez.
      p. cm.
   Includes bibliographical references and index.
   ISBN 0-415-93342-0—ISBN 0-415-93343-9 (pbk.)
      1. Urban economics. 2. Business and politics. I. Title

   HT321 .N474 2002
   330.9173'2—dc21   2002021348

Contents

Preface

In this book, I pose the question: Do companies, executives, and industry leaders in the software, entertainment, and tourism industries "do" local politics any differently than the traditional urban business community that dominated cities through much of the twentieth century? In the past, the defining feature of urban politics was systemic business hegemony rooted in the omnipresent threat of corporate withdrawal. What are the features now? The answer reveals a great deal about what has become of urban power in the new urban economy. Every research question originates in a specific place and time, and in my case, it starts in Santa Barbara, where I attended graduate school in the 1990s. A small coastal city in Southern California, Santa Barbara is known by many for its stunning coastal scenery and lively village quality. By the nineteenth century, Santa Barbara was already cherished by Native Americans, Spanish colonizers, Mexican *californios,* and Yankee newcomers, particularly in its contrast with its neighbor to the south, Los Angeles, then a small settlement. As Los Angeles developed in the following century into its now famous sprawl, esteem for Santa Barbara grew even more, as did reputations (not entirely warranted) of its socioeconomic exclusivity. "Paradise," residents and visitors have called it.

Any kind of community quality, much less one treasured as "paradise," rarely materializes on its own, as those involved in urban and environmental politics know. There is almost always struggle to counter the structural forces and recurring actors that transform places for the sake of profit, and coastal Southern California has been no exception. I studied the regional conflicts surrounding urban growth and industrialization: to stop the importation of Northern California's water supplies to Santa Barbara and adjacent San Luis Obispo Counties, to prevent the spread of offshore drilling off the California coast, and to contain the tremendous pressures for urban development in Southern California. Activists, their organizations, and political representatives in Santa Barbara and San Luis Obispo were largely responsible for these (not always successful) local efforts to stop "business as usual," and their energy and savvy quickly earned these places reputations as liberal or, depending on one's perspective, "anti-business" strongholds. Granted, their struggles hardly entailed the more life-and-death stakes encountered by environmental justice activists, and observers on the left and right have long derided how well-off residents regularly supported activists' efforts with money, time, and advocacy. Nevertheless, precisely because Santa Barbara and San Luis Obispo have attracted so many for both community and commodity, I discovered that these places provided a remarkable setting to study the forces of urban power and profit-making. Local activists became my regular informants, and, in return, I enthusiastically conducted opposition research on their behalf wherever I could help.

By the mid 1990s, after decades of struggling against big oil, big development, and big industry, the tone of local environmentalists' battles in Santa Barbara and San Luis Obispo shifted in unforeseen ways. New kinds of business actors appeared, including local software firms. These companies were smaller and, at first, less conspicuous in the landscape than the defense-related research and development firms that had long inhabited the region. Their workers, even their executives, hardly fit the conventional engineer profile familiar to Silicon Valley and the comic strip "Dilbert." Indeed, in contrast to the caricatured businessman of activists' wrath, the software worker or executive was more likely to resemble the stereotype of a Santa Barbaran: tanned, sandaled, comfortably but not conspicuously affluent, with perhaps a hint of a dope-smoking past. Meanwhile, the tourist economy had gained considerable steam along coastal California. Regional, national, and even international visitors filled the downtown sidewalks and beaches; new hotel proposals came before municipal planning commissions; and residents increasingly muttered to themselves how they just had to "leave town for the summer these days." Around this time, I moved down to Los Angeles, where I saw firsthand the new exuberance of the entertainment industry in local economies and landscapes. Santa Monica, a coastal municipality long known for its progressive rent control policies, seemed especially caught off guard by local growth in entertainment, software, and tourism. For two decades, the progressives in power had fought landlords, imposed unprecedented conditions on development, and proudly called their town the "People's Republic of Santa Monica." Now they looked on uncertainly as new media companies moved into warehouses and artist studios, screenwriters and dot-commers crowded the local Starbucks cafe, and visitors flocked to the rehabilitated pier and pedestrian malls.

For activists in these communities, there was confusion over whether these new economic activities constituted a problem. Some instinctively saw familiar enemies on the horizon. These companies and hotel developments meant an eroding local quality of life, new allies for their traditional business opponents, and the loss of grassroots control over the pace of urban development. Others were not sure the new money promised old battles. At first glance, the new guys on Main Street looked liberal enough, hardly the kind to mingle with local business conservatives. Far from rejecting the local quality of life, these companies and visitors came to appreciate it. Besides, activists confessed among themselves, the promise of "clean" and knowledge-based industries was an important incentive for locals to reject offshore drilling and unwanted development in previous battles. This new urban economy posed a "good problem," some activists argued, and now it was time to shift their priorities accordingly. As a Santa Barbara environmental organizer asked me, "So we've said no to everything else but this, so how do we learn to say yes to this, and what does that mean?"

As a student of urban power, I took this question and activists' broader uncertainty as another opportunity to conduct opposition research. Reviewing the literature on these industries, I found that it consisted almost entirely of either technocratic "how-to" guidelines for local economic development or narrowly cast evaluations of their socioeconomic and environmental impacts. Remarkably, no one to my knowledge had pursued a critical inquiry into the political interests that these companies have in the places where they do business. Most systematic analysis of the politics of new corporate elites focused on broader scales, like their political affiliations in national elections. No one had asked such questions locally and across the entire gamut of corporate power in urban affairs. Thus, I formulated my research question: Again, did software, entertainment, and tourism—all critical players in the "new economy"—"do" local politics any differently than the traditional urban business community? So phrased, this question addresses the practical concerns of activists who are well versed in taking on the old guys and who want to know what to expect from the newcomers. For evidence, I turned to the very places where these questions emerged: the three "quality-of-life" communities of coastal California.

I believe people can learn a lot from these places and Southern California more generally. (To San Luis Obispans who insist that they technically reside in *Central* California, I apologize for my geographical simplification on behalf of the non-local reader.) Yet, as I discovered, many people, not just outsiders, cannot see how Southern California illuminates their own lives and communities. In part, this might stem from deep cultural ambivalence that the rest of the world holds about Southern California, with its "idyllic" landscapes, lifestyles, and prosperity that Hollywood has projected into global consciousness. As a thirteen-year resident, I confess to my own love-hate relationship with this region. For example, thanks to a good number of friends and family who work in the entertainment industry, I have enjoyed Hollywood's glamour firsthand and vicariously. Yet, well before an entertainment lawyer's SUV rear-ended my car on Los Angeles's Wilshire

Boulevard—as he reached for his cell phone, no less!—I have shared the existential realization that Southern California can be a little absurd, to put it nicely. The region is also home to millions of people not often featured in Hollywood content: immigrants, people of color, and the poor and working classes. Although my attention in this book to the faces of power often leaves these groups only a supporting if crucial role, the less-fabled dreams they pursue in Southern California are as much the region's history as the living nightmares many often encounter there. If only for their sake, I would contend that anyone who entirely loves *or* entirely hates Southern California is out of touch with its reality.

Perhaps more seriously, some observers doubt that Southern California can be compared to cities, economies, and ways of life in other settings, American or otherwise. Their claims echo the traditional scientific concern for generalizability; Southern California (the argument goes) is atypical, a statistical outlier in the larger set of cities and regions from which social analysis can be validly drawn. In response, scholars in the self-styled "Los Angeles school of urban studies" and other fields have argued that the region indeed shows typicality, or at least a glimpse of the social patterns and processes emerging in other places, such as nonwhite majorities, growth from the urban periphery, polyglot neighborhoods, and economic and cultural reorientation toward the Pacific Rim. Although I sympathize with many of these arguments, this book does not stand or fall with them. I would contend that typicality is not always the most useful criterion with which to evaluate power, economy, and politics. Particularly for urban studies, any claims about "typical" settings must be literally placed within a framework of geographically uneven development, urban hierarchies and networks, and capitalism's incessant dynamism. In this book, the places I examine exemplify the cutting edge of economic restructuring, not its norm. Santa Monica, Santa Barbara, and San Luis Obispo are more than economic "best-case" scenarios; the prosperity and power wielded here touch down on other places throughout the world, perhaps more often to underdevelop and marginalize them than to model their potential futures. Politically, the three research sites have activist traditions that are rarely effective in the larger "race to the bottom" among localities competing for capital investment. Yet, because software, entertainment, and tourism industries have materialized in these places, they offer useful settings to investigate how "anti-business" politics affects new urban economy sectors: pushing them away for more "pro-business" locales, making them submit to local demands, setting in motion activists' own co-optation, or some other potential outcome. Whatever happens in these places will surely suggest the limits of the possible in more quiescent climates.

As I write, recent events like the dot-com crash of 2000 and the terrorist attacks on September 11, 2001 have seriously upset the fortunes of software, entertainment, and tourism companies; for some, this suggests that the inevitability of the new urban economy, as conceptualized here, is less than assured. This may well be, although in the final chapter I make the case that these events do not promise the end or wholesale transformation of these industries, as some observers have suggested. Yet, even if my specific claims about why software, entertainment, and tourism companies locate in particular places and how they consequently intervene in urban politics become outdated, as at least some certainly will, this book nevertheless reveals broader insights into how economic shifts bring about political reconfigurations. It is my hope that scholars, activists, and other citizens who are concerned about urban politics, but who live in places where the industries I study have no role whatsoever, can glean useful insights from the dynamics I describe here.

Acknowledgments

This book and my intellectual development have benefited from the insights of many colleagues, friends, and acquaintances. Richard Appelbaum, Thomas Beamish, Richard Flacks, Andrew Jonas, Harvey Molotch, Krista Paulsen, Jacqueline Romo, and two anonymous reviewers at Routledge read the entire manuscript at various stages of its development. James Birchler, Mitchell Duneier, Brian Godfrey, Richard Lloyd, Michael McGinnis, Britta Wheeler, Daniel Sullivan, Judith Taylor, Rikard Treiber, Peter Van de Loo, and Jessica Winston read portions of the manuscript. Pinar Batur, Howard Becker, Benjamin Bratton, Ron Breiger, Fred Bloch, G. William Domhoff, Norman Fainstein, Susan Fainstein, Noah Friedkin, Roger Friedland, William Hoynes, Jan Lin, John Logan, Guido Martinatti, Chris Mele, David Silver, John Sondquist, and Yu Zhou otherwise advised me on conceptualizing my argument and developing this book. In the field, David Gershwin, Greg Helms, Henry Hernandez, and Christopher Needham offered help that may not be reflected in the text but that facilitated this project nevertheless. Criticisms, encouragements, and suggestions by all these people made this book far stronger than it would have been otherwise, and to them I am unendingly appreciative. Of course, any flaws that remain are solely my responsibility.

This project was financially supported at various times by U.S. Minerals Management Service under contracts 14-35-0001-30796 and 14-35-001-30663; James Lima and Fred White were supportive liaisons there. I was also honored to receive the 2000 Donald Cressey Dissertation Award at the University of California, Santa Barbara; I thank its benefactor, Elaine Ohlin, for her generosity to young scholars.

Dave McBride at Routledge has been an extremely supportive and gracious editor; our conversations and correspondences improved this book immeasurably. Stephan Cox proofread the manuscript and made crucial suggestions when I had lost almost all objectivity. Gina Gambone and Ronald Armwood provided able research assistance. Meg E. Stewart stepped in at the last moment to furnish the excellent map.

Two mentors deserve special thanks. First, Harvey Molotch, who supervised this research when I was a graduate student, has placed his stamp on virtually the entire scholarly field in which this book is situated. Perhaps less well known, he generously shares his methodological savvy, writing expertise, practical assistance, and humor with his students. As a member of that fortunate group, I occasionally differed with his assessment of the problems we examined, and I am grateful that he took my conclusions seriously and collegially. That said, I am continually persuaded and instructed by his original insights on the places, perspectives, and issues we studied in common. Second, Richard Flacks has kept the political and emotional heart of this project beating. Perhaps more than any other scholar, he showed me how to integrate my life and community with my research to the improvement of all three. At a time when academics have become anxious or cynical about their social contributions, he made evident by his example and his uplifting words how "making history" in even the smallest way can have a genuinely large impact. It pleases me no end that he is still in Santa Barbara, staying involved in local politics and showing sociology students how to glean insights from their backyard.

I am grateful to my friends and family outside of academia for their support through the duration of this project. Michelle Barber was there in the beginning, and her love and material support made this book possible. Deborah Paredez, a scholar and poet, never let my spirits fail when the book reached its later stages. My sister Lydia, grandmother Virginia, and *tía* Georgia kept telling me I was brilliant, even though I believed otherwise. Finally, I dedicate this book to my parents, Leonard and Lela, without whose love and faith I could not have sustained the effort needed to finish this project.

Previously published work has been incorporated into this book. Chapters 2 and 8 were informed by a chapter I wrote for *Understanding the City: Contemporary and Future Perspectives,* edited by John Eade and Christopher Mele (London: Blackwell, 2002). Chapter 3 is based upon an article published in *Research in Community Sociology* 9 (1999): 185–215. Chapter 7 draws heavily from *Urban Affairs Review* 36 (2000): 197–227.

1

Corporate Power in the New Urban Economy

F or decades, city dwellers, activists, politicians, businesspeople, and
scholars have grappled with what an emerging "new economy" portends for urban life and politics. Most certainly, traditional manufacturing
has lost its predominance, at least in cities of the developed west. Corporations have laid off employees, sourced production out to suburban peripheries and overseas locations, and adopted other so-called flexible strategies
that signal the surrender of the stolid corporation to the competitive imperative. The local ties forged by factory town legacies have seldom outweighed
the bottom-line factors that motivate capital to relocate for more profitable
locales. As the deindustrialized landscapes of America's and western
Europe's rustbelts illustrate, the flight of industry has devastated many urban
economies and undermined the institutions and services that anchor local
life. These episodes underscore the current urgency and insecurity with
which localities seek to appease the rootless corporation.

In the wake of traditional manufacturing's flight, however, a closer look
reveals that some cities and regions have experienced new fortunes as locations for business services, technology and lifestyle sectors. In thriving regions like Southern California, local leaders have seen their communities
revitalized by the prosperous edge of an economic restructuring for which
they cannot claim credit, but from which they benefit nevertheless. Three
sectors are especially thought to provide fortuitous combinations of high
wages, environmentally benign industry, local tax revenues, and local job
creation. First, and perhaps most obviously, information technology has
transformed communities and economies the world over; as an industrial
sector, the design of software, computer architecture, and Internet infrastructure services (hereafter referred to as *software*) offers a fast-growing

1

source of job creation and skill enhancement. Second, motion pictures, television programming, and recorded music entertain and inform ever more of the world's inhabitants; the production and commercial release of this popular cultural content (henceforth, *entertainment*) stimulate an array of aesthetic, technological, craft, and management activities. Third, *tourism* accounts for an increasing amount of consumers' leisure and travel time, and the provision of tourism services circulates visitor dollars through local restaurants, hotels, stores, and services.

Although these three sectors have created important social and economic goods in the regions and cities they inhabit, how such goods end up being distributed in those places has long been an open question. Much research has shown that urban economies most often subsidize private profit through the political hegemony of the *traditional urban business community:* conventional industry as well as local firms in real estate, banking, utilities, business services, and retail, to name the major sectors. Less frequently, local wealth supports social services, urban amenities, and environmental quality, particularly when community activists successfully challenge the traditional urban business community's privileged role in local affairs. Economic restructuring has been thought to make such challenges less likely, since capital's rootlessness threatens the fiscal basis of liberal urban policies and legitimizes the conservative thrust of the entrepreneurial city. The transformations of urban life witnessed in economic hotspots like San Francisco and New York City suggest a dubious fate for them: widespread gentrification, unplanned redevelopment, and the erosion of distinctive places.[1]

However, it is unclear that cities and activists unambiguously lose out in the new economy. For some, fears of rootless capital are assuaged by the locational affinities of educated workforces and tourists for urban and environmental amenities. The 2000 U.S. presidential elections revealed unprecedented corporate support for liberal candidates, spearheaded by Hollywood and Silicon Valley contributors to Democratic campaigns. A recent upturn in philanthropy has given nonprofits and the media cause to celebrate the interests of the "suddenly wealthy" in traditional charities, higher education, and community organizations. As these trends suggest, not only the traditional urban business community views the local growth of software, entertainment, and tourism as a positive outcome. Even residents and community groups accustomed to struggling to defend a grassroots vision of community can pin great hopes on these three exemplary sectors, since in many ways they seem to legitimate efforts to preserve amenities and fight for urban justice.

Given these apparently contradictory expectations, an investigation of what new economy firms and corporate elites want from the places they do business is urgently needed, since both optimistic and pessimistic scenarios treat this issue as an unexamined assumption. What are the political interests of software, entertainment, and tourism firms in the cities where they locate? How do these interests mesh with the "pro-business" agenda of the traditional urban business community? Does the new economy sustain or transform the usual dynamics and constituencies of business-versus-grassroots politics? I pose these questions in the very places where new money has materialized on Main Street and begun to crowd out the traditional urban business community. In this book, I ask, *Do firms and business leaders in software, entertainment, and tourism behave in local politics any differently than does the traditional urban business community?* Because the traditional urban business community has long advocated a conservative agenda, this difference could mean more progressive possibilities for local politics.

TRADITIONS OF LOCAL BUSINESS GOVERNANCE

Socially enlightened, post-materialist, environmentally concerned, liberal—these are assorted traits that many activists hope, and many scholars hypothesize, characterize the "post-industrial" generation, if not its captains of industry.[2] Indeed, quite a few of the business leaders I interviewed for this book view themselves in such promising terms. However, I situate their claims to "enlightened" perspectives in a context of business interest to acknowledge how capital accumulation sets corporate priorities in at least the last instance. A century and a half ago, Karl Marx observed that capitalist competition forced employers, regardless of their altruistic inclinations, to exploit workers.[3] Since then, scholars have extended Marx's structuralist premise to examine how the competitive imperatives of capitalism influence a variety of arenas; in the urban political economy perspective that frames this book, the most relevant is the local economy, where parochial business serves local markets, and industry produces goods and services for export. As for the hopes placed on new corporate elites, Marx's insights suggest that any progressive or environmentalist convictions espoused by business leaders are so much empty rhetoric *unless the way they do business gives them a structural incentive to carry out their convictions.*

Why are the political interests of the traditional urban business community generally conservative? The explanation begins by deconstructing this group into its constituent fractions of capital based on specific ways of realizing profit that, with some oversimplification, correspond to local and non-local circuits of accumulation. In local circuits, firms in real estate, banking, utilities, routine professional services (like law, accounting, and insurance), and retail typically serve a market of residents and other businesses that concentrates around where firms are physically located; this quality makes these firms *locally dependent* upon the economy that anchors this market.[4] In non-local circuits of accumulation, firms in manufacturing and more specialized services export to consumers and businesses whose purchasing capacity is largely removed from firms' physical base of operations; the popular idea of industry as "big business" suggests this quality of local independence.[5]

THE TRADITIONAL URBAN BUSINESS COMMUNITY

In capitalism, increasing market size leads to greater profitability. For locally dependent firms, increasing market size stems from urbanization, local growth, and the production of physical space. These structural imperatives cast locally dependent firms specifically as *growth dependent*. For instance, developers, landlords, construction firms, and real estate agencies profit from rents derived from land; local growth and development make rents appreciate and thus increase exchange values for these businesses. Non-rentier industries like newspapers, utilities, and local banks profit from expanding advertiser and subscriber bases and therefore from local economic development and population growth. These firms have a concrete and direct stake in local politics, since their growth dependence makes them economically sensitive to local government's regulatory power over land use. Thus, their collective interests lie in promoting what is popularly called a "pro-business" climate that reduces as much as possible local governments' capacities to intervene into, and impose exactions on, business activities. (In this book, I leave quotation marks around the term "pro-business" to highlight its social construction, usually by conservative business interests.) Interventions targeted by the "pro-business" agenda include environmental regulations,[6] growth controls,[7] rent control,[8] mass transit bonds (except to bring suburban commuters into cities),[9] and at the political extremes even the very practice of land-use zoning.[10] Growth-dependent firms' interests in reducing governmental interventions are what make their politics conservative, although usually not to such a principled extent as to discourage governmental interventions *promoting* urban growth and private profit: for example, subsidies to developers, tax abatements for new industry, or bonds to secure infrastructure like highways and water.

In the urban political economy perspective, growth often comes at the expense of local residents by disrupting the settings for their local rounds, congesting traffic and schools, and reducing budgets for social services. Likewise, the "pro-business" agenda promotes an anti-democratic system of urban governance that dismisses non-economic concerns regarding the distribution of wealth. In this way, growth dependence reflects a structural contradiction between business and residential interests (or what neomarxists call the exchange and use values of places) that sets the stage for political conflict. Locally elected officials find themselves in a particular bind; although they can benefit electorally by riding the waves of voter mobilization against growth, their governments depend on growth, too, via tax revenues. A vast body of urban research suggests how they typically resolve this dilemma: elected officials usually join businesses in *growth coalitions* to promote the cause of growth, irrespective of other contentious, and less systematic, issues before local government.[11]

In even the most open of local governments, growth coalitions impose their agenda over opponents with what Clarence Stone has described as *sys-*

temic power, or the superior organizational capacity to capture the attention and agendas of local decision-makers.[12] Developers, for instance, hire technical experts and lawyers and court local business representatives who dominate discussions at city hearings by their (paid) persistence. Campaign contributions to elected officials, as well as a revolving door of employment between business and government, let growth coalitions diffuse their agenda throughout local government. Outside the governmental arena, business leaders are frequently active in local charities and other civic organizations where elected officials and other local opinion-setters can be found. Through these modes of participation, growth coalition members over time become repeat players in the formal and informal environments for local decision making. By contrast, few neighborhoods or communities that oppose growth can marshal the needed resources or access comparably privileged settings to counter growth advocates. Even successfully bringing a halt to a specific growth project does little to stop the promotion of growth in general.[13]

Of course, locally dependent firms vary in whether and how they participate in growth coalitions. Some businesses depend on existing environments—for example, a pristine outdoors for recreational equipment suppliers, an existing stock of vintage housing for architectural preservation specialists—that growth can impair. Many locally owned businesses compete with local branches of corporate chains, such as "big box" retail outlets or national banks. In the "quality-of-life" politics that galvanize many communities today, these issues often rally some businesses against particular forms of growth and potentially split growth coalitions.

For urban scholars, when, where, and how growth coalitions split is an empirical question that underscores how other structural imperatives besides growth dependence drive urban politics. Although the answer varies from place to place, the collected evidence reveals two factors that tend to minimize growth coalition divisions. First, these other business imperatives do not necessarily cut against a more abstract structural interest in growth. Potential business opponents can be appeased with promises of "smart" or otherwise preferable forms of growth: an increase of educated residents who prefer lively "urban village" settings or green products, for example. This is one reason why growth coalitions vary across places in the kind of capital investment they prefer; some seek out industries like high technology that pay workers good wages that allow for expensive homes and refined tastes, while others opt by choice or necessity for low-value development (e.g., waste landfills, noxious industry) with dubious employment and revenue benefits. Second, the dynamics of collective action in growth coalitions can undermine the ability of individual members to advocate dissenting agendas, as I explain later.

WHAT BIG BUSINESS WANTS FROM PLACES

How does industry relate to these patterns of community power? Export sales yield profits that enable further investment in production; when this investment needs a physical location, it is *inwardly invested* in places in the form of factories, branch offices, or other local infrastructure. In this way, capital investment by industry forms the primary base for the surrounding local economies, even though this is largely accidental and extraneous to corporate interests in particular places. In fact, rent, wages, and other locally set costs cut into profits, and so in a competitive environment, big business has a structural aversion to getting stuck in expensive sites of production. Nevertheless, at the onset of industrialization in the nineteenth century, other forms of local dependence often outweighed capital's interest in geographical mobility. Industry often sank substantial capital into massive physical plants (another reason why it was "big business") and depended locally on access to technological infrastructure, consumer markets, and labor markets.[14] Companies also had origins in particular localities where founders and executives were often regarded as local "first families"; sentimental attachments to their hometowns gave industry another source of local dependence.[15]

As communication and transportation innovations extended capital's reach across the globe, the rise of the multinational corporation brought an end to this era of local dependence.[16] During the second half of the twentieth century, economic restructuring further changed the guise and impact of big business in localities. Service sectors usurped the primacy of manufacturing in many urban economies. By the 1970s, competitive imperatives that scholars associate with "flexible accumulation" began to dissolve the organizational bonds of industrial activity; now, several small and specialized firms might perform the same work that in prior eras would be internalized within a single large enterprise.[17] Consequently, "big business" is not necessarily big these days, at least in terms of its workforce, capital assets, or scope of activities. Still, export-oriented firms (or what I will call *core firms*) continue to lay the primary base for urban economies, and growth coalitions still pursue their inward investments in order to set in motion local growth and profits.

Big business has different interests in local growth than growth coalitions. Occasionally the value of its real estate investments may be tied to local growth.[18] Otherwise, multinational corporations are not growth dependent in the local sense, since they produce goods and services for non-local markets. Instead, as Harvey Molotch observes, big business's "indirect interest is perhaps in the existence of the growth ideology rather than growth itself."[19] Big business benefits when growth coalitions seek to stimulate growth with a "pro-business" agenda of public subsidies, lower taxes, less expensive real estate, fewer regulations, lower wage levels, no unions, and so on, since these potentially reduce local operating costs. Furthermore, in its individual and aggregate dominance over local economies, big business has an advantage in power that can compel localities to meet its political demands.[20] If they fail to do so, big business can exercise another form of power: *exit*, or the influence that comes with its increasing capacity to pick up and move its operations elsewhere.[21] One result is that big business need not participate actively in growth coalitions to convey its demands but can opt instead for a more passive exercise of power.[22] Indeed, the traditional urban business community carries out its "pro-business" agenda as a proactive enticement for big businesses that have yet to invest locally.[23] At the global scale, corporations exploit "pro-business" climates to pit cities, regions, states, and nations against one another for the most advantageous terms.

When all is said and done, the demands of big business upon places mesh rather well with growth coalitions' interests. In what is sometimes called "enlightened self-interest," growth coalitions exert influence over local government and community affairs to make their localities more "pro-business" and (they assume) therefore more attractive to mobile capital— and to profit themselves from rising rents and larger markets as a result.[24] Consequently, the asymmetry of power seldom generates antagonism between big business and growth coalitions. Conflict instead is displaced between different growth coalitions that compete for the capital investment of big business.[25] Once a given locality succeeds in securing capital investment, big business and growth-dependent companies tend to share complementary interests *as a traditional urban business community*: in local exchange values for growth-dependent businesses, and in the political consent to operate locally without prohibitive governmental intervention or community conflict for big business.

This reciprocity of interests recurs so often that it supports a key premise in the theory of contemporary capital accumulation advanced by regulation theory. This school of thought contends that capital accumulation sets in motion systemic tendencies for structural contradiction. To manage this contradiction, capital regulates the modes and relations of accumulation with specific social and political norms. In the "Fordist" regime of accumulation that existed in the United States between the New Deal and the 1970s energy crisis, capital regulated its tendencies to provoke underconsumption and labor protest with a social contract of relatively high wages (at least for union workers, employees of military contractors, and others in primary labor markets), suburbanization and other new opportunities for consumption, and the promise of economic stability for workers, cities, and the welfare states of the west. Economic restructuring, triggered by declining corporate profitability, utterly overturned this social climate, as capital withdrew from the social contract it forged in the developed world and relocated to lower-cost sites.[26] In the urban arena, modes of regulation shifted toward neoliberal policies of "urban entrepreneurialism" ushered in by the 1980s Reagan and Thatcher administrations, as national governments abandoned urban aid programs and compelled cities to increase their attractiveness to capital.[27]

Regulation theory's explanation of such "post-Fordist" shifts are ubiquitous in the study of economic restructuring, even among commentators who otherwise avoid its highly abstract vocabulary and level of analysis. However, some scholars have charged that regulation theory glosses over diverse regulatory processes and political conflicts that occur beneath its macro concern for regimes of accumulation. The theory "explains economic continuity and change in terms of (among other things) political processes," but it "is not an explanation of those political processes," observes Joe Painter, one of its more sophisticated practitioners.[28] In response to such critiques, urbanists and other scholars have begun to redirect regulation theory away from its earlier macro focus; they now examine the ways that variation in institutional and geographical scale influences how capital accumulation creates structural contradictions and how capital seeks to regulate these contradictions. In this recent approach, modes of regulation are not singular and dominant entities, but rather collective processes that ebb and flow across time and space.[29]

COOPERATING IN A TRADITIONAL CIVIC NETWORK

This suggests that there is still much to be gleaned from smaller-scale investigations of the many contexts and problems that frame the big business–growth coalition alliance. For one reason, sharing interests in a "pro-business" climate is not the same as effectively mobilizing toward this end. The latter requires special efforts of coordination when the traditional urban business community members bring different backgrounds, assets, and methods to the local idiosyncrasies and bureaucratic inertia that frequently characterize local politics. This is the insight of urban regime theory, which examines how various ensembles of public and private actors come together to negotiate and execute different agendas for local politics, ranging from conservative growth agendas to the progressive provision of social services.[30] Following the lead of Clarence Stone, urban regime theory examines how governing public-private coalitions mobilize power in two phases. In the *social control* phase, or what can be thought of as the front stage of urban politics, individuals and groups mobilize scarce resources to preempt and weaken their opponents. For example, at the behest of non-local industry that promises inward investment, conservative politicians may direct funds and staff toward economic development schemes and away from social services. Although potentially available to grassroots and/or progressive coalitions, this kind of power is traditionally concentrated in fewer hands, usually a growth coalition of corporate and political leaders. By contrast, the *social production* phase reveals the back stage of power, where local politicians, civic leaders, growth-dependent companies, big business, and others must establish consensus and learn to cooperate, lest potential opponents exploit their disunity.[31] Urban regimes, then, are the different formal and informal arrangements that make local governance by coalitions of private, public, and community leaders possible.[32]

Although regimes vary by the political agendas that its actors pursue, not surprisingly the most common kind is the pro-growth regime enacted by a growth coalition.[33] Importantly, the pro-growth regime recurs most frequently in large part due to the stable and extensive ecology of institutions in which the traditional urban business community produces its social power. I call this ecology the *traditional civic network,* the local complex of interdependent relationships, networks, and organizations that encompasses developer and bank relations with clients, local business organizations, business access to politicians and government, and philanthropy and service to traditional charities—all arenas that I examine in this book.[34] The participation of companies, business leaders, and other potential regime members in these settings is often discretionary, informal, and mundanely "non-political." Yet in the aggregate and over time, the traditional civic network provides repeated opportunities for *systemic relationships:* "thick" relations in which participants deal with one another and thereby learn of shared interests, develop cooperation patterns, and establish norms about the means and ends of their political agenda. As colorfully evoked by the "old boy network" in the United States, systemic relationships in the traditional civic network sustain and reproduce "business as usual" far more effectively than, say, exclusive high-level contacts between a mayor and the CEO of a city's largest firm.

It is a sociological truism that members of a social network tend to share one another's perspective; in the traditional civic network, one reason is because the currents of power give members special opportunities to enforce consensus. If a business dissents from the collective agenda, it can face an array of sanctions in the traditional civic network, from being passed over for the board of directors at the Chamber of Commerce or United Way to having a developer or bank reject its business. Since companies often enter these relationships just to do business, even a single sanction can impose enough costs to deter defection; no "conspiracy" by the whole network is needed. Collective mobilization in the traditional civic network also works in a member's favor. Others may mobilize on behalf of a member's individual agenda, such as getting a "pro-business" reception in local government for one's development project, because they share a stake in preventing governmental precedents for intrusion and interventions into business activities. These dynamics of local business governance suggest three general expectations for traditional urban business community members' political interests: (1) overall support for the local "pro-business" agenda, (2) direct participation in local politics by a company when its business is sensitive to local growth or regulation by local government, and (3) at least indirect support for other companies whose business is likewise sensitive to local growth or regulation by local government.

WHERE DOES CAPITAL MAKE A LIVING?

The legacies of bottom-line interest and corporate power have led many to ask sardonically, How can capital live with itself? A question that is perhaps less pondered but equally relevant for urban scholars is, How does capital *live* at all? Given urban political economy's concern for how people's daily rounds suffer from the spatial contradictions of capital accumulation, it is a simple yet erroneous step to reify the distinction between exchange value and use value into capitalists and residents, respectively, and to forget that capitalists also reside somewhere. This issue requires clarification: As a social concept, "capital" is not a person or organization but an ownership relation to the means of production with a contextual logic based on its particular kind and stage in the accumulation process. This relation is vested into a social group, capitalists, who manage capital's investment and profit—it is in this sense that one can speak of the "interests" of corporate executives, entrepreneurs, and business leaders—but whose behavior cannot be reduced to the capital accumulation process. In the corporation, executives are capital's agents; although technically they do not necessarily own the means of production, the historical record shows that they serve as vigilant stewards of capital's bottom line.[35] Meanwhile, entrepreneurs and other owners of private firms remain bona fide capitalists, although in cutting-edge sectors, the means of production they own and (for urban economic development) the increment of capital they inwardly invest are dramatically smaller in value and influence than the big business of old.[36]

Capitalists are also people, and like everyone else their lives take place in particular settings. As residents and in other roles by which capitalists "get a life," what are their interests in place? Most scholarship regards capitalists as rootless colonists of place, extracting localities of all their productive value until an even more "pro-business" site turns up. Capitalists are thought to have no qualms about this process, nor sentimental attachments for places or even neighborhoods that they (often literally) secure for their residence. If price is no object, capitalists may make extended commutes from their homes, but when this becomes impractical, they are thought to dutifully move their families and themselves to the next place to exploit. The realms where capitalists more earnestly make their lives and commune with their class are conceptualized as exclusive yet somehow placeless settings for work (corporate towers, industrial parks, conference facilities), class reproduction (elite colleges, country clubs, exclusive shopping and vacation destinations), and transport between the two (first-class air travel, five-star hotels).[37]

The problem with this picture is not that it unfairly depicts capitalists' rootless lives and exploitative roles in places (although it certainly presumes a mindset that does not square with what many social psychologists believe about people's self-estimation). Rather, it fits uneasily with what new research shows about the relevance and binding qualities of place for capital. An entire corpus of research in economic geography has shown that particular locales have strategic importance for capital accumulation beyond the placeless logic of competitiveness. In very different ways, both the poststructural turn in urban studies and urban regime theory emphasize that localities imbue capital accumulation with place-specific meanings that cannot be reduced to abstract structural imperatives. Perhaps more to the point, recent attention has been called to how cutting-edge industries have apparent affinities for places that offer special lifestyle opportunities, cultural amenities, recreational opportunities, and other "non-economic" components of place distinction that attract managerial elites and technical workers. In different ways, these claims problematize the popular notion of rootless capital and need to be taken seriously. However, their insights into capitalists' interests in "getting a life," and, more generally, capital's relation to specific places must be reconciled with what has already been shown regarding capital's strategic need to exploit places.

LOCAL BUSINESS STRUCTURE AND URBAN POLITICS

The issues I have raised so far all touch on a key question: Do software, entertainment, and tourism sectors operate in a way that *allows* them to make a difference in local politics? A company has to work out of a physical setting, which means it has particular needs from a locality and engages in certain relationships and activities in order to do business there. This points to what I call a firm's *local business structure,* or the business-determined interests and activities specific to a firm working from a given locality. Local business structure lends a capitalistic rationality to particular modes of civic interest and participation that vary based on a firm's sector and location. I presume that any significant difference that the new companies and corporate elites make in local politics—i.e., any modes of civic participation that software, entertainment, and tourism firms undertake differently than the traditional urban business community, including taking no action at all—will reflect first and foremost the imperatives of local business structure, not personal dispositions or idiosyncrasies at odds with their business interests.

In this book I examine software, entertainment, and tourism firms and industry leaders' involvement and interests in five routine activities that indicate local business structure: locating a business, occupying a physical site, dealing with other local businesses, interacting with local government and officials, and supporting community nonprofits. These activities provide opportunities for software, entertainment, and tourism firms to show their difference from the traditional urban business community, which I observe by comparing the software, entertainment, and tourism firms with traditional urban community patterns and, where meaningful quantitative measures are available, local banks specifically. (See the Methodology Appendix at the end of this book for further discussion.) I now set forth the specific research questions that this book attempts to answer and discuss their relevance for urban politics.

1. LOCATIONAL MOTIVATIONS. Why do companies in the three sectors set up in particular localities? Much research explains their locational motivations in

terms of how firms weigh the benefits of access to local assets—external economies,[38] specialized business services,[39] and visitor destinations[40]—against tangible operating costs like prevailing wages and rents. Not yet integrated into this perspective, there is separate evidence that software and entertainment firms locate in places that satisfy the lifestyle preferences of their workers.[41] Why are these issues important for urban politics? Popular business wisdom holds that low costs of doing business, coupled with a local government willing to subsidize business infrastructure and lower tax rates, create a competitive, "pro-business" climate. When capital needs such an environment, its local business structure legitimates the efforts of the traditional urban business community to tilt the business and political climate as much as possible toward no land-use restrictions, no environmental regulations, "business-friendly" government, and a "supportive" (read: politically quiescent) population.[42]

2. SITE DEVELOPMENT. Once they decide on a general location, what kind of buildings do software, entertainment, and tourism companies need to occupy? Here the outcomes of corporate location take physical shape and mobilize the local development sector. One job of developers, landlords, land-use lawyers, architects, real estate brokers, construction firms, and related business services is to understand what companies need from their sites and anticipate shifts in industrial demand. As clients to the development industry, footloose companies gain a point of access to banks, legal services, insurance companies, and others in the traditional urban business community.[43] The kinds of sites that companies demand also point to what political difference they can make in at least two ways. First, conventional site needs legitimate the advocacy of developers and their business allies, who vigorously promote "value-free development" and traditionally exert dominance in community affairs to advance this collective goal, as well as their own projects.[44] Second, even if software, entertainment, and tourism firms do not have conventional site needs themselves, they might mobilize in "pro-business" solidarity around development controversies suffered by another in their industry.

3. LOCAL BUSINESS ASSOCIATIONS AND CAPITAL. Do software, entertainment, and tourism firms use local business groups and financing? In their general (e.g., chambers of commerce) and industry-specific (e.g., trade association) forms, local business associations provide their members networking opportunities, regional marketing and promotion, a collective voice before local decision-makers, and, in some cases, even vital industrial infrastructure. As more members use their services, local business associations achieve a network centrality that reinforces members' bonds to these organizations. Local finance, as provided by local banks or economic development organizations, achieves a similar integrative effect through capital flows.[45] To the extent

that software, entertainment, and tourism firms are embedded in these networks, they may be compelled to endorse the "pro-business" agenda that means business and politics as usual.[46]

4. CAMPAIGN CONTRIBUTIONS. Do software, entertainment, and tourism companies and elites support the kind of mayors and city council members favored by the traditional urban business community? Campaign contributions reveal how government intervenes in or impinges on a firm's operations.[47] At the local arena, a business contributor may seek to articulate concerns or introduce projects on which local decision-makers have yet to form opinions, or he or she may wish to overturn existing land-use or environmental restrictions.[48] Through the traditional civic network, contributors are likely to know who represents the "pro-business" candidate; supporting these candidates thus signals, and can serve to reinforce, business unity.[49] As I describe later, the places I examine in this book have long legacies of political conflict and liberal regimes in local government. Thus, beyond their obvious and direct impact on city hall, corporate contributions reveal whether software, entertainment, and tourism companies are concerned about the "anti-business" thrust of city hall.

5. PHILANTHROPY TO COMMUNITY NONPROFITS. Do software, entertainment, and tourism firms donate money and service to local charities? Are these the same as the ones favored by the traditional urban business community? Beneath the language of altruism and generosity, corporate philanthropy provides an opportunity for informal business networking on nonprofit boards and fund-raising events.[50] It can also embody a subtle strategy of political activism by making allies out of community nonprofits that can bestow upon their corporate benefactors a sheen of civic legitimacy through their association,[51] if not their outright advocacy.[52] Thus, philanthropy reveals the structural imperatives of network-building and profit-seeking that motivate "discretionary" corporate behavior.

(RE)ALIGNING URBAN REGIMES

In the following chapters, I elaborate upon the interests and behavior of traditional urban business communities for each component of local business structure in order to interpret the patterns I find for software, entertainment, and tourism firms and highlight the specific issues of scholarly and political interest they raise. However, the potential for repeated differences across the entire gamut of local business structure suggests a qualitatively different outcome: namely, broader departures from the arrangements and understandings that align private and public actors in urban regimes. This speaks to the concerns of urban regime theory, although mine is not a typical study of urban regimes. Many works in this field pursue a historical analysis of specific places to describe how regimes achieve, maintain, or lose political dominance over time, as local leaders emerge on and leave the scene, community demands surface and are met (or not), coalitions come together and fall apart, and economic conditions shift. By contrast, this book focuses primarily on the static organization and process of the three sectors' local business structure, and less on their subsequent effects on urban politics. For the places I studied, I treat the specific ensemble of local actors, community demands, and other business interests as empirical context but follow through much less on the three sectors' subsequent influence. As a result, my analysis does not dwell on the historical consequences of the three sectors for urban regimes.

However, beneath the historical framework of most regime studies lies a set of claims about the role of business in urban governance that this book reevaluates. Urban regime theory focuses on how collective process begets political agenda, especially via the mechanisms of collective action that sustain the traditional civic network. In this book, I update this premise for the "new economy." I examine whether firms in the three sectors share the same bottom-line outlook toward locality as traditional mobile capital—an orientation that legitimizes the "pro-business" agenda of the traditional urban business community. I investigate whether the five components of local business structure embed these firms in the traditional civic network, wherein they might face normative and structural pressures for consensus. I address whether political difference from the traditional urban business community signals a new business support for more progressive urban politics. In short, I take up the broader issue of whether economic restructuring sustains or undermines the alignments of business actors with each other and community actors in pro-growth regimes.

IS THERE A NEW ECONOMY?

The advent of software, entertainment, and tourism industries and their possibilities for social change are frequently associated with the "new economy," a term that is rapidly becoming commonplace in everyday language. However, some confusion remains about the criteria for a new economy. For one reason, although the three sectors assumed a new preeminence by the 1990s, they are not necessarily new. Southern California hosts a venerable regional industry: Hollywood, a neighborhood within the city of Los Angeles but also a synonym for the motion picture, television, and music industries. (In this book, "Hollywood" refers to this local entertainment industry, whereas "Hollywood proper" refers to the specific neighborhood within the city of Los Angeles.) Tourism dates back even further, and while the software industry has created a new generation of companies and activities associated with the Internet, computer networking, and digital media like mobile phones and personal digital assistants, these have precedents in the regional aerospace and defense industries that prevailed during the Cold War. It is beyond the scope of this book to resolve whether a "new economy" really exists or not; more to the point, my analysis does not necessarily require a position in this debate, which is a task I leave to the reader. Below, I explain what is in fact new about software, entertainment, and tourism: that is, how they characterize the urban economies that have emerged since the 1990s.

THE PROBLEM OF THE "NEW ECONOMY"

Perhaps long before Karl Marx described the rise of an industrial capitalism in which "all that is solid melts into air," social observers have attributed social change to structural shifts in production and consumption, thereby initiating a project of describing a "new economy." Tracing this concept's etymology warrants its own book; my review here is necessarily selective and begins with the post-World War II era. It emerged alongside other concepts, usually modified by "post," that public intellectuals and social movements introduced to explain their changing society and, in some cases, wrestle with the political and intellectual ghost of Marx haunting Cold War society. Amidst the increasing prosperity and environmental concern of the 1950s and 60s, "post-industrialism"[53] and "post-materialism"[54] connoted the apparent transcendence of material scarcity and its sociopolitical manifestations. "Flexible accumulation,"[55] "post-Fordism,"[56] "disorganized capitalism,"[57] and, most popularly, "globalization" evoked conditions emerging by the 1970s such as the functional disintegration of large corporations, capitalism's unprecedented scale, the flight of industry for places with more quiescent workforces, and the decline of the welfare-state social contract in the developed world. In all of these works, references to a "new economy" suggested the stakes of and gave urgency to theorists' claims, although rarely did the term frame an entire theoretical perspective. By the 1980s, the "new economy" usually meant any economic activity or sector that appeared as the military-industrial economy shrank: disarmament, industrial disinvestment, services.[58]

By the 1990s, claims about a "new economy" resurfaced with greater prominence. Among social theorists, the most important one to take the idea seriously has been Manuel Castells, whose theory of the "network society" describes an economy that is informational in its productivity, global in its scale, and networked in its form. In its leading-edge sectors, the organization of production has moved out of the individual corporation and into the business project, whereby an ad hoc group of firms, contractors, labor, and finance creates a specific good or service at a specific time, only to dissolve once the product is finished (as a one-off or small batch) or becomes less profitable to produce (as a mass commodity).[59] For Castells, corporate demands for such flexibility have transformed and reduced professional-managerial, industrial, and service workers into two classes: *self-programmable labor,* which innovates and adapts to market demands and economic conditions, and *generic labor,* the routine work of which is increasingly performed by lower-skilled workers or mechanization.[60]

Far more than Castells or other social theorists, however, the business press, managerial researchers, and mainstream economists have made the "new economy" a problem of the highest order, and can claim substantial responsibility for popularizing the concept. For these organic intellectuals of capitalism, the new economy is both a macro and micro concept; they reach little consensus on any one criterion partly because each addresses different constituencies, from economic policy-makers to the would-be entrepreneur. At the macro level, the concept refers to assorted business processes, cycles, and "rules" that are thought to lack precedent in capitalism. For many economists, the new economy refers to increased labor productivity in the 1990s that appeared to break the typical cycle of productivity followed by inflation. By the end of the twentieth century, economists and historians hotly debated the empirical existence of such productivity gains[61]; soon thereafter, recessionary trends slowed the American economy's expansion and made the debate somewhat moot. Another conceptualization emphasizes the qualitatively new *sources* of productivity gains, such as technological innovations,[62] cultural-organizational transformations in the workplace,[63] the expanding stock market, or some combination of these.[64] At a more micro level, the new economy refers, first, to distinct sectors like high technology, business services, and media that emerged out of the consolidation of economic restructuring to specialize in high value-added activities. As "old" Fortune 500 companies acquire firms in these sectors, this understanding of the "new" has also lost some currency with business observers, although it remains a popular wisdom. In a more sophisticated conceptualization that pertains to both old and new companies, the new economy has come to refer to new kinds of competitive strategy, such as e-commerce,[65] consumer-driven production,[66] and niche marketing.[67] These exemplify the larger strategy of competing on value, in which firms identify and reorganize around core competencies that cannot easily be routinized and thereby relegated to lower value-added activities that compete on price.[68] Although there is debate whether this strategy is new or was merely overlooked in prior eras, competing on value certainly accounts for much of the turbulence in corporate form, industrial organization, and labor employment that is popularly attributed to the new economy.

Defining the "new economy" is one matter; agreeing that it exists is another. For scholars, the issue is complicated by capitalism's innate tendency to creative destruction; when a system regularly reinvents its rules, what counts as new? Most agree that the informational mode of development—one in which the production, analysis, and circulation of information and expertise drive economic productivity—distinguishes the contemporary economy from the prior industrial mode. But does this mean the "rules have changed," as many in the business world insist? If new forms of capitalist organization still reflect the need to appropriate ever greater surplus value from labor, there is good reason to be skeptical that capitalism has really changed.[69] Furthermore, what process epitomizes the informational mode of development: scientific innovation in information and biological technologies, or the resurgence of "artisanal" work in high value-added technical and creative sectors? From several vantage points, recent developments in economies, work, and consumption can credibly be deemed new when compared to their predecessors. Yet the new is also always in a state of emergence; it develops alongside and in dialectical engagement with the old, often to the benefit of capitalist accumulation, as the notion of uneven development implies.[70]

Despite this scholarly debate, the term's recurrence in the business world sheds ethnographic light on the changing nature of corporate power. A quick review of the business press shows that the "new economy" is most frequently invoked to suggest peril for the keepers of tradition and promise for the opportunistic. Hence the colorful dichotomies of the business press between corporate "dinosaurs" or "elephants" who are "slow" and "stolid," and the "insurgents" or "Young Turks" who "race" to gain "first-mover" advantage. The recessionary consolidations of 2000 have disabused most businesspeople of the idea that small and young firms have consistent advantage over their big and old counterparts. Still, the widespread perception that "the rules are changing" in a "new economy" echoes the belief of corporate elites, business leaders, and the media that the cutting edge of capitalism has, in fact, become less amenable to conventional strategies of technocratic management. Although I do not take a position on the "new economy," I nevertheless find it useful to pay heed to the *perception* of a new economy as a sign that the agents of corporate power view economic change as unprecedented and inscrutable.

TRANSFORMATIONS OF URBAN POLITICAL ECONOMIES

For the purposes of this book, an important context for this perception is capital investment in space, an activity that has long been subject to technocratic management by industry and growth coalitions. Industry quantifies its material operating costs fairly easily and compares the suitability of potential locations across the globe. Growth coalitions compare the prosperity and "pro-business" suitability of their own locales against other places with which they compete for capital investment. The spatial environment for capital investment is sufficiently transparent, and the motives for intervention predictable enough, that industry and growth coalitions alike can refer to their consequence: a global hierarchy of places stratified by variation in business climate, as perceived by capital.[71] This global hierarchy sets the playing field for subsequent rounds of interurban, interregional, and international competition for capital investment. As transportation and communication innovations reduce the friction of space, capital can negotiate for better terms in the remaining costs of doing business, such as wages, rents, and governmental exactions; increased automation in the production process makes sites of lower-skilled labor all the more suitable. The result is the familiar story of globalization: Industry flees for localities with more advantageous business climates, often in the developing world, leaving behind only corporate headquarters and management branches in the deindustrializing developed world.

It is important to note that this conventional dynamic of capital investment is for the most part *exogenous* to the workings of any particular sector. It is informed by an industry-general currency of cost differences across local business climates, and it presumes that production is largely carried out by generic labor that is interchangeable across space—often the case for routine manufacturing and service activities. Furthermore, this conventional dynamic is hardly fading into obsolescence. Many corporations perceive an interest, at least for short-term profits, in transforming as much of their activities as possible into generic processes that can be carried out by generic labor in potentially interchangeable locations, in keeping with the new economy strategy of competing on value.

However, economic restructuring has brought to bear two new spatial contexts that, I contend, do fundamentally "change the rules" for inward investment and local business governance, even as they emerge amidst the traditional hierarchy of places. First, a *new industrial space* of production and labor reproduction has emerged in which capital investment is driven by dynamics *endogenous* to particular sectors.[72] Certain high value-added activities take place in particular settings characterized by dense agglomerations of firms, flexible production networks, access to vital infrastructure, special interpersonal networks, and other locational qualities that are essentially specific to industries themselves and have little to do with growth coalition overtures for capital investment. In the next two chapters, I elaborate on the dynamics of location and expansion in this new industrial space for software, entertainment, and tourism. Importantly, these dynamics make firms locally dependent on places that are not necessarily competitive in terms of material cost factors, at least as traditionally conceived. As Castells observes, "The work process is interconnected between firms, regions, and countries, in a stepped-up, spatial division of labour, in which networks of locations are more important than hierarchies of places."[73] Over repeated rounds of capital investment and business activity, the new industrial space coheres and expands atop the traditional hierarchy of places, inscribing it with a new geography of haves and have-nots.

Second, the conditions for local governance have changed in what I call the *new urban economy*. When pressed to defend their legitimacy, growth coalitions have long claimed that local growth brings overall prosperity and demonstrates their can-do efficacy; in a political culture like the United States that privileges urban entrepreneurialism and "running government like a business," this rhetoric is highly persuasive.[74] However, places with conventional "pro-business" advantage are potentially handicapped if they cannot support the new locational demands of cutting-edge firms and industries. Consequently, in the dynamic and often inscrutable new industrial space, many growth coalitions cannot even show growth for their efforts. Additionally, in many communities, they must contend with political backlash by residents against growth impacts, corporate chain investment, and environmentally degrading industry. These constraints set the political terms for the new urban economy, which alters the conditions for business community hegemony in local affairs and leaves growth coalitions with great uncertainty as to how to proceed. Should they ignore residential dissent and try to attract industries, such as mall development, distribution warehouses, or prisons, which seek a conventional "pro-business" climate? Those industries profit by competing on price, are sensitive to local costs of business, and therefore provide unsustainable engines of economic development. Alternately, growth coalitions can try to harness the new industrial space that for the most part expands without their intervention, and to stimulate the growth of higher value-added industries. The high priority in contemporary growth strategies for sectors that bring better-paying jobs, more-educated workers, "greener" industry, and more-sustainable sources of economic development reveals what is really "new" about software, entertainment, and tourism. In the new urban economy, these sectors take on new prominence as potent and desired engines of economic development, even when they are not so new, historically speaking.

THE RESEARCH SITES

In the places I examine in this book, the three sectors have emerged largely independent of any overtures by traditional urban business communities. The reasons why, and the consequences thereof, are the crux of my study. My original data come from Santa Monica, Santa Barbara, and San Luis Obispo, three communities along the Southern California coast (Figure 1.1) where I interviewed roughly one hundred business and community representatives, conducted field research, and collected secondary data between 1996 and 2000. (Unless otherwise indicated, all quotations in this book come from my interviews and fieldwork; see the Methodological Appendix for more discussion.)

Readers familiar with these three places or Southern California more generally might argue that they hardly characterize the economies, politics, or cultures of most American cities. This is largely true; these places comprise a sample of locations where capital investment in software, entertainment, and tourism has actually taken place—in short, the new industrial space—and not the larger set of places potentially available to capital investment. Additionally, their small-to-middling sizes resemble the scale of most American cities without the fiscal resources or infrastructure that make metropolises and large cities more enticing places to do business. Their traditional urban business communities have historically endorsed a pro-growth agenda common to many American cities.

Figure 1.1

The research sites and major California metropoles.

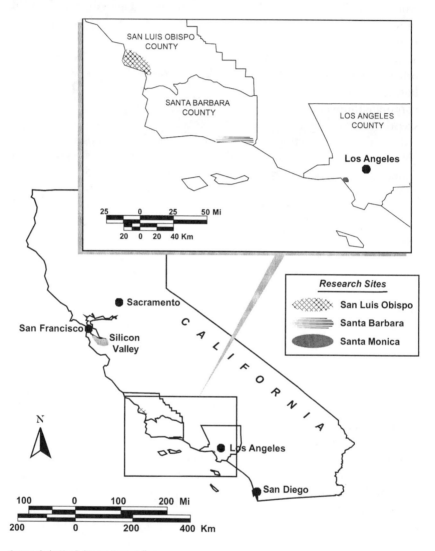

Cartography by Meg E. Stewart, Vassar College

Perhaps most importantly, their strong liberal and environmental traditions in local government and community groups have made them notoriously "anti-business" in regional, national, and international business circles, a quality that offers a unique methodological advantage. Companies in Santa Monica, Santa Barbara, and San Luis Obispo have historically had to assert "pro-business" demands vigorously against a countervailing liberalism in local policy and community sentiment. Should the business climate frustrate software, entertainment, and tourism firms or leaders, then, quite likely, they would mobilize the traditional urban business community, for example, by pressuring local business leaders to lead the charge against land-use restrictions. At least some component of local business structure should reveal this activity; for instance, a firm might back "pro-business" candidates for local office, or join the local chamber of commerce to voice concerns about the business climate. Insofar as these apparently "anti-business" places make such corporate interventions likely, my choice of sites to study should increase skeptics' confidence in whatever political differences I find.

SANTA MONICA

Santa Monica (2000 population: 84,084) offers a vibrant and architecturally contemporary landscape for cutting-edge economy and beachside lifestyle. Most outsiders know the city for its coastal attractions (the beach, a pier with an amusement park, temperate weather), popular retail-entertainment districts like the Third Street Promenade (a pedestrian district of specialty stores and cinema complexes), and art centers like the Bergamot Station complex. More perceptive visitors also notice the many public amenities that residents enjoy, like street-side art and numerous parks. Moving east away from the beach and toward Los Angeles, generic industrial areas and warehouses dot the landscape; although older light manufacturing firms and artist studios still occupy some of these spaces, increasingly they house small and often inconspicuous software and entertainment companies. In addition to software, entertainment, and tourism, the local economy includes health care and professional service (architects, law firms, and finance) sectors, a modest amount of light manufacturing, and the Rand Corporation, a Cold War–era think tank. The city's community college is America's second-highest granter of associate degrees to foreign students, while the University of California at Los Angeles is about five miles away to the east. In 2000, twenty-eight percent of the population identified themselves as non-white—a considerable amount, but significantly less than in the surrounding Los Angeles County.

Before the late 1970s, business exerted political hegemony over city affairs. After the city was linked to U.S. Interstate 10 (known regionally as the Santa Monica Freeway) in 1966, the traditional urban business community looked to further the city's rapid growth with a radical development agenda that at one time included an attempt to replace Santa Monica's famous pier with a high-rise resort island. Then, in 1978 Santa Monica earned its current reputation as a flagship progressive city with the ascendance of Santa Monicans for Renters Rights (SMRR), a municipal political party that established rent control ordinances without parallel in Southern California.[75] While word spread nationally about the "People's Republic of Santa Monica," SMRR leaders realized that only a healthy tax base could finance their ambitious set of social programs.[76] Consequently, they rarely opposed urban development and growth in principle, but only imposed rent control, levied fees on projects to pay for public amenities, regulated projects' environmental impacts, and channeled growth into particular revitalization zones.[77] Despite its apparent success in handling the city's economy (which received an extremely favorable triple-A credit rating in recent years), SMRR remains in a precarious political position. On the left, its growth-with-equity policies frustrate some progressives who contend that the community has suffered because of development encouraged by the SMRR-led city council. On the right, social services (particularly for the homeless) and the remnants of rent control galvanize steadfast opposition by business leaders, landlords, and homeowners who currently unite under the "Coalition for a Safe Santa Monica" moniker.

SANTA BARBARA

Separated from Los Angeles's sprawl by coastal and agricultural expanses, the Santa Barbara area (which includes the namesake city and adjacent communities of Goleta, Montecito, Summerland, and Carpinteria, for an estimated 2000 population of 173,000) has long fostered economies and civic sentiments that thrive in their distance from the metropolis. The namesake city offers a Spanish colonial milieu of cultural refinement with its 1820 mission, the "Mission Revival" architectural motif mandated in most downtown buildings, numerous "paseo" outdoor shopping plazas, and an annual "Old Spanish Days" festival. Nature also sets the local tone. Through coastal views, neighborhood flora, parks, and (for some, particularly in upscale hillside and clifftop neighborhoods) palatial estates and country clubs, residents can enjoy the beach, undeveloped mountains, and the pastoral agriculture of avocados, oranges, flowers, and grapes. As far back as the nineteenth century, Santa Barbara's economy has turned on these community amenities through the industries of tourism and retirement. The 1954 expansion of a University of California campus made education the area's largest local employer (thanks also to the community college), and put in motion new local economies, such as aerospace and defense research and development that set up in the surrounding Goleta community. Most recently, in addition to the three sectors I study here, the city has lured headquarter offices for Tenet Health Care and a few other major corporations. Census statistics show a socioeconomic diversity that is obscured by the area's reputation as wealthy and predominantly white; for example, Hispanic populations range from five percent in exclusive Montecito to twenty-seven percent in Santa Barbara to thirty-six percent in Carpinteria.

Local politics have long pitted industry and growth against residential quality of life. Slow-growth sentiments date back at least to the 1920s, when civic leaders promoted the city's Mission Revival architecture, village atmosphere, and surrounding wilderness as a distinction of Santa Barbara's superiority to bustling Los Angeles.[78] Local elites quickly moved to preserve the amenities that now comprise Santa Barbara's tourism attractions, for example, purchasing the beachfront (later sold back to the city) to spare it from further development.[79] Oil drilling in the Santa Barbara Channel has been a long-standing controversy well before the dramatic 1969 oil spill, which some nevertheless credit with sparking the modern environmental movement.[80] Since the 1970s, a new generation of politicians, organizations, and voters has sought to slow urban growth by approving growth control ordinances, rejecting imported water supplies (until 1991), and mandating urban limit lines to stop the sprawl of the South Coast. Except during the 1969 oil conflict, Santa Barbara's traditional urban business community has opposed and tried to undermine most of these restrictions on business. By the late 1990s, while something of a political calm existed in the city, and a handful of liberal politicians and environmental organizations sought to "build the bridge" to the business community through various community organizations and forums, many activists were again challenging the forces for urban growth, embodied this time in technology sectors and chain hotel/retail development.

SAN LUIS OBISPO

Surrounded by mountains and large ranch estates, the San Luis Obispo area (which includes the namesake city and smaller communities of Baywood Park, Los Osos, Morro Bay, Avila Beach, Oceano, Shell Beach, Pismo Beach, Arroyo Grande, and Grover City, for an estimated 2000 population of 115,000) is a favorite place for state residents and others to "get away from it all." The outdoors and the natural environment figure in many local attractions and activities: uncrowded beaches, a downtown pedestrian plaza (with a Spanish mission and meandering creek), hiking, animal watching, dune buggying, deep-sea fishing, wine tasting, and hot springs. These amenities notwithstanding, the city of San Luis Obispo is the seat of a mostly agricultural county, and the surrounding economy reflects the absence of urban industry. The biggest county taxpayer is the Diablo Canyon nuclear power plant. The largest employers are government and education, the latter represented by a state polytechnic university and a community college. The least racially diverse of the three Southern California places, the area's Hispanic population ranges around ten percent in San Luis Obispo to over thirty percent in small working-class communities like Grover Beach.

Much as in Santa Barbara, politics in San Luis Obispo pivot around environmental and growth issues, as an early cadre of residents who opposed growth were reinforced on the left in the 1960s by an expanding university population. In the 1970s, national demonstrators descended on San Luis Obispo to protest the construction of the Diablo Canyon nuclear power plant.[81] On the other side, the traditional urban business community has fought residents over the pace of growth since at least the 1950s, when business leaders proposed paving over the downtown creek with parking spaces.[82] Recently, business and community have reached consensus on certain environmental issues; the chamber of commerce criticized federal plans for offshore oil drilling and endorsed an unsuccessful ballot initiative to authorize public purchase of undeveloped mountainside property, while many local businesses have joined environmentalists in opposing "big box" retail projects. Yet, although both sides in principle prefer tourism and high-tech to "dirtier" industry, they still differ on particular visions and developments, such as expanded downtown parking, golf courses, and high-tech industrial parks.

THE NEW URBAN ECONOMY SECTORS

In these three Southern California communities, software, entertainment, and tourism have assumed a greater role in local economic development since the Cold War ended in 1989. Table 1.1 illustrates their preeminence for the surrounding counties, which only underestimates these sectors' concentration since traditional manufacturing is more dispersed.

Otherwise, firms in the three sectors vary in size, specialty, and age across the three places. Below, the statistics that I report for total local firms in each sector have also been incorporated into quantitative measures that I present in subsequent chapters (see Methodology Appendix for further discussion). Many of the firms have folded, relocated, "rolled up" into larger firms, or otherwise disappeared since I studied them. I discuss these recent trends in the final chapter; for my purposes here, this is one reason why I refrain from identifying company names in this book, except where the public record or narrative flow warrants it.

SOFTWARE

Although software is far more economically important in Northern California's Silicon Valley, it nevertheless represents a vibrant growth sector in the state's southern half. In 1996, this and other non-defense high-tech industries (like telecommunications and biotechnology) generated Southern California's third largest manufacturing payroll at $5.01 billion, just behind a declining aerospace sector.[83] Table 1.2 shows the size and concentration of this sector in the three places. Santa Barbara has the most software firms, a status behind the city's nickname of "Silicon Beach"; its county has also ranked eighth in regional density of commercial Internet domain names for the United States, three places ahead of the Los Angeles-Riverside-Orange County region.[84] However, Santa Monica's second place status masks its central position in the thriving software district of Los Angeles's Westside (which also encompasses Culver City, Marina Del Rey, Venice, and El Segundo). A 2001 study of regional technology firms found that "despite the sprawl of L.A. County, the tech community is actually tightly knit in and around Santa Monica. Over fifty-five percent of the companies that received funding were located within ten miles of Santa Monica."[85] In last place, San Luis Obispo has what local business leaders concede is a

Table 1.1

Economic restructuring in employment, by county

	Los Angeles County				Santa Barbara County				San Luis Obispo County			
	1997 employ-ment	Change from 1989	Ratio to manufac-turing	Change from 1989	1997 employ-ment	Change from 1989	Ratio to manufac-turing	Change from 1989	1997 employ-ment	Change from 1989	Ratio to manufac-turing	Change from 1989
Software	47,335	43.3%	0.07	87.8%	2,018	23.0%	0.13	60.9%	920	405.5%	0.15	413.4%
Entertainment	190,911	41.0%	0.29	84.7%	574	6.5%	0.04	39.4%	343	16.3%	0.06	18.1%
Tourism	274,819	8.5%	0.41	42.1%	16,084	13.3%	1.00	48.2%	10,281	14.0%	1.66	15.8%

SOURCE: U.S. Census, *County Business Patterns*, 1997.

Table 1.2

Number of local software firms

SIC	Description	Santa Monica	Santa Barbara	San Luis Obispo
3571	Electronic computer manufacturing	4	5	1
3572	Computer storage devices manufacturing	0	1	0
3577	Computer peripheral equipment manufacturing	2	3	1
7371	Computer programming services	54	69	28
7372	Prepackaged software	6	8	2
7373	Computer integrated system design	6	9	0
7374	Computer processing & data preparation	26	31	18
7375	Information retrieval services	1	1	1
7376	Computer facilities management services	0	0	0
7379	Computer-related services	9	14	5
	Total software firms	**108**	**141**	**56**

SOURCE: Select Phone, 1999 version, InfoUSA Inc., Omaha, Neb.
NOTE: Firms with multiple SICs are categorized according to the first reported SIC. Different branches of the same firm are counted as separate firms.
SIC, Standard Industrial Code.

rather modestly sized sector; the emergence of technology companies is slow and for many imperceptible.

Most software firms are concentrated in computer programming services and computer processing and data preparation, categories that typically correspond to firms that sell services to local firms and consumers, not the core firms that export products or services to a global market.[86] The latter include the stars of the local software industries. In Santa Monica, these tend to be "new media" firms that provide e-commerce and Internet content and design video games, as well as a handful of more conventional software firm branches. In Santa Barbara, the most important firms with global markets are software "tool-makers" specializing in graphics, business utilities, and Internet applications. Also notable in Santa Barbara are the few research and development branches for aerospace and defense manufacturers (listed in Table 1.2 under the two-digit 35 Standard Industrial Code), now regarded as economic "dinosaurs" by industry boosters who place their hopes in the newer generations of software firms. In San Luis Obispo, the most important software firms design hardware and operating systems for computers, peripherals, wireless phones, and other digital media, and a few work in new media niches like video games and Internet content. None of the firms I studied approaches the size of Silicon Valley's giants, although they do include branches of those companies.

ENTERTAINMENT

Long an economic motor for Southern California, entertainment became the region's primary manufacturing sector with the post–Cold War decline of the aerospace sector. In 1996, entertainment generated the largest manufacturing payroll in Southern California, at $8.92 billion.[87] Table 1.3 shows the sector's size and concentration.

Only Santa Monica claims a critical mass of entertainment firms, particularly in the motion picture and television industry. Strictly speaking, the city's film studios are distributors and marketers in the independent or subsidiary range, not the "big boys" with extensive soundstage properties that are found in nearby entertainment centers like Burbank, Universal City, and Hollywood proper. However, Santa Monica holds important post-production facilities, special effects houses, and production companies, as well as branches or headquarters for record companies, cable channels, and magazine publishers. Other important institutions in Santa Monica include the National

Table 1.3

Number of local entertainment firms

SIC	Description	Santa Monica	Santa Barbara	San Luis Obispo
4832	Radio broadcasting stations	5	6	13
4833	Television broadcasting stations	1	3	3
509909	Records, tapes, & compact disc—wholesale	7	2	1
738947	Recording studios	13	12	2
7812[1]	Motion picture & video production	169	51	18
7819	Motion picture production services	25	12	5
7822	Motion picture & videotape distribution	11	1	0
792201	Professional talent management	4	1	0
792205	Television program producers	29	4	1
792206	Talent agencies & casting services	4	2	1
	Total entertainment firms	**268[2]**	**94**	**44**

SOURCE: Select Phone, 1999 version, InfoUSA Inc., Omaha, Neb.
NOTE: Firms with multiple SICs are categorized according to the first reported SIC. Different branches of the same firm are counted as separate firms.
1. In their study of Southern California's motion picture and television production, Storper and Christopherson operationalized this sector as SIC 7813, 7814, and 7819; Michael Storper and Susan Christopherson, *The Changing Location and Organization of the Motion Picture Industry: Interregional Shifts in the United States* [Los Angeles: School of Architecture and Urban Planning, University of California, Los Angeles, 1985.]. However, the database that I used to count entertainment firms listed no firms under 7813 and 7814.
2. A Santa Monica city-sponsored study counted 118 firms and organizations under the category of "motion picture, television, recording, and multimedia production and support." The study derived this smaller entertainment firm count by using different sources (telephone surveys and city tax records). See AMS Planning & Research, *The Economic Impact of the Arts in Santa Monica* (Petaluma, CA: AMS Planning & Research, 1997).

Academy of Recording Arts & Sciences (which sponsors the annual Grammy music awards) and events like the American Film Market, an annual conference where international movie studios, distributors, and investors review the latest films available for commercial release.

Although their numbers pale next to Santa Monica's, entertainment firms have recently come to Santa Barbara. The area has a sprinkling of high-profile postproduction facilities, digital effects firms, and production companies. Perhaps a more common entertainment "industry" has been the frequent use of Santa Barbara as a film location; for this reason, the local conference and visitors bureau employs a full-time "film commissioner." Finally, San Luis Obispo's entertainment industry is practically negligible, although it has at least one manufacturer of entertainment production technology.[88]

TOURISM

The three Southern California communities share similar environmental and visitor amenities, although tourism's absolute impact is greatest in Santa Monica and, more generally, the Los Angeles area. In 1995, tourism's payroll in the metropolitan area totaled $4.86 billion.[89] By 1997, tourism employed over 253,000 workers in Los Angeles County, making it the area's third-highest employing sector.[90] Furthermore, the three places cater to different kinds of tourists. Santa Monica brings in the most out-of-state and foreign tourists. Santa Barbara follows closely behind, although most of its visitors come from the Los Angeles region for the day or weekend. Regional visitors comprise an even more primary market for San Luis Obispo. Table 1.4 shows the current size and concentrations of this sector in each place.

Although they seldom attract visitors directly, companies that provide lodging, food, and drink deserve special attention because they are the primary forms of visitor expenditures and therefore have the largest economic impact in local tourism sectors.[91] San Luis Obispo has the most lodging establishments, although, with one or two exceptions, these tend to be mid-sized hotels (around fifty rooms) or smaller motels offering modest rates for highway travelers and regional visitors who (according to tourism officials), on average, stay one and a half days, engage mostly in beach recreation, and spend only $75 a day. By contrast, the other two places have larger hotels and (in Santa Barbara) the golf courses that cater more to upscale visitors and business functions. Restaurants reveal a similar divergence between Santa Monica and Santa Barbara, on the one hand, and San Luis Obispo on the other. Santa Barbara (with the most restaurants) and Santa Monica are especially noted for fine dining venues that feature "nouvelle California" cuisine, celebrity chefs and owners, and perhaps a chance to mingle with the rich and famous. For the epicurean visitor, these restaurants emanate a uniquely Southern Californian ambiance, as much as any natural amenity, and are an important destination in themselves.[92] By contrast, San Luis Obispo restaurants tend to offer more affordable meals for price-conscious visitors and locals.

Table 1.4

Number of local tourism firms

SIC	Description	Santa Monica	Santa Barbara	San Luis Obispo
4725	Tour operators	5	14	4
5812	Restaurants	371	518	372
5813	Alcoholic beverage drinking places	17	30	18
7011	Hotels, motels & tourist courts	36	100	130
7996[1]	Amusement parks	3	1	8
799972	Tourist attractions	0	0	1
	Total tourism firms	**432**[2]	**663**	**533**

SOURCE: Select Phone, 1999 version, InfoUSA Inc., Omaha, Neb.
NOTE: Firms with multiple SICs are categorized according to the first reported SIC. Different branches of the same firm are counted as separate firms.
1. Although firms under SIC 7996 reported their business as meeting an "amusement park" definition, most (e.g., an aquarium, a skateboard park, camping grounds) did not fit the common notion of this setting. Only in Santa Monica did these firms actually work out of a bona fide amusement park, a two-acre boardwalk on the city-owned pier with eleven rides, assorted midway games, and no entrance fee.
2. Table 1.4 may underestimate the relative vitality of Santa Monica's tourism sector in at least two ways. First, since the average Los Angeles County tourist visits 3.6 areas other than the one in which their hotel is located (David L. Gladstone and Susan S. Fainstein, "Tourism in U.S. Global Cities: A Comparison of New York and Los Angeles," *Journal of Urban Affairs* 23 [2001]:26), a popular destination like Santa Monica does not have to provide as many tourist services for its visitors, because it "shares" a tourism sector with the rest of the Los Angeles area. By contrast, Santa Barbara and San Luis Obispo must provide relatively more tourist services, since these localities are relatively distant from other tourist destinations. Second, millions of Los Angeles residents live within driving distance of Santa Monica and can therefore partake of its tourist services and attractions with relative convenience.

Although local hotels and restaurants in the three places cater to (or at least seek to attract) non-local and especially foreign visitors to varying degrees, local and regional markets remain quite important. As "hospitality" (an alternate term for tourism) can suggest, local residents also patronize local restaurants and bars, and local firms and organizations give hotels business by scheduling festivals, conferences, dinners for annual fund-raisers, and the like.[93] During the winter off-season, many out-of-town visitors consist of business travelers referred by local firms and residents, which again makes restaurants and hotels depend on a local market.[94]

ORGANIZATION OF THE WORK

Having introduced the issues, places, and sectors to be examined, the rest of the book follows these across the five components of local business structure. The next two chapters address locational motivations in the new industrial space. In Chapter 2, I examine industrial locations familiar to scholars of these sectors, with an extended discussion of how corporate locations work in Silicon Valley for software and in Santa Monica/the Los Angeles metropolitan area for entertainment and tourism. From these and other centers, industry process and contradiction expand the new industrial space to include a new kind of industrial location, the quality-of-life district, which I describe in Chapter 3, using the examples of Santa Barbara and San Luis Obispo. I conclude Chapter 3 with a review of the locational sentiments that frame the local perspectives of companies and business leaders in the three sectors.

Chapters 4 and 5 address how local business is done in the new industrial space. In Chapter 4, I look at corporate interests and mobilizations around development issues. I discuss software, entertainment, and tourism firms' real estate needs and how these entail particular kinds of systemic relationships to the local development sector. I review case studies of local development projects to see whether executives from the three sectors differ from the traditional urban business community in the kinds of development they advocate and the degree of unity with which they support other firms' local projects. In Chapter 5, I look at how and why firms use local business organizations, capital, and industry-specific associations. I examine whether these local institutions provide opportunities for the traditional urban business community to shape the new corporate elites' urban politics.

Chapters 6 and 7 address activities that are apparently "discretionary" yet motivated by compelling features of local business structure. In Chapter 6, I analyze campaign contributions to local mayoral and city council candidates to see whether firms and industry leaders in the three sectors engage in local politics in the same manner as the traditional urban business community. I identify the kinds of new corporate elites who are especially involved in local politics and examine their motivations. In Chapter 7, I examine the new corporate elites' local philanthropy in traditional charities, environmental organizations, and higher education with an eye to how this reinforces or undermines the traditional civic network. I also review their advocacy of efforts by environmentalists and higher educational institutions and discuss how these business–nonprofit alignments change the nature of urban power in the three Southern California communities.

Chapter 8 addresses the effect of political and economic upheavals since the year 2000 on the three industries and then outlines the larger lessons suggested by the new urban economy. With a different set of land-use practices and a new concern for environmental and urban amenities, companies in software, entertainment, and tourism do not share the interests that customarily unite urban business communities and reinforce the global stratification of places. Although these patterns support an optimism for progressive urban futures, at least in those places privileged by economic restructuring, the new urban economy in fact relies upon more ominous trends in globalization. I conclude with a new theory of corporate power that situates elites' personal attachments to places alongside capital's continuing interest in a world without geographical constraints.

2

Centers of the New Industrial Space

If there is any promising sign for would-be entrepreneurs outside [Silicon Valley], it is that the Internet is reducing the importance of geography in the high-tech world, said Esther Dyson, a Silicon Valley veteran who in recent years has helped entrepreneurs in Eastern Europe find funding and markets for their ideas.

"I just funded a company based in Prague that's doing Java development tools," Dyson said. "I don't think they're under any big disadvantage. You can create a presence over the Internet."

Still, she said, "it can't replace going out to lunch in Silicon Valley. And at some point, you're going to have to travel there."[1]

Many view the "new economy," especially as it intersects with globalization, as creating a world without geographical bonds where capital and information move instantaneously to find their most advantageous location. In some ways, their fears find support in the rhetorics of the software, entertainment, and tourism sectors, as spokespeople claim that their industries provide the world information and leisure without concern for the "parochial" interests of localities. These statements echo the findings of those who have studied what happens when global capital overshadows local families in the ranks of local business communities: Typically, social attachments to the locality decline.

While mobile capital is certainly a real phenomenon, conceiving of it in this way neglects the human setting for corporate power. At a very minimum, corporate elites need a physical base more permanent than traveling conferences, business hotels, and first-class airline seats. However, their choice of particular places in which to do business and exercise corporate power is little understood except in economic terms—for example, to exploit a locale's "competitive advantage"—that subordinate the human face of corporate elites to the corporate rationale. Does this rootless corporate logic explain the reasons why software, entertainment, and tourism firms locate in particular places?

TRADITIONAL CORPORATE GEOGRAPHY

The study of how industry and economies locate in space conventionally juxtaposes what *capital* needs from space (i.e., the fixity and mobility of firms and economic activity) with how *space* manifests and shapes those needs (i.e., the construction and influence of spatial economies and spatial divisions of labor). Regarding the latter, classical location theory posits that natural endowments like deep water ports or transportation junctions give places particular competitive advantages that tilt the distribution of industries across space.[2] The proposition is valid insofar as some industries have physical constraints on their locations; shipbuilders, for example, need access to places with ports, and brick-and-mortar retailers need optimal access to the widest possible consumer markets. However, a focus on places' physical endowments inaccurately puts the locational cart before the horse. To a great extent, social actors like industries and growth coalitions *develop* material endowments in particular places, while their counterparts elsewhere fail to do so effectively; cumulatively, these efforts produce the geography of industries and economies.[3] For a critical geographical analysis, the key empirical issues then revolve around the mechanisms that construct a location's competitive advantages.

To understand the locational motivations of software, entertainment, and tourism firms, it is useful to compare the new industrial space that these sectors form to the prior corporate geography reflecting the bygone era of American industry that scholars describe as Fordist.[4] Before I do, some caveats are in order. First, although I speak in the past tense to facilitate my comparison, the "old" geography produced by traditional locational motivations has not altogether disappeared in the current moment. Rather, the new industrial space has inscribed itself upon the old and transformed locational motivations, particularly in cutting-edge sectors.[5] In fact, many industries continue to operate well within the Fordist logic of traditional corporate geography. Second, corporate concerns for location, the topic of this and the next chapter, are not the sole factors that produce the economic geographies of software, entertainment, and tourism. Other institutions (like states and capital flows) at other geographical scales (like the nation and the region) also have roles that I cannot adequately describe in this book.[6] Finally, industrial geographies are not entirely functional in the capital accumulation process, although the reader must wait for the next chapter to examine these geographical contradictions as I focus here on the assorted and complex locational motivations of software, entertainment, and tourism firms.

HOW INDUSTRY TRADITIONALLY PROFITS FROM PLACE

In any era, the need to be productive, competitive, and profitable drives corporate locational motivations. In the Fordist era, these concerns were characteristically enacted in corporate strategies to command and control the organizational frameworks for labor activity and consumer demand. Profits chiefly materialized through economies of scale, as firms produced goods in "Taylorist" (highly regimented to maintain labor productivity) assembly lines for mass markets. As vertically integrated firms, companies internalized much of the sequence of activities that creates commodities—that is, the "value chain" from research and development to manufacturing to marketing and even to retail. Capital in these firms was predominantly physical, usually in the form of large factories and properties housed in no more than a few corporate plants. Expressed in the corporate bottom line as fixed costs, this capital intensity made profits highly sensitive to operating costs, such as wages and rents, that varied across regions.

This highlights a general principle behind capital's fundamental concern for what political economists sometimes call the global exchange of labor power: Firms have a structural interest in transforming the means of production so that work becomes more deskilled and mechanized, workers provide more generic labor, and capital extracts greater surplus value. Consequently, firms are structurally averse to dependence on particular workforces and methods of production, which would limit labor supply and drive up business costs. With regards to locational motivations, firms avoid dependence on particular *sites* of labor, since wages and other local costs of doing business vary across the landscape of uneven capitalist development, and thus the rootless firm can obtain lower production costs elsewhere. However, whereas this abstract interest portends a placeless world of mobile capital, historically firms have always had to struggle with their countervailing and concrete tendency to localize industrial activity.[7] That is, big business cannot always relocate its activities to other sites, even if it would like to. For one reason, physical plants often cannot be moved easily; these sunk investments make big business locally dependent on these spatially fixed assets.[8]

For another reason, when businesses cluster near one another in particular places—the process of industrial agglomeration—they generate and profit from external economies that boost their individual productivities. For instance, when outside contractors add inputs and outputs to the value chain, these *traded interdependencies* are most profitably exchanged through close proximity, which reduces transaction costs associated with time. Consequently, lead manufacturers often trigger the growth and clustering of smaller suppliers and come to rely on these territorial concentrations of industry. In other cases, industrial agglomerations result from the presence of state activities, not a lead manufacturer.[9] A notable example of this pattern is Southern California's aerospace industry, which emerged largely around military bases and defense contracting sources.[10] Whatever their origins, agglomerations provide increasing returns, such as the speedy provision of inputs and productive rapport between suppliers and contractors, that give local firms a competitive edge via increased productivity. However, they also incur costs like tighter labor markets and rising real estate costs. The bottom-line issue for big business, then, is whether the benefits of agglomeration outweigh the increased costs associated with agglomeration. When higher productivity results, corporations generally consider staying put in agglomerations to be the cost-effective locational decision.[11]

Viewed as simple expenses, wages and rent do not fully explain the locational dilemma that firms face; they must be understood as embedded in particular kinds of social relations of production. First, consider the secondary consequences of industrial agglomeration. Rising productivity and the proliferation of firms absorb greater amounts of labor; industrial agglomerations therefore attract workers who get paid and local service firms that employ other workers. In turn, local incomes and corporate expenditures sustain local economies. Workers and their families make their lives in these places. This process of urbanization, initially incidental as to why firms locate in industrial agglomerations, feeds back to alter the social relations of production for firms and the agglomeration as a whole. In industrial agglomerations, demand for labor often outpaces supply, which gives workers a negotiating advantage in the labor market. Once hired, workers maintain the pace and productivity that sustain agglomeration economies, which gives them at least a potential source of power in the workplace. Thus, agglomeration creates potential problems of *labor control* for the corporation.[12]

Although local dependence on industrial agglomeration compels many major businesses to stay put, history shows many ways that capital transforms the means of production to manage the problems associated with this local dependence. For vertically integrated firms, one strategy has been to internalize the division of labor in order to obtain greater control over operating costs and greater independence from particular locations and workforces. In its infant era, the film industry did just this when studios collectively moved from New York to Hollywood in the 1920s to build soundstages on cheaper real estate and also to escape labor unionization by theater actors' guilds.[13] The Fordist firm also typically hired workers through closed labor markets, such as the corporate hierarchy or exclusive labor unions, that reduced operating costs by effectively training and socializing workers into specialized job skills and norms. Collectively, internal labor markets also divided the working class, giving job security and benefits to many white male workers while relegating most women, minorities, and immigrants to less-than-desirable workplace conditions and employment terms.

Fordism's uneasy capital-labor détente later collapsed to capital's benefit, once transportation and communication advances diminished the frictions of time and space associated with industrial agglomerations.[14] Technological advances have thus made yet another strategy, geographical exit, available to a greater number of firms. Consequently, a new corporate location appeared: the *satellite platform,* in which a branch factory or office is geographically isolated from others and obtains inputs and outputs exclusively from remote suppliers.[15] As illustrated, for example, by manufacturer Motorola's historic role in Phoenix, Arizona, the economy of the satellite platform can be driven by a single company, which gives it political leverage over the local regime.[16] More generally, geographical exit has allowed companies to seek out ever more "pro-business" sites, which started with an industrial exodus from the U.S. Northeast to the South and West. In the conservative political climate of these Sunbelt cities, growth coalitions readily met the political demands (against unions and environmental regulations, for tax incentives) of companies like aerospace and defense contractors that in fact depended too heavily on their sunk investments and skilled workers to reasonably threaten exit.[17] The dispersal of branches by a single multinational corporation illustrates how the modern firm exploits spatial variation in business costs *across* different locations yet simultaneously *within* the corporation's tariff-free internal environment. Globalization connotes only the most extensive terrain (to date!) in which business avoids local dependence on particular methods and resources of production.

THE R&D EXCEPTION

A very different locational motivation appears in the research and development (R&D) branches of multidivisional firms. R&D poses a different set of problems for big business, since its payoff is often long-term, and its process is characteristically uncertain and not easily amenable to corporate planning and Taylorist oversight. It also poses a special problem of labor control because it is performed by scientists and other highly skilled technicians whose labor is hardly generic; indeed, they foreshadow the self-programmable labor that for many observers characterizes the "new economy."[18] Since the ideas and products they develop are highly proprietary and, in the case of defense-related sectors, sometimes vital secrets of national security, big business must obtain loyalty and secrecy from its R&D workers, which renders traditional labor control strategies untenable. As a result, R&D workers usually get special privilege in the corporate hierarchy, receiving pay and workstyles commensurate with the professional labor markets from which they usually come.

Spatially, R&D divisions are often set in pastoral or campus settings, in part keeping with the conventional wisdom that a pleasant environment without urban distractions enhances knowledge workers' creativity. The location of R&D again varies by sector. In more consumer-oriented sectors where R&D emphasizes product development or applied research, corporate headquarters often set up R&D divisions close by, in order to facilitate productive communications.[19] By contrast, where basic research is emphasized,

R&D tends to be located in places distant from corporate headquarters and other production activities. Defense and aerospace corporations and defense-related think tanks, for example, typically located research campuses in pastoral settings at (then relatively unurbanized) locales such as Columbus, Ohio; Boulder, Colorado; and Salt Lake City, Utah, where residential amenities and scientific institutions were paramount.[20] Quite often, R&D and science branches from other firms follow to the same location; the resultant cluster corresponds to another locational type, the *innovation center.* With its early defense-related aerospace and electronics R&D activities, Santa Barbara exemplified such an innovation center.[21] In 1955 Raytheon chose to locate its R&D branch in Santa Barbara over rival sites, according to one official, for its special environmental and cultural amenities. Other defense-related R&D branches followed thereafter, triggering modest growth in small electronics design and light manufacturing firms.[22] Although the Cold War's end brought layoffs, mergers, and reorganizations to the original cohort of R&D branches, some still reside in the Santa Barbara area.

The innovation center thus illustrates the exception to corporate concerns for avoiding dependence on particular labor forces and particular industrial locations that otherwise inform the traditional corporate geography. It resembles the satellite platform insofar as the multidivisional firm isolates R&D branches away from industrial agglomerations. However, because big business cannot transform R&D work into generic labor, the tone of labor control in the innovation center differs dramatically. Companies grant science workers unprecedented autonomy over their work process and significant perks in their residential quality of life that acknowledge their self-programming capacity. In return, science workers concede loyalty and secrecy to the firm, rarely sharing ideas and switching jobs across other R&D branches that might cluster in the innovation center. Thus, whereas the satellite platform typically illustrates capital's advantage in the struggle for labor control, R&D location reflects capital's concession.

AMENITY INFRASTRUCTURES

Locational motivations in tourism deserve their own discussion because of the special nature of this industry, its actors, and their relations to place. Tourism is essentially a service sector, yet there is a difference between eating a fine meal in a tourist destination and in one's hometown. That difference is a symbolic component, the sign value of a place, that is independent of and external to the use value of the services that tourism firms sell visitors.[23] Furthermore, tourism is typically a labor-intensive business, yet its local viability requires prior investments in capital-intensive transportation (from airports and highways to parking lots) and amenity infrastructure (theme parks, sports stadia, urban entertainment districts, convention centers, etc.).[24] Sometimes tourism amenities occasionally appear due to natural providence, historical accident, or some other form of "place luck," as the beaches of Southern California or the cultural attractions of Paris illustrate.[25] However, even a "natural" destination must be socially produced through the concerted actions of social actors in urban political economies.[26] Even with a deep-pocketed multinational corporation or developer, few firms can afford to develop an amenity infrastructure alone, or even in concert with other local tourism firms. For these reasons, the creation of large-scale destinations and amenities is usually facilitated by public-private partnerships with local government and business, a topic which is beyond the scope of this book.[27]

Once amenity infrastructures are in place, tourism firms are ready to move in and serve visitors. They can represent another corporate division of the amenity developer (as with the Disney Corporation or Club Med), but usually they are separate and often local firms specializing in individual tourism services: hotels, restaurants, tour operators, and so on. Their work consists largely of generic labor, and most tourism workers hold manual service jobs as front desk operators, hotel maids, janitors, waiters, or kitchen help. Labor costs predominate in corporate bottom lines.[28] Consequently, like big business, tourism firms have a structural aversion to depending on particular skills, workforces, or settings that might trap them into higher operating costs. Unlike big business, however, tourism firms cannot usually move to more competitive sites because they depend on the amenity infrastructures that are fixed in place; locating in a more "pro-business" city or neighborhood just outside the tourist destination may not suffice to attract customers in sizeable numbers.

Because of its differences from conventional big business and the distinct nature of the localized assets that they exploit, the tourism industry does not easily fit the locational patterns of the traditional corporate geography described earlier. Still, the geography of the tourism industry—its local successes, failures, and absences—reveals a similar rootlessness of capital. Tourism gives an "industrial" face to the entrepreneurial localities whose economic fates in the global hierarchy of places are ultimately determined non-locally. In this case, however, places compete to attract the capital of visitors, not big business. Otherwise, tourism firms make profit in very conventional ways, by economizing on material cost factors like rent and wages. Furthermore, local dependence on amenity infrastructure may preclude tourism firms from exiting the locality, but it still leaves open spatial jockeying *within* the locality, as well as a variety of more conventional political options, as Chapter 4 discusses. In these ways, tourism is perhaps the most conventional of the new urban economy sectors.

THE NEW INDUSTRIAL SPACE

Although scholars debate the nature and extensiveness of transformations to the traditional corporate geography, they generally concur that a new set of spatial dynamics has emerged to drive competition in capitalism's leading-edge sectors and activities. These changes entail a strategic shift toward *flexibility* in which corporations abandon command-and-control strategies and embrace the uncertainties associated with incessant technical and aesthetic innovation, the economies of small-batch production, and the breakdown of mass markets into both narrow demographic niches and international markets.[29] Corporate shifts toward flexibility most likely began after 1948 anti-trust legislation ordered U.S. film and television studios to divest themselves of their theater and media distribution outlets.[30] They accelerated in the 1960s and 70s, when Fortune 500 firms responded to symptoms of economic malaise (declining productivity and profitability, the OPEC oil embargo, 1970s inflation, etc.) by relocating production to low-cost labor sites, first in the developed world, and later in Third World countries.[31] By the end of the Cold War, signs of changes in corporate organization became incontrovertible, as the torch of high-tech employment passed from defense-dependent technology sectors to computer and software sectors and, geographically, from Southern California's aerospace industry and the defense contractors of Massachusetts' Route 128 to Silicon Valley.[32]

In the contemporary economy, competitive pressures compel firms to reevaluate the various "value-added" activities and human skills by which they produce commodities and services. Using flexible strategies, firms re-organize their division of labor, retaining core competencies that cannot be easily routinized, and outsourcing lower value-added activities where productivity or profitability suffers. In many cases, these disintegrated activities move to sites of lower-cost labor, either in overseas satellite platforms or, as in the case of designer fashion industries, to First World sweatshops of immigrant labor. This is consistent both with the thrust of traditional corporate geography (to make production amenable to generic labor performed in non-specific sites) and the erosion of place difference to a global currency of competitiveness. However, the conventional struggle between capital and labor does not fully explain this process, since now, even the work of capitalists—that is, executive and managerial services—can be routinized and outsourced. The new industrial space radically changes how firms work with one another and even organize their form in a particular location; as the integrated firm managed by corporate elites no longer controls long-range strategy, the function of space shifts from a location for firms to a medium for disintegrated production and multicephalous coordination. Consequently, geographical location plays new roles in setting the context for firms' business and political interests in places, a point that I develop through the next chapter.

INDUSTRIAL DISTRICTS AND REGIONS

Flexible production systems have revived the centrality of industrial agglomerations, especially the type known as the *industrial district*. This type, in fact, preceded Fordism; its current form, therefore, warrants distinction from its classical predecessor. Associated with many nineteenth-century industries, like cotton textiles in Lancashire and silk in Lyon, the classic industrial district typically housed a self-contained sector. Described by the classical economist Alfred Marshall, the classic industrial district clusters firms, usually small and locally owned, whose input-output linkages are locally contained.[33] In addition to the external economies that these traded interdependencies achieve, the absence of a single lead company gives competitive value to the flow of workers and expertise across firms. This and other *untraded* interdependencies create external economies that seem to hang "in the air" of the classic industrial districts. Because of their small economies of scale and comparative failure to develop the means of production, early industrial districts became vulnerable to competition by Fordist firms' mass production techniques. Decades later, the strengths of the Fordist firm in turn became a liability, as production networks have again reorganized most profitably into localized agglomerations of small to medium firms.

The contemporary or flexible industrial district differs from its Marshallian predecessor and more generic industrial agglomerations in at least three ways. First, the flexible district encourages a more cooperative ethos, as joint ventures between firms and with non-economic institutions (like trade associations, research institutions, or political entities) govern local industrial organization in order to spread risk, stabilize markets, and share innovations.[34] Second, new efficiencies are achieved in untraded interdependencies, such as highly skilled labor markets, the emergence of specialty services (e.g., venture capital, marketing), and shared conventions for developing, communicating, and interpreting knowledge.[35] Third, these first two aspects combine with the imperative for technological innovation that pervades industries like high technology and entertainment to generate a whole new level of industrial dynamism. As the exchange of expertise and workers fuels innovation in industrial processes and products, flexible districts transform their industries in path-dependent and utterly *local* ways, thereby locking competitive advantage into specific places.[36] They spatially embody the cutting edge of their industries in ways that cannot be recreated wholesale elsewhere.

To be sure, individual firms in these industries can and do appear outside of flexible districts. Those that provide low-cost sites for routine production or sell relatively unspecialized goods and services can compete on price from a variety of locations. Others can pursue the industry cutting edge in or out of the flexible district, competing on value by taking advantage of company-specific expertise or clienteles. When planning horizons grow longer (as, for instance, government contracting allows), effective competition on value becomes more viable further away from established industry centers. More generally, advances in transportation and communication technologies, like the digitization of services into forms that can be transmitted across phone lines, continuously reduce the frictions of time and space and make geographical proximity to input and output providers increasingly unnecessary for any single activity.[37] What the flexible district offers that few other locations can, however, is simultaneous external economies in a variety of activities, which becomes increasingly valuable when firms eschew long-term planning or cannot predict what products the market will demand. Thus, for most companies on the "bleeding edge" of innovative industries, it still pays to locate in the flexible district.

Perhaps the exemplary flexible district is Northern California's Silicon Valley, arguably the birthplace of microelectronics technologies like the electronic transistor and the personal computer. The local number of computer, software, and other technology firms is unparalleled; the region is headquarters to most of the dominant firms in these sectors, and firms headquartered elsewhere (e.g., Microsoft, Dell) maintain active branch plants there. The division of labor is astonishingly deep, with particular strength in specialized business services (like venture capitalists, law firms, accountants, real estate firms, and executive headhunters) and new ideas and workers emerging out of the area's research universities and institutes. Silicon Valley's vitality is all the more remarkable for surviving the end of Cold War–era defense contracts and the flight of its namesake industry, semiconductor manufacturing, to Asia. The latter is especially telling of how the region has maintained its competitive edge. As semiconductor manufacturing became sufficiently routine for production costs to outweigh the benefits of location in the region, it and other physical manufacturing almost totally disappeared from the Valley. So, too, did the labor conflicts associated with the sizable, significantly female, and undocumented industrial workers these activities employed—an intended goal, to many observers' thinking.[38] Silicon Valley now essentially specializes in the production of technological innovations more than actual goods and services, since the latter can usually be produced more profitably elsewhere once their innovative component has been routinized.[39] This is reflected in Silicon Valley's remaining primary labor force, which has grown more homogenously well educated, skilled, and well paid.

Silicon Valley's geographical links to other industrial locations now include mostly satellite platforms and developing world sites for manufacturing and assembly, as well as smaller flexible districts specializing in different value-added activities: Seattle (an outgrowth of Microsoft's demand for software suppliers and services), San Francisco's "Multimedia Gulch," the financial and media service niches of New York's "Silicon Alley," the Internet–telecommunications cluster of Northern Virginia, the wireless technology clusters of Helsinki and San Diego, and so on. In this book, the "Digital Coast" of Southern California merits special mention for specializing in the production of entertainment and creative content for embedding in digital media. Santa Monica is the Digital Coast's geographical center, where the concentration of software, entertainment, and new media firms creates a pull on other firms seeking to access the networks of this growing niche. For instance, IBM recently located some three hundred employees doing "e-business" R&D into a local four-story building:

> Why base this somewhat experimental operation in Santa Monica? [An IBM executive] says the main reason is the environment that exists in the booming beach town with all of its production studios and artists contributing to a creative community, along with the numerous new media companies that have recently moved in—a trend that shows no sign of abating.[40]

Southern California hosts another exemplary flexible district in a different industry: Hollywood, where entertainment content is produced in the form of films, television programs, and recorded music. At its highest levels of value-added activity, Hollywood is a hiring hall of white-collar offices where corporate heads, talent agents, independent producers, and other executives coordinate production, as well as an industrial environs for specialized services and production facilities for the entertainment industry. Hollywood's geography also illustrates how the industrial district grows into an *industrial region,* as different industrial niches move out to different neighborhoods to create an expansive spatial division of labor. Film services tend to cluster in the east-west corridor between Santa Monica and Hollywood proper; film studios, animators, multimedia firms, and music labels cluster in the north-south corridor between Hollywood proper and the San Fernando Valley, and smaller production and postproduction units (many sustained by the pornographic video industry) cluster in the San Fernando Valley.[41]

ECOLOGIES OF FLEXIBLE RECYCLING

It is hard to exaggerate how dramatically the competitive pressures and localizing tendencies associated with flexibility have transformed the quest for profitability among firms at the cutting edges of capitalism, and not simply because agglomeration brings high costs. The medium of industrial space, not corporate bureaucracy, now enables new levels of productivity and sustains growth in even mature sectors.[42] This insight has become so axiomatic that many Silicon Valley firms resign themselves to organizational impermanence amidst a competitive local ecology of "flexible recycling."[43] As production revolves around fluid constellations of human capital, firms view competitive advantage less as material assets to be owned and amortized and more as organizational competencies that are transient within, or even incidental to, the firm. For instance, a small software firm may create a successful product, license or sell it to a larger company through a merger agreement, then retain and reconstitute its original employees in a new firm that designs a new product. Such strategic lateral moves let the business project withstand the vicissitudes of the companies with which it is associated.[44]

Although a small core of venture capitalists and large firms dominates in financing, distribution, marketing, and other essential activities in the commercialization of a product, the highest "value-added" stages of industrial production are often performed by small and impermanent companies that achieve scale through joint ventures, mergers, or other means besides internal growth. With the capacity for "virtual company" management by venture capitalists, lawyers, and other flexible district specialists, firms can flexibly abandon the conventional bureaucratic concern for organizational survival.[45]

In Hollywood, ad hoc organizations have usurped the role that film studios and television networks once filled to coordinate actual film and TV production. Motion pictures and television shows, for example, are initially developed by private production companies that are essentially vehicles for producers, directors, writers, actors, and other talent with sufficient industry status and influence to "make deals." These production companies initiate the search for financing and distribution, pitching their projects to studios or networks that then assume control of production (e.g., subcontracting to craft workers, legal firms, and talent agencies) to varying degrees.[46] Sealing their relationships, the talent, studios, and companies involved in any film project usually form a limited liability company for the duration of production.

As dynamism and specialization transform innovative industries, the processes for each value-added activity tend to relocate to new places where the new balance of productivity and costs is optimal. Thus, the same competitive imperative that agglomerates innovative and high-value activities also disperses routine and low-value activities. Goods and services are now produced in *global commodity chains*, spatially dispersed production networks that link several firms in diverse sectors across different places. Flexible districts concentrate the most innovative activities; activities of a cross-industry nature (like legal services) often cluster in their own industry agglomerations; more routine activities disperse to satellite platforms of less specialized labor. Thus, a software design firm might house its headquarters/R&D functions in Silicon Valley, obtain legal and accounting services in New York, subcontract for routine coding in Ireland, and have the software imprinted on CD-ROMs in an East Asia platform.

In the case of entertainment, Hollywood is no longer a necessary location for actual filming. Even though the largest entertainment conglomerates maintain soundstages for motion picture and television filming in the area, such as Disney, NBC, and Warner Brothers in Burbank, and Vivendi Universal in Universal City, these large facilities are becoming artifacts of a bygone era. Thanks to technological advances in on-location shooting and, some industry leaders contend, Los Angeles's high costs and red tape, filming has increased in other U.S. sites (Florida, North Carolina), Canada, New Zealand, and other foreign locales.[47] In 1998 alone, the U.S. lost an estimated $2.8 billion and 23,500 entertainment jobs in film and television production.[48] So, too, music for commercial release can be recorded in commercial and (increasingly) home studios around the world, not just in music industry centers like Los Angeles or New York City, although the most successful recording studios are still found there.[49]

HOW LABOR SUSTAINS THE NEW INDUSTRIAL SPACE

In addition to firms and places, a third actor organizes the new industrial space: *workers* and, more specifically, their collective organization in labor markets. Be it the old economy or new, wages still make up the largest cost in corporate bottom lines, and capital and workers still struggle for advantage when negotiating income and benefits, the pace and kind of work, and other terms of labor. Outside of the workplace, labor markets are the most important setting where this antagonistic negotiation unfolds. They replenish the workforce, set the basis for employment and remuneration, and shape the level of labor control that firms can exercise over workers. Since Fordism's decline, the competitive pressures of flexibility have diffused the conditions of secondary labor markets up the occupational hierarchy to even managers and executives.[50] Although the advantages in cost containment and labor control are obvious, companies have nevertheless had to adapt to this decline of workforce stability.[51] Automation and routinization of the labor process offer one solution, since getting productivity out of generic labor requires less firm-specific skills and attitudes. Moving production to satellite platforms in industrial peripheries is a second solution often used in tandem with the first; where labor markets hold vast reserve armies of labor, as in developing nations, firms get the benefits of a stable Fordist workforce without the costs of high wages and other labor market concessions. Still, flexible competition entails a great degree of technically sophisticated and innovative work that requires self-programmable labor.

DEMANDS FOR EXPERT LABOR

Software and entertainment labor markets illustrate the central roles for expert self-programmable labor that can inject value-added inputs of technical expertise or aesthetic creativity into a product. The centrality of these self-programmable workers in software and entertainment production makes these sectors talent-intensive (which is not to be confused with their labor-intensity, since the ratio of capital to labor costs is skewed toward the former in many of these firms). Software is characterized by two kinds of talent, the first and most familiar being scientific-technical expertise. The great bulk of workers in Silicon Valley and other high-tech districts use software programming, microelectronic engineering, or other forms of scientific-technical expertise in the design of software, computer architecture, and Internet infrastructure services. However, in contrast to the R&D branches of old, the occupational settings in which scientific-technical talent currently exercises its expertise are no longer entirely rarified professional realms. Indeed, a great need for software coding and debugging has turned many highly educated workers into the high-tech equivalent of assembly line workers. Accordingly, firms tend to outsource these "routine" activities to lower-cost expert labor elsewhere (often overseas to places like Bangalore, India), and leave the more innovative activities for self-programmable labor in Silicon Valley and other industry centers.[52]

A second and more recent form of talent in software is entrepreneurial expertise. After the Cold War, the demand for technological research and development moved out of the long-term horizons of defense contractors and moved into the more uncertain, short-term realm of the market. As large corporations broke up and spun off into disintegrated production networks, their R&D functions and entrepreneurial risk have been increasingly assumed by small firms, as well as non-economic entities like research universities.[53] Perhaps best illustrating the exuberance and chaos of high technology's new entrepreneurialism is the late 1990s proliferation of "dot-com" firms that sold Internet-based goods and services in the hope of satisfying untapped consumer demand, only to meet widespread failure in consumer and investor markets. Software districts tend to concentrate entrepreneurs, where, in many cases, they are newly minted MBAs or seasoned executives from other industries. The dynamism and newness of the software sector give a special texture to entrepreneurial talent in Silicon Valley; with little corporate tradition and a libertarian ethos of market-determined meritocracy, the success of entrepreneurs is measured less by traditional corporate status and more by pure commercial success.[54]

Entertainment privileges workers who wield at least one of three kinds of expert knowledge. First, deal-making expertise—the authority to assemble financial and organizational resources, access to the industry's "movers and shakers," and the know-how to put together projects—is concentrated at the highest industry levels. More than just the management of actual production logistics, deal-making involves the project-based arrangement of financing, distribution, and exhibition.[55] By monopolizing and synergizing their expertise, studio and record label executives, producers, talent agents, managers, and elite lawyers control and coordinate knowledge- and commodity-production at all levels below.[56]

Second, the aesthetic creativity of screenwriters, directors, talent, musicians, animators, and other content producers drives the continuous production of content in all its forms: films, television programs, recorded albums, and other consumer commodities.[57] Although industry insiders and critics may lament the debasement of "real" creativity in entertainment, aesthetic production still gives entertainment commodities their distinguishing character. Aesthetic workers gain labor market status based on the commercial success of their work and through their access to deal-makers. Whereas would-be and up-and-coming creators and talent scramble through the Hollywood hierarchy, their higher-status counterparts are rewarded considerably, not only in their pay, but also in their ascendance to the realm of deal-makers.[58]

Third, and overlapping somewhat with aesthetic talent, is a growing scientific-technical component, thanks to the prominence of special effects, digital animation, computerized editing systems, and other technical innovations in motion picture and television production.[59] Of entertainment's three talents, scientific-technical expertise most resembles the labor markets of software and "new media"; in some fields, entertainment competes with these industries for the same workers. Film and TV craft workers like cinematographers and editors wield technical knowledge that is somewhat less high-tech, but no less rarified; in the music industry, recording engineers and producers work in a comparable technology-heavy niche. These technical workers derive their demand more through their collective restriction of the labor pool (through unionization and apprenticeship) than a shortage of skilled labor, but the result is the same: labor market advantage in the form of high income and employment security.[60]

ENABLING PRODUCTIVITY

As with other untraded interdependencies, talent not only concentrates in the flexible district, it also *inheres* to the district—or, more specifically, local labor markets of skilled workers.[61] In the software industry, the high demand for technical and entrepreneurial talent has led (at least before the 2000 dot-com crash) to a boom in specialized "headhunters" (recruiting firms), and human resources departments have assumed strategic importance in most medium-to-large firms.[62] Conversely, talent shortages threaten the competitive productivity of the flexible district. In 2000, the mere possibility of an actors' strike brought many entertainment projects to a halt before they ever began, lest even more unacceptable costs be incurred once projects got underway. Likewise, in the late 1990s, a high-tech talent shortage led Silicon Valley firms and political action committees to lobby the U.S. Congress to increase immigration of skilled foreign workers.[63] The dot-com crash of 2000 has since loosened the labor market, but with mixed results: talented labor is more plentiful and less costly, but many workers now avoid the job insecurities associated with the Internet economy and especially its small firms.[64] Especially for start-up firms, then, the primary question an entrepreneur most likely faces is "who are the immediate people you can grab who are really interested in this with the money you've got?" as a software CEO told me.

This is not just an issue of which company to work for, but where to look for work. To understand how workers' locational motivations sustain the competitiveness of flexible districts, consider a highly skilled software programmer as she looks for employment. Whether she hails from across town or overseas, she faces a critical decision: Is her first priority to be paid the top market wages for her skills? If so, the labor market compels her to work in an industry center like Silicon Valley, the site of the highest wages for the industry and much of the broader economy as well.[65] As thousands of skilled workers repeat her decision, the immigration of talent to the flexible district advances the fortunes for the three kinds of economic actors. First, the firm can find the best workers money can buy with minimal search costs. Second, the region further develops the specialized labor pools that reinforce its indispensability in the global sector. Third, the worker reduces the risk in her career path; with a critical mass of employers, Silicon Valley offers her a "safety net" should her first job not pan out as expected. As a San Luis Obispo CEO observed, "If you're insecure, it's difficult to think of leaving an area like Silicon Valley. People up there are used to being able to go right down the road and find another job in five minutes if something happens to their company."

The flexible district's pull on talent illustrates a crucial aspect of the new industrial space. When corporate impermanence is the rule of the day, as in Silicon Valley's flexible recycling or Hollywood's characteristic one-off project, talented workers anchor the intellectual assets of an entire sector by bringing their expertise from one employer to another.[66] At the same time, the clustering of highly skilled workers makes firms all the more dependent on a particular workforce and a particular region, and compels them to pay higher wages and rents. This is precisely the bottom-line dilemma that, in other contexts, motivates companies to reorganize their activities and outsource their lower value-added activities in order to lower costs. Yet when it comes to competing in the most innovative and highest value-added activities, most firms accept the costs of flexible district location in order to avail themselves of the externalized economies, specialized division of labor, and cutting-edge innovations that are only available there.

The persistence of proprietary information and anti-union sentiments in Silicon Valley, Hollywood, and other centers of the new industrial space suggests that firms still seek to control the self-programmable capacity of human talent. However, they do so only at the risk of harming this critical labor force's productivity. As Castells has observed, "Technical labor in these industries, because of their unique capacity for symbol processing, will require special methods of generation and reproduction."[67] Most industry insiders and some scholars contend that the presence of interesting and challenging work (which also implies opportunities for career and financial advancement) offers its own reward and deters talent turnover in Silicon Valley firms.[68] Still, given talent's advantage in the labor market, attempts to control labor through intrusive oversight or stifling workplace cultures bring potentially serious costs to firms: Skilled workers may lose morale or quit, bringing production within the firm to a halt. The local clustering of potential employers only makes this scenario more likely.

Therefore, to stabilize their workforce in a tight labor market, firms in the flexible district have an interest in obtaining an edge in attracting workers and securing morale. In addition to offering competitive salaries, stock options, and other income benefits, high-tech firms have increasingly refashioned the workplace to meet the lifestyle preferences of the labor markets; hence the now-clichéd "hip" environment characteristic of the dot-com firm, with its informal dress code, cutting-edge architecture, game rooms, and so on. This strategy has assumed notoriously exuberant forms (e.g., flashy company parties in exclusive nightclubs) in the urban environs of San Francisco's Multimedia Gulch and New York City's Silicon Alley:

> Today, the twenty-something execs of Silicon Alley are rewriting the book on office culture, and for good reason. Their employees are in such high demand that they don't have to—and wouldn't—put up with tyrannical working environments. (And let's face it, something has got to keep them from noticing that they're trading life for work, or at least keep them from complaining about it.)[69]

As this quote suggests, workplace amenities also facilitate labor control (for example, by compensating employees for longer work hours) and reflect the corporate preference in many sectors for younger hires with less experience of job security. Nevertheless, they represent unprecedented concessions of corporate hierarchy and "professional ethos" to a tight labor market.

THE COMPANY TOWN

In the flexible district, business does not stop at the firm door, but pervades the restaurants, bars, parties, fitness centers, and other places where industry workers gather. This makes possible another locational asset, the creative milieu.[70] Here, workers share their workplace ideas and problems, learn of and evaluate other firms and competing products, and socialize one another into the norms and attitudes that permeate the flexible district, in what one Silicon Valley observer breathlessly calls "the 24/7 professional-merging-with-personal life of the Valley."[71] Hollywood's creative milieu illustrates how firms and workers combine working and living in specific local settings and activities, or what insiders call the "company town."[72] A motion picture director told me, "There is a thing [in Hollywood] about how you bump into people at restaurants, you go to parties—in that sense, [it is] a social part" of the entertainment industry. A talent agent described how extensive and extra-corporate networking is in her field:

> My job is seven days a week, and there is no division between the social and business. Everything, it's all combined. Yes, there is a lot of socializing—I would say about five out of seven nights a week during the busiest part of any given season, and a fair amount during the weekends, although I try to limit that.

Barbed portrayals in movies like *The Player* and *L.A. Stories* capture the company town's environs more or less correctly: restaurants, cafes, and exclusive beach clubs in affluent communities on the Westside; film premieres at historic Hollywood theaters; fund-raising events in posh ballrooms; cocktail parties at large houses (ideally with a commanding urban or ocean view); and after-hours barhopping in West Hollywood for the younger set.[73] Music industry elites are more likely to mingle with music fans in the city's many clubs along the "Sunset Strip" of Hollywood proper, where artists are showcased on stage and in VIP rooms.[74] Executives and talent involved in the growing motion picture soundtrack industry might occupy both film and music settings. Although most of these settings are open to anyone willing to pay for admission, a meal, or a drink, insiders patronize a specific ecology of restaurants, bars, hotels and clubs that keeps the industry culturally insulated from other Angelenos. A music industry executive observed, "There are certain restaurants that I'll take my clients to, and it's usually because they're better restaurants, although a local taco stand might be just as good [as], if not better, than some of the chi-chi restaurants." This cultural insularity may reflect a norm specific to entertainment, where "there's kind of a standard you're expected to meet" in choosing settings for business that contrast with the prosaic bars and strip mall eateries favored by Silicon Valley workers for socializing.

In both entertainment and software, informal networking pervades the creative milieu. Whereas Fordist firms with closed corporate cultures, including many in technology sectors, often seek to prevent this informal networking, most firms in the flexible district encourage it in order to facilitate the flow and innovative recombinations of expert knowledges.[75] "The high-tech industry is notorious for turnover; it's almost cultural," a San Luis Obispo CEO observed. "That process, however, is what makes this industry tick." In Hollywood, informal networking centers less on brainstorming the latest innovations, as it does in Silicon Valley, than on entering and protecting relationships behind the latest entertainment projects. Networking is not a casual affair in entertainment, despite its apparent ubiquity and informality. As the record of legal battles over stolen screenplay ideas and broken verbal contracts suggests, getting access to the right information and individuals is fraught with high stakes. A talent agent explained:

> There are a million different ways to say "yes," and a million different ways to say "no." Deals are undergoing negotiation for months or sometimes years at a time, but you don't have the sort of situation where, when one company is acquiring another company, there is a sort of due diligence that has to be done, in terms of, say, the Securities [and] Exchange Commission. There is no governing board; there's no one who looks over our shoulder, so to speak, in terms of how agents transact business. There's enormous conflict of interest, because things have become so centralized that you have both attorneys and

agents representing parties on one side of the situation, and their associates are representing parties on the other side.

As in Silicon Valley, networking in the company town simultaneously advances workers' interests by permitting the exchange of job opportunity information.[76] At the bottom of industry hierarchies, up-and-comers live "on call," going to auditions and waiting for news from their agents or unions. Their in-demand counterparts learn of new projects more casually. A line producer described this process:

> [In other industries,] most people look for a job every five to seven years. In this business, it can be [ten] to [twenty] times a year. The way the system works is through extreme networking. And it's built in that everyone is using each other. You develop a finely honed survival skill. So the last week on a film, most conversations are: "So, what are you doing next? Will you mention me to him?" It's difficult in the beginning to, but you learn.[77]

Within the company town, most entertainment workers do not live in the fabled Hollywood Hills, Beverly Hills, or Malibu, but rather in less exclusive areas differentiated by lifestyle. Younger workers with a taste for the bohemian lifestyle have helped gentrify older neighborhoods around Hollywood proper, such as Los Feliz and Silverlake; older actors with families may choose "suburban" communities like Brentwood or Sherman Oaks; West Hollywood remains a popular residence for gay and lesbian workers. As a residential area, Santa Monica seems to attract younger, mid-level executives with children seeking two- or three-bedroom houses with a garage and proximity to progressive private schools, and good public schools, and sophisticated stores and services. One Santa Monica neighborhood popular with entertainment workers is Sunset Park, which was developed in the 1920s to house employees of the (since departed) Hughes and McDonnell Douglas aircraft companies:

> Lisa Gaynor moved to Sunset Park ten years ago with her husband, Kerry, so that their three children could attend the schools.
> "Most of the teachers here get their teaching credential[s] at UCLA, which has quite a famous teaching program," Gaynor said. "The Santa Monica school district gets to hire the cream of the crop of teachers who graduate from UCLA."
> The Gaynors paid $310,000 for their fifteen-hundred-square-foot home. The first thing that struck Gaynor about Sunset Park when the couple moved into the neighborhood was that a number of the dads work at home.
> "They work in entertainment, or are a therapist like my husband, or do some sort of entrepreneurial thing," Gaynor said. "So many of the dads are around."[78]

Altogether, these company town neighborhoods offer a complete and some-what hermetic setting for work and life. One record company executive told me she can work, live, and take her child to school all within the Santa Monica city limits. Another insider revealed that actor Arnold Schwarzenegger lives in neighboring Pacific Palisades, has an office and restaurant on Santa Monica's Main Street, and even "goes to his kids' t-ball games" in Santa Monica. As entertainment workers regularly run into others at the farmer's market, PTA meetings, or the cinema, their daily rounds fuse with neighborhood ambiance in their own minds as well as the public's. Hence, Santa Monica and other chosen communities become synonymous with the company town.

ELITE WORKERS

In talent-intensive sectors, corporate power accrues to the workers with potentially commercial ideas, a resource that few firms can keep in executive hands. Consequently, the entrepreneurial energies of many software and entertainment workers have blurred the occupational and status distinctions that traditionally separate them from their corporate superiors. For instance, a non-executive software designer can work at one firm, become a director on a second firm's executive board, consult for a third, and then leave the first to start a fourth firm. Likewise, an actor who traditionally answers to the producers, directors, and studio heads who manage movie production can create his own independent production company and assert creative and managerial control over future projects. Reinforced by the impermanent forms that flexible firms adopt, this fluidity of human talent helps make the business project, not the firm, the fundamental organizational form in software and entertainment.

These examples also illustrate how talent has become less uniformly subordinated to corporate executives. Notably, in the start-up software firm or independent film, the manager-worker distinction often collapses into a small cadre of employees sharing both sets of duties. Consider also the example of a corporate software designer deciding whether to go it alone with a new product idea that she has developed. If her current employer can satisfy her demands for project autonomy and expected rewards, she channels her entrepreneurial energies within the firm, in effect receiving a promotion within an internal labor market. If she does not receive a positive reception, then she quits the firm and redirects her entrepreneurial energies toward starting her own company. If any software or entertainment worker with a commercial idea is potentially her own boss, her entrepreneurial energies manifest opportunities for free agency coordinated by industry labor markets.

This suggests that, in flexible sectors, a central dimension of the capital relation—i.e., control of the means of production, in this case toward a specific product—has spread through the upper tiers of industry labor markets. That is, the organizational power to manage production has diffused out of the control of firm executives and financiers to include other *elite workers,* like would-be entrepreneurs, celebrity talent, project-based free-lance workers, and others down the labor market hierarchy with potentially commercial ideas. In a context of flexible production, elite workers' capacity for commercially tested self-programmable labor gives them a degree of control over entertainment and software production. They derive this power by exercising their entrepreneurial energies or negotiating with employers in the labor market, which results in high salaries, special entitlements to product royalties and licensing income, and/or autonomy over work. Labor shortages are not an essential condition, although they no doubt enhance elite workers' advantage in the labor market.

Crucially, elite workers do not seem to regard their power as corporate beneficence or an opportunity for adversarially "getting over" any particular employer, in contrast to what many studies of highly bureaucratized workplaces in "old economy" sectors would suggest. In sectors like software and entertainment where creativity and experience are valorized, elite workers instead tend to adopt an individualized, "post-material" perspective toward their careers.[79] For example, many use their time between jobs for personal "recharging" and self-examination. Before one San Luis Obispo CEO assumed leadership at his current company, he "retired" for eight months: "I did nothing but travel and have a good time, and drive my wife crazy." According to cultural observer David Brooks, such an outlook reflects the "Bobo" (or bourgeois bohemian) ethos endemic to talent-intensive industries:

> Workers in this spiritualized world of Bobo capitalism are not the heroes of toil. They are creators. They noodle around and experiment and dream. They seek to explore and then surpass the full limits of their capacities. And if a company begins to bore or stifle them, they're gone. It is the ultimate sign of privilege— to be able to hit the road in search of new meaning whenever that little moth of tedium flies in the door. Self-cultivation is the imperative. With the emphasis on the self.[80]

Thus, the emergence of elite workers in software and entertainment labor markets recasts an important debate about worker autonomy in post-Fordist sectors. Many companies embrace the language of worker empowerment and adopt worker feedback, "quality circles," and other non-Taylorist techniques of workplace organization to improve firm productivity and worker morale.[81] When these are used within conventional corporate hierarchy and managerial planning, it can reasonably be argued that "worker empowerment" merely hides a traditional corporate interest in labor control.[82] However, the emergence of elite workers suggests that firms have sacrificed a real level of labor control for the more-than-compensatory benefits of flexible agglomeration. Indeed, flexible recycling and the devolution of corporate entities suggest that there is hardly a conventional firm to control labor anymore. This does not mean that the issue of labor control disappears in the flexible district, only that it loses its characteristic prevalence *within the workplace.*

TRADITIONAL COSTS OF LABOR

Still, in satellite platforms and other conventionally "pro-business" locations for software and entertainment production, exercising labor control within the workplace remains a key motivation for corporate location. Indeed, entire sectors of the "new economy" remain largely untouched by the industrial factors that give rise to elite workers. Tourism is one such sector. Although its work is largely performed by generic labor, the industry's local dependence on amenity infrastructures prevents it from exercising labor control through geographical exit. In Southern California, firms compensate by hiring the bulk of their workers from peripheral labor markets— usually Latino and Asian workers, especially for behind-the-scenes work.[83] Tourism depends on global flows of unskilled and often undocumented labor, and industry associations regularly lobby national legislators (albeit with less visibility than their high-tech counterparts) to sustain these flows amidst pressures to limit immigration.[84] However, *individual* firms do not search for workers globally. Instead, they impose the "opportunity cost" of the job search onto workers and industry trade associations and only scan local labor markets to fill low-skilled jobs.

Tourism firms also require managerial talent who come from one of three labor pools. In the first and most rarified, celebrity chefs, hoteliers, and entrepreneurs lend their name, experience, and/or prestige to their businesses. This group thus resembles elite workers in software and entertainment, although their participation is by no means an essential component in the tourism industry. Second, corporate and/or large hotels and restaurants may fill the top two or three managerial slots from labor pools that are international in scale. Although the industry occasionally shows some concern over the shortage of managerial hotel talent, these shortages do not occur in a flexible industrial environment that gives rise to elite workers analogous to software and entertainment. Third, all other hotel and restaurant managers tend to come from local labor markets; entrepreneurial firms are often started and managed by local businesspeople.

The economics of tourism largely derive from the profitability and amortization of physical capital, not the innovative recombinations of human talent. Thus, the provision of tourism services remains bound to the inflexible firm, not the impermanent business project. Locational motivations in tourism, then, make sense only in terms of corporate rationale, not workers as well. Tourism firms select a place first and foremost on "location, location, location"; after that, their choice hinges on a favorable balance of material cost-factors. These two factors can occasionally be at odds when a place has an "anti-business" climate that might squeeze profits. For example,

Santa Monica and many other Southern California municipalities ban cigarette smoking in indoor public settings like restaurants and bars; tourism firms in these places often fear losing customers to neighboring municipalities without such restrictions. Perhaps more to the heart of their bottom line, tourism firms have an interest in avoiding unionized workforces that can raise local operating costs. In 1997, Santa Monica's only unionized hotel held a successful decertification election that employees subsequently appealed; a year later, the National Labor Relations Board overturned the election due to the hotel's illegal harassment of union leaders. The decertification controversy caught regional attention and sent tremors through the local hotel industry, which organized to quell potential union organizing in other hotels.

COMPETITION AND POWER AT THE CENTER

This review of locational motivations offers mixed support for fears that economic shifts portend a world of ever-more-rootless capital. On the one hand, in order to compete in capitalism, firms must extract greater surplus value from their workforces, which motivates them to relocate production to ever-cheaper sites of labor. On the other hand, the competitive pressures associated with flexibility have transformed locational motivations in sectors like software and entertainment, and have generated a new industrial space. Firms now use spatial forms, most notably the flexible district, as organizational media to coordinate production. The concentration and configurations of skilled workers also usurp important coordinating and innovating functions from the firm; elite workers' new centrality gives them organizational power and labor market advantage. Consequently, firms in the flexible district can strategically devolve, focusing around their core or higher value-added activities, and outsourcing lower value-added activities to other sites at a variety of distances. To be sure, even flexible firms consistently scrutinize their activities to reduce this local dependence by routinizing and outsourcing as many activities as they can; such organizational dynamism is part and parcel of "flexibility." Yet because at least their higher value-added activities achieve external economies when they cluster, only individual bankruptcies or industry-wide transformations will release firms from this compelling cost advantage. By contrast, tourism firms take a bottom-line orientation to profiting from place, and their conventionally *corporate* rationales for location highlight just how dramatically the organizational autonomy of human talent has transformed software and entertainment. At this juncture, the only similarity that tourism firms show to their counterparts in the other two sectors, or at least those located in flexible districts, is their fixity in place, at least as long as rootless visitors make them their destinations.

Not surprisingly, the economic development strategies to which most growth coalitions subscribe put great emphasis on efforts to become "the next Silicon Valley" and stimulate the growth of their own specialized industry centers. The reasoning behind such strategies is obvious enough: In a turbulent economy, the flexible district offers the most compelling way to root firms to places, create jobs (many of them high-paying), and sustain local economic development. However, such growth coalition efforts misunderstand the nature of the new industrial space, and, for this reason, are likely to fail. The dynamics that imbue the flexible district with competitive advantage do not derive from the qualities or actions of localities; rather, industries create their own geographies and industrial settings through their collective interaction. Tourism's workings may be more accessible to growth coalition efforts; yet, building a viable amenity infrastructure is not the same as attracting visitors to it. Not all places are fortunate enough to be literally placed in the paths of these expanding industrial and consumer geographies, as Santa Monica has been. The next chapter shows how Santa Barbara and San Luis Obispo, hardly conventional centers of the new industrial space, have had such place luck.

3

Spaces of Lifestyle

The software engineers at Alias |Wavefront have it pretty good.

It's not just the handsome salaries, flexible hours and casual, footwear-optional dress code—perks like that are now all but standard in the industry.

These engineers, who develop special-effects software for the film industry, enjoy something far more unique: a physical setting that puts even the loveliest parts of Silicon Valley to shame.

For some, the commute to work is an eight-minute downhill bike ride from a hillside canyon home; for others, it's a roller blade trip on quiet, tree-lined streets. No traffic. No smog.

Many spend their lunch breaks surfing, windsurfing or jogging on a beach that's just two blocks away. Or they can grab a bite in a thriving, yet uncrowded, downtown area, with its plethora of cafes, restaurants, shops, bars and movie theaters.

Welcome to Santa Barbara, Southern California's newest high-tech mecca. The unparalleled Mediterranean setting and upscale mix of urban and rustic lifestyles that has attracted movie stars and celebrities for decades is now luring software and telecommunications companies by the dozens—and they're helping to revitalize the area's economy.[1]

Recently, urbanists have debated whether knowledge-intensive industries have some affinity for places with urbane cultures, environmental quality, residential amenities, and other attributes that constitute a "high quality of life." Beyond its ramifications for economic development strategies, this quality-of-life affinity would suggest that, at least in certain cases, capital puts down roots in locations other than industry centers like Silicon Valley. Since the politics in places with high qualities of life tends to emphasize environmental preservation, social services, and other checks on business as usual, evidence for this affinity supports a critique of the practice by which localities "race to the bottom" for capital investment.

The debate hinges upon the claim that the residential preferences of elite workers influence companies' locational motivations, not *vice versa*. On the one hand, proponents of this claim point to assorted studies that show how knowledge workers are "very sophisticated consumers of place."[2] A meta-analysis of twenty studies on the role of quality of life in corporate locations revealed that knowledge-intensive firms favor good schools, public safety, environmental quality, cultural amenities, and proximity of housing to work. Interestingly, when high-tech firms are singled out, environmental quality moves to the first rank.[3] Recently, statistical correlations have been found between prosperous technology regions and the presence of gay, bohemian, and foreign-born communities.[4] In a provocative interpretation of these studies, Joel Kotkin and Richard Florida argue that places with visible and distinct lifestyle opportunities and qualities of life *attract* workers (and subsequently, firms) in talent-intensive sectors, producing a "new geography" where high quality of life and economic prosperity go hand in hand.[5]

On the other hand, critics of the claim that elite workers' residential preferences influence companies' locational motivations offer three rebuttals. First, "quality of life" is a notoriously subjective concept for academics who study it as well as for workers who seek it, and studies like the aforementioned hardly share uniform criteria to define it. Even more, proponents ignore the possibility that for some people, income, work, domestic arrangements, and other aspects of "quality of life" may have nothing to do with place *per se.*[6] Second, even if many workers perceive certain high-tech locations to have a high quality of life, *corporate* interests explain the location process. In either classic R&D innovation centers or urban agglomerations, the presence of amenities valued by workers is a coincidence, or even the result, but not the cause of firm locations.[7] Third, most proponents have not explained the mechanism that links workers' locational choices to corporate interest. Granted, some executives acknowledge the primary influence of non-economic residential preferences of managerial elites, but such cases are so idiosyncratic as to represent only "random locational effects."[8] By failing to take into account more systematic corporate interests in location (like those described in the last chapter), proponents appear to resurrect old and discarded theories of residential migration that underestimate the power of capital to constrain labor's residential choices, and to create the "market" of locations from which both workers and firms choose.[9]

These rebuttals identify important shortcomings in the claim that workers' residential preferences influence corporate locations—and yet here I will advance just this kind of claim, albeit narrowed to explain a specific mechanism of corporate location illustrated by Santa Barbara and San Luis Obispo, as well as other places that I will occasionally reference. Critics' arguments set forth three questions that my account will answer. First, how do elite workers in software and entertainment as well as tourists come to understand "quality of life" as traits of places, such as local environmental, urban, and cultural amenities? Second, how does this understanding of quality of life lead to the growth of software, entertainment, and tourism firms in places like Santa Barbara and San Luis Obispo? Finally, how do executives and entrepreneurs in software, entertainment, and tourism use quality of life as an asset in the larger issue of corporate locational motivations?

CONTRADICTIONS OF THE CENTER

Quite often, explanations for how quality of life influences corporate location betray the whiff of a "virtuous capitalism" argument in their contention that "nice" places attract the most coveted engines of economic development. Local boosters and business cheerleaders may have no qualms with the tone of this claim, but it neglects starker realities like the geography of uneven development that capital produces. Additionally, these explanations can erroneously project the interests of capital onto the "logic" of the capital accumulation process. Such a functionalist fallacy overlooks how the larger process may undermine the conditions under which capital enacts its interests. Thus, the analysis of how quality of life influences corporate location must be guided by a critical perspective on uneven development and structural contradiction. The problem of labor control best frames this approach.

THE INDUSTRIAL CONSTRUCTION OF QUALITY OF LIFE

Quality of life's role begins not in amenity-rich settings off the industrial map, but back in the centers of the new industrial space, where the success of prior industrial agglomeration, economic development, and urban growth generates a structural contradiction that is expressed in the physical and social environment.[10] The history of Silicon Valley, software's undisputed geographical center, provides the archetypical case, which I supplement with evidence from Southern California to make the case for entertainment. Over decades of industry growth and worker migration, poor regional planning has exacerbated infrastructure and environmental strains in Silicon Valley.[11] Local housing is extraordinarily costly; Silicon Valley's 1997 median home prices ranged from about $250,000 in San Jose (the region's lower-income residential center), to $490,000 in Palo Alto (home to Stanford University), to over $1,000,000 in Los Alto Hills (the priciest enclave for the region's movers and shakers).[12] The scarcity of affordable housing in turn promotes residential sprawl, long commutes, and air pollution. Frequent employee turnover prevents most workers from using car pools or mass transit for long, if at all, which further crowds freeways. Regional schools, infrastructure, and services are often stressed beyond capacity, as are more discretionary amenities. As a software CEO complained, "It bums me out when I'm in [Silicon Valley's] Mountain View that I can't drive 20 minutes and go to a restaurant where I can get a table and have lunch in an hour and be done and back at my office."

Industry leaders know well the implications of these problems for business: "All the very productive industries here depend on human capital. If the quality of life deteriorates, that human capital walks out the door."[13] Indeed, the exodus of elite workers from Silicon Valley produces software industry growth in Santa Barbara and San Luis Obispo, although the process is subtle and not easily observed at first glance. For one reason, physical strains have not raised the cost of doing business sufficiently high to drive firms out and diminish the region's agglomerative value. Nevertheless, certain *workers* experience the brunt of the region's structural contradiction in their domestic and personal lives—a phenomenon known in Silicon Valley as "technostress"[14]—and decide it is time to "get a life" somewhere else. To understand how the actions of labor in industry centers create industry growth elsewhere, I now follow the contingent decisions that workers make in this process.

One reason that a high quality of life is attributed to areas like Santa Barbara and San Luis Obispo is because the "push" pressures out of flexible districts also derive from place traits, in this case, the region's quality-of-life crisis. However, before they follow the "pull" of places with a higher quality of life, potential emigrants must first experience life and work as a *problem,* specifically, as an existential dilemma—do the benefits of staying put outweigh the personal costs?—to feel the "push" out of flexible districts. It is time now that I address that nebulous concept, "quality of life," not to provide a comprehensive theory of its many meanings, but rather to explain the factors that encourage a place-based understanding for certain groups.

Environmental risk, it has been said, is democratic.[15] However, although the rising costs of living and daily stresses in Silicon Valley may be inescapable, they do not compel many people sufficiently to motivate them to leave. "I think that quality of life is a perspective," a CEO told me; "I work with a lot of high-tech people who think quality of life is a Mountain Dew and a window to the outside world." There are a number of reasons why many in Silicon Valley and other flexible districts show such effective indifference to local strains on living and environment. After all, the first pull of the flexible district, especially for elite workers, is income. Living in the flexible district also offers workers a career safety net of multiple employment opportunities. Such rational incentives for workers to stay constitute the common wisdom among urbanists like Manuel Castells and Peter Hall about the flexible district's attraction for the best and the brightest:

> [For workers in the flexible district,] milieux of innovation are a goal in themselves. People do not live in them because of the quality of their life or the

beauty of their nature; quality of life is a highly subjective attribute, and many areas in the world are of startling beauty without having much chance to become technological or industrial centers. If young business talents continue to overcrowd the already overcrowded, unpleasant areas of Central Tokyo or Manhattan, it is not to enjoy the rarity of the singing of a surviving bird. It is to be part of, and be rewarded by, the world's financial centers. If film makers and music composers spend their lives on the Los Angeles freeways, it is not to catch a last ray of the sun through the ultimate toxic smog of Southern California; it is to be in the networks of the milieu generated from Hollywood [sixty] years ago. Similarly, the attraction that Silicon Valley continues to exercise over the high-technology researchers and entrepreneurs of the entire world relies on the simple and fundamental fact of being the depository of the most advanced knowledge in electronics and on its capacity to generate the next generation of such knowledge by processing the flows of information through its social networks and professional organizations. Silicon Valley's fate is to live up to its own historic role as a milieu of innovation of the latest industrial revolution—whatever the consequences for its land and for its people.[16]

There are also rational *disincentives* for leaving Silicon Valley. First and foremost are the material constraints of class. One of the most acute contradictions of the new industrial space is that as local residence becomes unaffordable for schoolteachers, public employees, and consumer service workers, Silicon Valley teeters on the verge of pricing out the industry's external "support labor" to the region's commuting peripheries. The same happens in the work-life hotspots of the Hollywood company town; in Santa Monica, some residents believe that the rising property values triggered by the entertainment industry influx threaten local renters more than years of landlord antipathy toward rent control. Yet, although these strains affect lower classes most dramatically, these groups are at the same time less able either to afford to move or to find comparable work and pay in places with less vibrant bases of potential employers. Workers, especially those with dependents, may also suffer if they uproot their daily rounds (child care, schools, personal networks of friends and family) from particular community settings. Thus, acting upon the push pressures out of Silicon Valley is a luxury affordable only to some. For this reason, the rest of my discussion focuses on elite workers, who have sufficient status in industry labor markets that they can reasonably expect to find work elsewhere or bring it with them as freelancers and entrepreneurs.

In addition to "inherently" rational reasons to put up with life in the flexible district, industry practices and cultures also encourage workers to ignore the push out. Software and entertainment sectors notoriously discriminate against older workers on the basis of employer preferences for the latest skills, worker "adaptability," and generational proximity to young consumers.[17] This labor market premium for youth may limit the number of opportunities for older elite workers with families to find work elsewhere. Also, the ethos that challenging and innovative work is its own reward is heavily ingrained in the "cyber-nerd" culture.[18] Gendered discourses may reinforce this ethos among male workers:

> Engineers have this idea that you are out there and you are building something and these small companies are going to do huge things and lots of people are going to get rich and it's gonna happen because we are great. Even under normal circumstances when there are no extraordinary demands, you see people working thirty-six hours straight just because they are going to meet the deadline. They are going to get it done and everybody walks around proud of how exhausted they were last week and conspicuously putting in wild hours. It's a status thing to have pizza delivered to the office. So I don't know why it happens, but I really feel like it is kind of a machismo thing—I'm tough, I can do this thing. Yeah, I'm tired but I'm on top of it. You guys don't worry about me—I can get my thing done.[19]

It becomes clear that certain groups are likely to experience the flexible district's quality-of-life crisis as a problem requiring a migratory solution. First, those who can afford to move and face the risks of finding another job are likely to act upon the push pressures; elite workers are highly represented in this group. Intersecting with them, those who can withstand the industry practices and cultures that encourage commitment to living and working in the flexible district are likely to act. Speculating on the type who might fit this profile, a San Luis Obispo software CEO mentioned "people who have gone through rapid acceleration in their career and have gotten into more of a maintenance phase, maybe sitting back and reflecting a bit about, 'Why do I have to run so hard and so fast?' " Since the Internet economy deflated, some in this group may be even more sensitive to their quality of life:

> Some dot-com execs—when they realized they weren't going to get fabulously rich or saw their paper wealth evaporate—remembered that they had neglected to cultivate their minds, their bodies or their families and communities. Now, those who have the free time and the cash are going on long vacations to surf in Bali or hike in the Andes in an effort to shock their systems into some kind of spiritual, physical, and emotional balance: In essence, they are looking to be reminded that they are actually alive and not just automatons with no other purpose but to make money.[20]

Other potential migrants include workers who are young, are new to the region, have families, or have some other experience that lessens their internalization of industry norms.

Although the simultaneous and continuous arrival of newcomers and jobhoppers attracted by high pay and challenging work obscures the departure of quality-of-life migrants, signs of the Silicon Valley exodus are nevertheless becoming evident. A study conducted in 1999 (a full year before the dot-com crash) showed that the region's population dropped for the first time in five years; roughly thirteen thousand people (not necessarily all technology workers) moved out for other parts of the United States, even as 11,800 others arrived from overseas.[21] Although Silicon Valley's industries will almost certainly withstand this flux, elite worker exodus hurts individual firms through workforce turnover that halts projects and threatens the viability of start-up firms. For firms that relocate to quality-of-life districts, a Santa Barbara CEO explained, "Turnover is enormously expensive, because it's not only expensive to go recruit new people and train them and get them going, it's expensive in terms of the experience and the knowledge that people gain over time that they leave with. And it could even be so far as competitive intelligence type stuff." The evidence from Santa Barbara and San Luis Obispo suggests that firms likely to migrate include start-ups at critical stages of product development, "toolmakers" and other companies creating proprietary products, and firms that have some degree of autonomy from venture capitalists or other external managers based in flexible districts.

Besides having to manage employee turnover, executives and entrepreneurs may themselves feel the push pressures that come with life and work in industrial centers. One entrepreneur described his revelation at a previous company in Los Angeles: "After a year of commuting, I just got sick of it. I told my partners, 'Either we move, or I move.' " As a corporate strategy to control labor by accommodating elite workers' preferences to move out of industry centers, firms can set up corporate branches in places that meet certain place-specific quality-of-life criteria (which I discuss below). Alternately, elite workers can themselves decide to bring the industry with them in the form of entrepreneurial ventures and freelance work. These strategies may not be widespread in Silicon Valley, yet their very existence reveals the recurring problem of labor control in locations where firms depend on elite workers.

The overall effect of these locational strategies is usefully framed by regulation theory, particularly its recent concern for how geographical and institutional scale regulates contradictions in the capital accumulation process. Conventional and alternate modes of regulating labor control correspond to the scales of the region and the firm, respectively. The norm of a work-for-life trade-off is the conventional regulatory mode that no one firm or elite tends; it inheres to the cultural milieu of the flexible district proper. However, because not all workers have or are willing to make this trade-off, this mode of regulation does not effectively serve the competitive interests of all firms, particularly those that depend upon low workforce turnover or particular workers. These firms avail themselves of an alternate and deliberate mode of regulation: the relocation of corporate branches and entre-preneurial activities to places where employees can "get a life" and still work.

Some scholars contend that the capacity of at least certain workers to make companies locate based on employee preferences reflects a new demo-cratic era of economic and technological change. Rebutting explanations to the contrary, Richard Florida argues, "By insisting that these social changes are somehow imposed on us," so-called determinist theories of technologi-cal change "avoid the real question of our age: Why are we *choosing* to live and work like this? Why do we want this life, or think that we do?"[22] I agree that certain groups of employees have the collective power to make compa-nies move to their location, even if I believe this power is limited to elite workers and not the broader "creative class," as Florida contends. However, the occasion in which elite workers exercise their locational power—namely, environmental and cost-of-living strains generated by capital's agglomera-tion in the industrial district—is hardly within their control. Although cor-porate location may follow the cue of elite workers in certain sectors, this development permits capital to externalize the contradictions of its geo-graphical strategies. Indeed, employee turnover and corporate exodus in industry centers and sectoral growth in the quality-of-life district manifest two poles in a *spatial structure of regulation* for the industry problem of labor control.[23] Through collective denial as well as deliberate "imposition," then, capital continues to set the structural basis for the geographical decisions of labor, in this case for elite workers. As I describe below, the rhetoric of their decisions very much upholds values of individual choice. Yet this locational process raises the question: Although elite workers may get what they want (out of work, lifestyle, and location), does all of society really want, much less control, what elite workers get?

QUALITY-OF-LIFE DISTRICTS

If the aforementioned set of factors motivates certain elite workers to leave the industry center, a different set influences their choice of destination. The first is labor market status, which shapes the life-for-work trade-offs that elite workers can entertain. The most privileged may opt out of the indus-try altogether, like many "suddenly wealthy" technology workers who cashed out their stock options before the 2000 dot-com crash. After years of "paying dues" and accruing wealth, this group can either switch to a less hectic livelihood or retire completely, which gives them the widest array of possible destinations.[24] Others find work in established locations where the industry edge may not be so cutting, but the living is easier; for instance, they may exchange the career safety net of the flexible district for corporate loyalties in the branch plants of the "technoburb."

The growth of software and entertainment firms in Santa Barbara and San Luis Obispo reflects a middle path between these two decisions: elite workers bring the industry to places where it did not exist before. I call these places *quality-of-life districts* to highlight how place-based amenities valued by elite workers make these locations strategic in the new industrial space. Outside of the Fordist innovation center, amenities hardly constitute "corporate" locational assets. However, "people don't move here for rational reasons," a San Luis Obispo executive explained. "They move here for all kinds of qualitative reasons." The quality-of-life district reveals how, among flexible firms, the centrality of talent transforms what count as corporate (i.e., "rational") criteria for location. Now, "qualitative" factors (i.e., elite workers' demands, locational or otherwise) are compelling interests for capital.

Potential quality-of-life districts must meet two conditions before elite workers move. First, the organizational forms of flexible industries must make these locations viable places to work. To begin, only elite workers with corporate authority, labor market privilege, or entrepreneurial savvy can reasonably expect the industry to follow them if they choose to set up in remote locations. Thus, a small cohort of *pioneer migrants* generally arrives first. Consisting largely of entrepreneurs and "owner-founder[s] who have the authority, money, and will" (in the words of a San Luis Obispo pioneer migrant) to move a company, they provide opportunities for other workers subsequently making the same migration. In software, pioneer migrants have typically achieved status through previous work with companies in Silicon Valley or other fast-paced industry centers. They see their migration decision as an entrepreneurial risk, but also a self-reward for years of hustle and bustle. "I think it's just guys like me," observed a San Luis Obispo software CEO when describing the executives who brought their companies to the area. "They came here, they had an idea they wanted to do something, and they just got it done, you know?" In entertainment, the move hinges more narrowly on the migrant's status in production networks and industry hierarchies. Said a film director who built an editing facility in Santa Barbara, "It had to do with the success of my career, so if the director wants to edit in Santa Barbara, they're going to let him edit in Santa Barbara."

Second, more concrete industrial and technological infrastructure to link quality-of-life districts to the new industrial space must also be present. At a minimum, software and entertainment firms need high-speed telecommunications capacity and proximity to airports and freeways that can shuttle them back to industry centers. "I [still] find myself driving up to Silicon Valley at least once a week, if not twice," a San Luis Obispo software CEO told me; "there's just so much going on up there." Nearby universities that provide research opportunities or skilled entry-level labor may also be needed. Even this modicum of infrastructure may not suffice to make all industrial activities feasible, given the face-to-face interaction and quick turnaround that drive the "bleeding edge." A review of the software and entertainment activities carried out in Santa Barbara and San Luis Obispo suggests which kinds of work are most viable. Software firms tend to specialize in R&D (either under the aegis of a corporate branch or as their own speculative enterprise), e-commerce and other activities that use the Internet as their retail interface, or input provision with medium- to long-term turnaround (e.g., special effects and custom multimedia toolmakers for Hollywood films). Notably, in these activities, the most common medium for industry transactions tends to be digital (and thus conductible by high-speed telecommunications infrastructure) or spatial (e.g., proximity to nearby research universities). In San Luis Obispo, the relatively few firms that design or add inputs to physical components often complain of distribution problems, since the area is hardly a major node of shipping traffic. For this reason, an executive observed, "Numerous times, we just looked at giving up, but we believe that ultimately the lifestyle will be better than Los Angeles. So, like everything else, you tough out the hard parts to ultimately enjoy the good parts."[25]

In entertainment, elites have made Santa Barbara a second home for most of the twentieth century; more recently, comparable Hollywood getaways have been established in remote places like Aspen, Colorado, and Jackson Hole, Wyoming. However, work activities tend to be limited to the pre-production stage, since screenwriters, musicians, independent producers, and other talent can easily add their input or review potential projects from their homes until deadlines arise. Even in these relatively discrete tasks, the industry's networking requirements do not make remoteness feasible for everyone. "If, say, you're writing all day, you're working in isolation," a veteran talent agent explained. "So you have to go to the right clubs and the right parties."[26] With rare exceptions, such social events do not take place outside of Hollywood; optimal networks rarely materialize in places where people go to *leave* the company town. Santa Barbara has virtually none of the talent agencies, film studios, record labels, and television production companies that make Los Angeles entertainment's preeminent hiring hall.[27] Although many live in Santa Barbara, deal-makers who are perennially on call and sought after by others prefer to leave their work in offices back in the industry zones of Hollywood. Recently, a handful of Hollywood moguls have set up new entities like independent production companies and editing facilities in Santa Barbara. However, the projects carried out here, either by the moguls or others leasing the facilities, tend to be feature length or big budget, and allow for slower turnaround than the television shows and commercials that are a mainstay of Hollywood facilities.[28]

After they decide for themselves to move, all but freelance pioneer migrants must also consider the viability of the firms or branches that they bring with them; their personal motivations must also square with their interests as corporate managers and talent recruiters. Pioneer migrants must be able to lure sufficiently skilled workers in development, marketing, and management, as well as workers with more routine or entry-level skills. In some cases these kinds of workers are available locally, as with the reputable computer science and engineering departments at Santa Barbara and San

Luis Obispo's universities. More often, pioneer migrants recruit their work-force from the labor markets centered back in flexible districts. "It's a fairly gutsy thing" for lower-level employees to leave the flexible district's safety net and creative milieu, a San Luis Obispo CEO observed. "I've literally had people walk in my door looking for a job, saying, 'We have moved,' or 'We are moving, and we're looking for a job.' . . . It's always amazing to me how many people up and move and *then* try and figure out what they're going to do." Pioneer migrants gamble that residence in the quality-of-life district is its own recruitment incentive. "When I talk to Santa Barbara–based en-trepreneurs," a software executive told me, "I think virtually all of them have made a decision that they want to be in a place with a high quality of life for their family. Basically, they make the decision for their family, and then sub-sequent to that, they say, 'Gee whiz, if it appeals to me on this level, it will probably appeal to employees on this level.' "

Without these organizational conditions and infrastructure, places that suit elite workers' lifestyle preferences may make poor industry locations. Otherwise, pioneer migrants can move to the quality-of-life district, bring-ing the corporate branch or their own start-up firm with them. Not all of these early firms survive, for reasons that may or may not (usually the latter, it seems) have to do with their geographical distance: They are effectively outcompeted, market opportunities fail to materialize, and so on. Those who succeed, however, bring visibility to their firm, the quality-of-life district, and their locational strategy; in turn, this makes future hires easier by creating a pull for other quality-of-life migrants at the elite worker levels.

As in other industries, executives and entrepreneurs in software and entertainment rarely migrate before starting up and staffing a company.[29] However, an exception to this pattern, a San Luis Obispo video game design firm, suggests the less systematic opportunities that make remote settings work. Conceived by Los Angeles area entrepreneurs, the start-up firm could only secure the requisite financing from a Denver-based investor who was simultaneously funding a non-technology company in San Luis Obispo. The condition he attached was that he wanted to show both companies to his clients on business tours up the coast of California. For the entrepreneurs, that meant "we needed to take a look at San Luis Obispo," a place they had previously only known as "a sign on the road." Now, "We're here to stay. I'm not giving up this town—this is a find."[30]

Then there is the question of local start-ups. CEOs in Santa Barbara and San Luis Obispo repeatedly insist, "There's only two reasons people are here: They either decided they wanted to get out, or they didn't want to leave." The latter path suggests that some "migrants" never leave the quality-of-life district; they graduate from local universities or return to these places as hometowns after graduate training elsewhere, and then find local employ-ment or start a firm. These local residents have created a significant num-ber of firms in the quality-of-life district (up to one-half of 1997 Santa

Barbara firms, by one estimate), and so not surprisingly local industry advocates proudly describe their enterprises as "spin-offs" reflecting localized economic opportunities. This may be true for some firms, especially the local service providers that constitute most of the local industry (see Chapter 1, Table 1.2). However, the quality-of-life district model offers another explanation for these local start-ups. Recurring claims that "with my skills I could easily work in Silicon Valley," and reports that local firms employ "some pretty world-class computer guys" suggest that these locals have already experienced the labor market pull exerted by Silicon Valley. Many hometown entrepreneurs, especially the pioneers of the local industry, are actually hypothetical Silicon Valley migrants, due to their elite worker status. They make the same trade-offs (in terms of lower income and more difficult business prospects) in Silicon Valley labor markets as bona fide quality-of-life migrants, even if they never leave their hometown.

More generally, the formation of quality-of-life districts should not be mistaken for the initial conditions of flexible districts. Although service firms have emerged to provide elementary inputs, quality-of-life districts do not otherwise witness the deepening division of labor and local specialties that usually follow the agglomerative pull of lead firms. The "stars" of their local industries tend to transact primarily with firms in Silicon Valley and other industry centers; "our customers are not here," I was regularly told by local executives. Nor does the quality-of-life district compete like satellite platforms by satisfying "pro-business" needs for corporate isolation and low costs.[31] For most firms, the quality-of-life district serves no recognizable corporate criteria of competitiveness, save securing the lifestyle satisfaction and workplace morale of elite workers. That this has become a strategic goal for many firms underscores the primacy of elite workers in the new industrial space. It reflects individual solutions by firms and elite workers to a crisis of labor reproduction that the collective industry is unwilling or unable to address back in industry centers.

LIFESTYLE TASTES

Industry organization aside, what qualities of life appeal to elite workers? Here I take account of elite workers' diverse yet patterned tastes in lifestyle and residence, albeit not to argue that they vary more or in qualitatively different ways than among the population at large. What makes elite workers' lifestyle tastes relevant to my argument is their capacity to make certain places desirable destinations and thereby expand the geography of the new industrial space.

Among the various factors that shape lifestyle preferences are workers' life stages. Elite workers with families (particularly for those from places with low costs of living) may be used to owning large homes that they can afford on one or more salaries. This and other family concerns motivate quality-of-life migrants to find a destination where spacious estates are sim-

ilarly affordable. Also, elite workers may seek to maximize their spouses'
career opportunities, which favors a destination with industries besides software. Metropolitan areas most easily meet this criterion, rendering the quality-
of-life migration a move to a slightly more "liveable," but no less suburban,
setting than the residential communities surrounding Silicon Valley or
Southern California.[32] These settings often rank highly in business media
indices of "best places to do business":

> Highly skilled engineers tend to be family folks looking for great quality of
> life. So for tech firms who want to attract top talent: Head for the Suburbs.
> OUR TOP PICK: Route 202 corridor, Philadelphia.
> With its great schools and affordable housing, Philadelphia's Route 202
> is a magnet for engineering firms. The bucolic lifestyle and strong business
> climate have created a high-tech haven.[33]

Alternately, elite workers for whom city living does not detract from quality of life but rather constitutes it (in the form of nightclubs, cultural opportunities, and so on) are likely to prefer urban settings. For this reason, firms
that place a premium on cutting-edge creativity, aesthetic experimentation,
and (sub)cultural savvy tend to cluster in revitalized city centers like San
Francisco's South of Market district, New York's Silicon Alley, or Chicago's
Wicker Park.[34] So, too, wilderness and other natural amenities appeal to
many, but single and/or younger workers most likely to make regular outdoor recreation a priority may consider this a more important factor in their
relocation decision. Elite migrants may also move based on more idiosyncratic sentiments about places, like ties to their hometown or a particular
local culture. In Microsoft's fledgling years, founders Bill Gates and Paul
Allen moved the company from its original New Mexico locale to Seattle in
order to work and live near their families.[35] Likewise, in Salt Lake City,
Utah's technology sectors benefit from the locational attachments of Mormon
elite workers. And this brief review hardly exhausts the lifestyle tastes that
elite workers display.

What kind of lifestyle opportunities do the three Southern California
localities make possible? Santa Monica is certainly a flexible district, yet
because firms can find agglomerative centrality from many metropolitan
locales, its special attraction is heavily lifestyle-oriented. The weather and
beach figure prominently in elite workers' descriptions of Santa Monica's
allure. A software CEO emphasized its cultural, recreational, and consumer
amenities: "It's sunny, there's an ocean, and the lifestyle is freer and easier,
more open to younger people than a lot of places you can think of." The
organizer of a local software business group cited "the beach, that it's its own
community—that it *is* a community. There's nothing else in Southern
California that really is a community, except maybe Carlsbad [outside San
Diego] and a couple of towns along the coast." Whether these amenities

successfully entice elite workers also depends on their life stage, which influences their domestic needs. Those with families who live in Santa Monica either feel especially comfortable living in apartments or can afford the still-high (although lower than Silicon Valley) costs of even median-cost housing: $395,000 in 1997. For this reason, software firms here tend to orient their workforce around employees in their twenties and early thirties; many older workers with families eventually leave Santa Monica companies for jobs closer to their suburban residences.

In Santa Barbara, with its distance from the Los Angeles metropolis, the quality of life is far more crucial for software and entertainment firms. Tellingly, many migrants described first discovering this place as a vacation destination. Its appeal includes outdoors and cultural opportunities, which are plentiful and do not require traveling to Los Angeles. As a software executive noted, Santa Barbara "is fun, it has great weather, it has access to recreation, you can walk all over downtown." Its small size is another factor, observed another CEO: "People like to feel they make a difference, and that's easier in small communities." Additionally, the perceived lack of crime is another important asset, particularly for companies where employees work nontraditional hours at all times of the day. With a 1997 median home price of $345,000, Santa Barbara's cost of living is less than most of Silicon Valley's, but still sufficiently high that it raises obstacles for firms recruiting elite workers who are used to larger homes and lower costs of living outside Southern California. As in Santa Monica, then, Santa Barbara software firms also tend to orient their workforce around young employees. However, local firms face a particular shortage in experienced managers; since it lies just outside the metropolitan career safety net, moving to Santa Barbara brings an extra degree of risk to which elite workers over thirty and/or with family may especially be averse.

Instead of Santa Monica's urban glitz or Santa Barbara's exclusive ambiance, San Luis Obispo provides a rustic coastal setting for elite workers to "get away from it all"—a distinction for which it received the highest rank in 2001 by the business periodical *Industry Standard*.[36] As in Santa Barbara, many migrants accidentally discover San Luis Obispo; a characteristic account I heard was, "My wife and I stopped at this bed and breakfast, we went to the wineries, and we thought, 'Why don't we move the company here?'" The area offers quality-of-life migrants proximity to a scenic coastline, the chance to own undeveloped land for ranching or beachside meditation, access to horse stables and other rural forms of recreation, and a Western milieu in which to wear cowboy boots or drive big trucks. Still, executives are sure to pitch the area as combining the cultural sophistication of a major university with a small-town flavor in a relatively undeveloped coastal region: "The population is, say, forty thousand people, yet it has the culture of about a 200,000 population center." Its cost of housing is the most affordable of the three research sites, with a 1997 median home price of

$175,000.[37] A smaller population, healthy tax base, and higher-than-average education levels have produced local schools with high standards and substantial parental involvement. Finally, almost everyone who has lived in major cities—which, as many claim, accounts for most of the area's residents—points out the area's lack of crime. For some, its relative racial homogeneity may be an additional, if often unspoken, attraction. These local qualities appeal to many technology workers raising families, thereby filling a lifestyle niche that contrasts with the generally young/single orientation of Santa Monica and Santa Barbara. The small town/family appeal is particularly important when local firms try to recruit senior management, the workforce segment most lacking in the local labor pool.

PRODUCING DESIRABLE PLACES

The characteristic feature of the new industrial space is that endogenous mechanisms of industrial activity organize and extend capital investment in space. How does tourism, an industry in which profits are sensitive to traditional cost factors and the exogenous currency of "pro-business" climates, exhibit this feature? Tourism does not generate quality-of-life districts insofar as the latter embody flexible *production* in space; tourism's endogenous mechanisms are industry structures for place *consumption* by visitors. Still, the ways in which tourism destinations attract visitors shed light on how elite workers in software and entertainment come to value quality-of-life districts.

THE CONSTRUCTION OF PLACE DESIRABILITY

How do locales become desirable places for visitors and competitive sites for tourism firms, particularly if, like Santa Barbara and San Luis Obispo, they lack extensive investment in amenity infrastructure? Recall that a symbolic component, the sign value of a place, makes a particular setting more desirable for the consumption of tourism services than other potential ones.[38] However, aside from theme park designers, tour operators, and the businesses that market holiday and tour packages (none of which predominate in the three Southern California places; see Chapter 1, Table 1.4), not many tourism firms substantially engage, at least individually, in this symbolic work for any setting outside their property lines. Most tourism firms tend to be small and focus their marketing efforts on distinguishing their business from competitors *within* a given locality. Except for the relatively few (albeit disproportionately influential) corporate chains and large-scale establishments, most tourism firms cannot afford to advertise extensively outside their locality. As with the *material* construction of amenity infrastructures, then, most tourism firms depend upon the external *symbolic* construction of local desirability.

Concretely, this means that tourism firms tend to rely on visitors and conference bureaus, chambers of commerce, and other collective entities to promote the locality. In this way, tourism's promotional efforts resemble the collective mobilization of growth coalitions to attract capital investment—by consumers, in this case. Not surprisingly, growth coalitions in Santa Monica, Santa Barbara, and San Luis Obispo, as in other places, have been instrumental in putting their localities "on the map" of visitors' attention. As early as 1896, Santa Monica boosters promoted the city as a beachside resort after an urban trolley system brought the metropolis to its then-unurbanized doorstep.[39] Also common to other places, growth coalitions lobby higher levels of government for aid in promoting tourism. Most prominently, California's central coast cemented its reputation as a travel destination after the state established Pismo State Beach in 1935, designated Hearst's Castle as a state monument in 1958, and completed its scenic coastal highway (California Highway 1) in 1964.

Although collective efforts by growth-dependent actors do much to forge a place's identity, they cannot make tourists prefer one place over another. Ultimately, localities depend upon non-local place representations to persuade potential visitors (as well as residents and industry) to choose them as a destination.[40] National media have been kind to the three coastal localities in this regard. In the early 1870s, travel journalist Charles Nordhoff publicized Santa Barbara as a place of healing in *Harper's Bazaar*, thereby triggering the first of many migrations by wealthy easterners and midwesterners; to this day, the three places remain frequent topics of travel and airline magazine articles.[41] Arguably more important in constructing the desirability of my research sites has been Hollywood, which has depicted and publicized these places in on-location settings for film production, and as fictional settings for various films and TV shows. As of this writing, international visitors continue to arrive in Santa Monica and Santa Barbara looking for the places depicted in the internationally syndicated television shows "Baywatch" and "Santa Barbara," respectively.

Media representations do not articulate the desirability of places in a vacuum; instead, their claims become credible by engaging prevailing discourses of urbanism.[42] For the three Southern California places, the most relevant discourses pertain to Los Angeles as site of both attraction and repulsion. Almost as long as LA boosters have peddled images of edenic nature and lifestyle reinvention, tourists, residents, and business have searched for newer locales within the region to avoid the "problems" associated with Los Angeles: the general tropes of congestion, pollution, crime, and racial and ethnic others, as well as LA's specific "ills" of riot, earthquake, flood, and fire. Much of Southern California's urban sprawl can be explained through the recurring story of local boosters exploiting the region's original allure and subsequent fears to attract growth outside the city center.[43] At different times, each of the three places has offered residents and visitors sites to "get away from it all" at distances sufficiently remote from the perceived stigma of Los Angeles, while still enabling opportunities to partake in its socially constructed desirability. Up through the 1970s, Santa Monica first profited from this metropolitan construction of desirability and repulsion; for many, Santa Barbara is approaching the limits of reasonably sustaining this dual construction, while San Luis Obispo appears poised to profit from this construction at least into the near future.

Although by this measure, the desirability of these Southern California areas increases the further one travels out of the metropolis, by another measure, all three have fared well relative to neighboring locales at comparable distances within and away from the metropolis. This is due to their natural amenities and local ambiance that many believe emanate coastal California's "uncommon" beauty and glamour, but that other coastal communities have lost to urbanization. Here it is useful to recall John Urry's crucial insight that, in its various historical incarnations, the tourist gaze "depends upon what it is contrasted with; what the forms of non-tourist experience happen to be . . . particularly those based within the home and paid work."[44] Thanks largely to efforts at environmental protection, growth control, and support for urban services, Santa Barbara and San Luis Obispo in particular contrast with the homogeneous sprawl and congestion that characterize many Southern California localities. Even bustling Santa Monica has preserved a "specialness" that is not found in many other Los Angeles communities.

WHAT CREATES QUALITY-OF-LIFE ADVANTAGE?

To be sure, getting away from it all is not the primary goal for most visitors to Southern California. Proximity to a critical mass of attractions and amenities remains key to the fortunes of visitor destinations; for this reason, the economic vitality of tourism declines as one travels further away from the Los Angeles metropolis. Nevertheless, the dominance of urban destinations in Southern California's tourism industry does not harken back to an era of mass tourism. Industry analysts point out that tourism localities and firms now compete to attract niche tourist markets that vary by demographic, scale of travel, and recreational pursuits.[45] In this context, place differentiation and distinction become strategic for local tourism industries. Urban tourism remains vital because it offers multiple and diverse—not mass and homogeneous—settings to consume goods and services and to appreciate places, landscapes, and lifestyles. Yet for this same reason, more remote and smaller-scale tourism industries in non-metropolitan places like Santa Barbara and San Luis Obispo also have industrial and theoretical significance by offering distinct consumption and aesthetic opportunities. Tourism growth in these "getaways" reveals that amenities and "desirability" become differentiated through expansion to the periphery as well as concentration in the center.

The differentiation of tourist destinations is only half the story. The increasing sophistication with which tourists distinguish and evaluate particular destinations in turn reflects the construction of the consumer—

particularly the place consumer—as an increasingly significant social identity.[46] The relevance of this identity in the new industrial space becomes clear through a comparison with locational motivations in software and entertainment. To the extent that tourism involves the consumption of places, tourists are necessarily engaged in distinguishing and evaluating place-specific qualities of life—landscapes, townscapes, ethnic groups, lifestyles, historical artifacts, bases of recreation, or simply "sand, sun and sea"—as desirable objects for consumption.[47] By contrast, elite workers are *not* necessarily engaged in these pursuits; for them, "quality of life" can just as easily mean career reward, domestic happiness, or other activities that do not engage the place consumers' gaze. However, when elite workers in software and entertainment *are* so engaged, when they consume "quality of life" as place characteristics, then their pursuit can produce industry growth in places where that quality of life is perceived to be available for consumption.

It is perhaps no coincidence that Santa Monica, Santa Barbara, and San Luis Obispo show vitality in all three new urban economy sectors, since tourism firms commodify the same kinds of place-specific distinctions of desirability that software and entertainment firms capture as locational competitiveness in the quality-of-life district.[48] These distinctions are ultimately made by individuals who collectively direct capital investment to places, albeit by different mechanisms: the consumer market for tourism services, and the labor market for elite workers in software and entertainment. These non-local structures touch down in new settings as a result of two particular forces: environmental and cost-of-living strains in industry centers, and place representations that frame such strains as quality-of-life "problems" for those with the ability to go elsewhere for permanent or temporary quality-of-life "solutions."

Two points follow from this claim. First, the conditions of "demand" for desirable places are not intrinsic to places themselves. As I have described here, localities do not *create* growth in software, entertainment, and tourism; their growth instead manifests the expansion of non-local labor and consumer markets. There is historical and geographic irony in this process. Despite the credit taken by local boosters who promote a "pro-business" climate, and by local liberals who struggle to preserve amenities, neither group actually attracts capital investment; at best, their efforts only create the potential conditions for place desirability. Ultimately, it takes non-local industrial geography and place representations to render these places as, respectively, feasible and desirable sites for quality-of-life-based industry expansion.

Second, although I have focused here on how industrial features like flexible accumulation influence locational preferences, this process is by no means totally economically determined. Particular locational and lifestyle preferences also derive from the culturally patterned tastes specific to particular social groups, of the kind that Pierre Bourdieu and others have theorized as "habitus." Interestingly, in his seminal work, *Distinction,* Bourdieu gave much attention to "symbolic" sectors like media, advertising, and design, since they offer certain venues to express tastes and lifestyles by the social classes (the "new bourgeoisie" and "new petit bourgeoisie") that they employ.[49] Although those sectors do not conveniently overlap with software, entertainment, and tourism (at least as I have defined them), the latter are also symbolic, insofar as they embed aesthetic design and creative effort into work process and final product. More generally, the Bourdieuian analysis of habitus can conceivably be extended to elite workers and tourists' locational and lifestyle preferences. While others have pursued such a project,[50] I refrain from it here. My argument concerns less the mapping of social classes' cultural capital (which, among other things, would confine my analysis to the specific qualities of life consumed in Southern California) and more the explanation of the endogenous processes by which software, entertainment, and tourism *industries* produce these spaces of lifestyle.

QUALITY OF LIFE AS LOCATIONAL ASSET

As the new industrial space expands to quality-of-life districts, software, entertainment, and tourism executives show business interests in and personal attachments to those places that break in important ways from conventional locational motivations. Below, I review these new locational sentiments, although I do not want to overestimate the distinctions I make between them. For one reason, executives often combine them in seemingly contradictory outlooks. For example, in interviews some voiced strident slow-growth sentiments, then later expressed skepticism or even irritation with the local activists who promote slow growth. I find it more useful to consider the different sentiments as motifs in a larger and more ambiguous discourse about the competitive value of places' qualities of life.

THE LIFEBOAT MENTALITY

For some software and entertainment executives in Santa Barbara and San Luis Obispo, quality of life is a wholly personal good. I heard this theme repeatedly:

> I'm here for a reason other than business. I'm here because I like living here. It's the old lifeboat syndrome: Too many people climbing in the lifeboat, and it sinks.

Remarkably, this "lifeboat mentality" betrays little concern for how the local quality of life and its preservation might impinge on business. A few executives recognize how unconventional such an outlook on location is:

> I'm not a pro-growth person like most people in business often are, and we would prefer to see it go the other way, really . . . I suppose that bringing businesses to the area is important, but it's the kind of thing where we're here now, we lucked out [chuckles], and we're not trying to close the door on anyone else; but on the other hand, we'd like to see it remain the kind of place it was when we moved here.

As these comments suggest, the lifeboat mentality departs strongly from both agglomerative and "pro-business" interests in corporate location. For a few proponents, it legitimates a defense of community that entails governmental regulation, land-use restrictions, and other "anti-business" activities. Not surprisingly, many environmentalists express optimism when they hear local executives voice such extraordinary sentiments.

Importantly, the rhetorical subject of the lifeboat mentality is the elite worker, not the firm. For those who espouse this perspective, perhaps the strongest limit to their place attachments comes not from concern for the corporate bottom line, but rather from the impermanence of their stay in the quality-of-life district. One San Luis Obispo executive told me,

> [My firm's parent company] would love to have me in Vancouver, but I wrote it into my contract that I can't be moved to an office more than twenty-five miles away. If I didn't have that in my contract, I guarantee you that I would have been moved. I mean, I wouldn't have moved; I would have just resigned. With the people who live here, a lot of us, it's here or nothing. I wouldn't even consider moving.

Conceivably, few other elite workers demand such clauses in their contracts, and so their length of stay is more likely determined non-locally by promotion, corporate mergers, or entrepreneurial failure. Such circumstances test the strength of their quality-of-life attachments. Precisely because the lifeboat mentality is essentially personal, elite workers weigh their place of residence alongside job opportunities, family interests, and other lifestyle features. Some may decide it is time to "get off the ride" when their careers or companies experience upheaval, no matter how pleasant their stay in the quality-of-life district may be.

QUALITY OF LIFE AS BUSINESS GOOD

More commonly, software and entertainment executives view quality of life within a corporate framework. Typically, they acknowledge that local quality of life offers a "reliability wage" to sustain employees' morale.[51] The personal costs of migration and the smaller career safety net that elite work-ers find in the quality-of-life district minimize problems of labor control in the firm:

> The reality is, being in Santa Barbara is an advantage to us because if we recruit people here, and they love the lifestyle—which virtually everybody here does—they don't want to leave. And in the high-tech business, if you understand the high-tech business, there's a shortage of help. In Silicon Val-ley, everybody's a free agent. Free agency is the order of the day, which means people walk into your office—let's say somebody's making $70,000 a year—and say, "I just got offered $85,000 and $5,000 in stock options to move to another company. Match it or I'm out of here." I don't have that kind of stuff going on here.

A few executives admit that they can pay workers less in the quality-of-life district than they would in other industry centers.

Quality of life also serves as a valuable marketing tool to raise awareness of the location. A software executive related what he told Santa Barbara politicians who sought advice on promoting the area's high-tech industry:

> When I was asked probably six years ago, "What is it that is our differentiator [sic] here in the county?" I said, "Walk over to the window and look outside. There's your differentiator. There's not many people that have the coastal resource, the mountains and the ocean, and the city environment that Santa Barbara does. That's what you can use as the basis for attraction."

In speaking of amenities that "not many people" have, his comment illus-trates how quality of life attains competitive value through non-local per-ceptions of place distinction. Industry leaders who champion Santa Barbara and San Luis Obispo partake in urban discourses originating in the nine-teenth century that construct these places as the opposite of Los Angeles and its perceived urban ills. Other Southern California high-tech regions, even quite urbanized ones, emphasize their contrast to Los Angeles as well. A human resources spokesperson in San Diego observed that recruiters there refrain from associating their region's high-tech growth with Los Angeles, since the latter evokes "earthquakes and guns, which is a drawback. They would worry that it would taint what we are pushing, which is the quality of life here."[52]

In contrast to the more extreme lifeboat mentality, executives who regard quality of life as a business good contend that its preservation should be suf-ficiently "sensible" to allow their businesses to prosper. Particularly in exclu-sive places like Santa Barbara, a relevant issue is whether the high cost of living hurts firms' ability to recruit talent. As a CEO stated, "From a quality-of-life perspective, it's easy to get people to live here. From an expense perspective, it's not, because it's so expensive to buy housing." Several executives support expanding the local housing stock; a few even attribute housing shortages to growth controls and governmental regulations, a stance that moves them closer to the traditional urban business community's "pro-business" agenda and neglects how their industry creates the impetus for population growth.

In Santa Monica, a flexible district with quality-of-life appeal, software and entertainment executives do not necessarily view their location as a place to "get away from it all," in contrast to many of their Santa Barbara and San Luis Obispo counterparts. For some, the urban milieu is the primary locational asset, given the gregarious nature of creativity and production:

> I think as long as people are interested in working with people—actors, directors, and writers—they sort of need to smell each other. With Internet stuff, you're just designing stuff that's coming up Xs and 0s, and it's not important, other than just having people give you feedback on whether it's working or not. A writer can go off and write anywhere, but maybe he needs to be in the middle of New York to get the right feeling . . .

Other Santa Monica executives regard the trade-off between the benefits of critical mass and burdens of traffic, lack of parking, noise, and the high cost of living as a necessary sacrifice. For instance, a Hollywood television producer resigns herself to escaping to her second home in Santa Barbara on weekends. She explained the difference between the two locations:

> It's very different [in Los Angeles]. This is an industrial area. People want jobs and work. There [in Santa Barbara], they want to limit the amount of growth; they don't like people coming in from other places. Here, the city survives on that.

Still, the urban milieu proved sufficiently repellent to motivate at least one software executive I interviewed to move his company *from* Santa Monica *to* Santa Barbara.

THE PLACE CARETAKERS

Whereas tourism's sensitivity to cost factors and growth dependence might suggest "pro-business" locational concerns, executives in this sector generally recognize that competitive value ultimately derives from a location's desirability to visitors. When the features of desirability are the natural amenities and "community feel" that many Southern California locales have lost to sprawling development, then tourism executives acknowledge that preserving these local assets so that visitors can enjoy them makes good business sense. On this point, tourism leaders in Santa Monica, Santa Barbara, and San Luis Obispo are in remarkable consensus. Some even espouse what might be called an environmentalist stance. In Santa Monica, the setting for "Baywatch," the manager of the largest hotel told me,

> We were sort of concerned when the quality of water in the [Santa Monica Bay] went down, just for PR . . . I remember [NBC news anchor] Tom Brokaw speaking right in front of our hotel—and fortunately he didn't show it—saying how polluted Santa Monica Bay was. That's not what you want on national television. So I think the efforts [to clean the bay] have been very, very good, and it has [sic] kept the negative out of the national news.

Tourism firms generally oppose offshore oil drilling, for fear of a devastating oil spill or (in places without offshore rigs, like Santa Monica or San Luis Obispo) the taint of an industrialized coast. Tourism firms in Santa Barbara and San Luis Obispo have expressed concern for development encroaching onto the scenic landscapes that travelers view on their drive to the localities:

> We want to maintain the character of [San Luis Obispo] as being something different from where [visitors] are coming from . . . I think that in this town, there's a genuine recognition on the part of people involved in tourism as to why people are coming here. They're coming here to this town because of the ambiance of it, which is the result of some of the policies that people might label as "no growth."

As with software and entertainment executives who regard quality of life as a business good, tourism executives recognize that their dependence on local amenities leads to an unconventional business and political agenda. A San Luis Obispo hotelier offered an important distinction: "If this were a town . . . where the hotels are just taking care of business travelers, and they're here to do business with the government or other businesses, I think you might tend to see them more supportive of growth-oriented policies." However, the industry's concern with visitors' quality of life is not always so progressive or ecologically sensitive. In Santa Monica and Santa Barbara, many tourism firms endorse efforts to keep the homeless out of visitor zones. And in San Luis Obispo, tourism leaders staunchly support the controversial use of dune buggies on the coastal park because this recreation also makes San Luis Obispo "unique," as the only public park in California to allow motor vehicles on the beach. Their stance rejects the worries of many environmentalists that dune buggying endangers coastal ecosystems and indigenous species.

THE AMBIGUOUS QUALITY-OF-LIFE DISCOURSE

In important ways, the role of quality of life in software, entertainment, and tourism locations mitigates the placeless rationale of the new economy, in which firms and industry rootlessly span the globe with only "rational" bottom-line concerns for the places they inhabit. Corporations that move to Santa Monica, Santa Barbara, and San Luis Obispo looking for a "pro-business" climate can only find frustrations. Also, Santa Barbara and especially San Luis Obispo can hardly boast a critical mass of firms and the agglomerative pull of a flexible district. Small wonder, then, that some scholars can only cite "random locational factors" to explain why a software or entertainment firm would move to, or start in, places like Santa Barbara or San Luis Obispo that offer no apparent competitive advantage.

In fact, quality of life primarily serves the locational interests not of firms, but of another key actor in the new industrial space. In software and entertainment, this actor is the elite worker whose status and power have risen vis-à-vis the corporation because of entrepreneurial opportunities and labor market demand for flexible skills. In tourism, it is the visitor who seeks a place-based experience unavailable in his or her home and most other places. That the firm accommodates the locational motivations, even partly (e.g., in Santa Monica, which also offers agglomerative advantage), of elite workers and tourists underscores the fundamental roles these actors have to enable productivity (in software and entertainment) and fuel demand (in tourism). It is beyond the scope of this book to conclude whether place-based quality of life will prove an enduring dynamic in the new industrial space. Yet, at least at the end of the twentieth century, it has offered a firm-level solution to a collective problem created elsewhere: the crisis of labor control exacerbated by environmental strains in Silicon Valley and other centers of the new industrial space. For this reason, places endowed with desirable amenities attract certain elite workers and tourists, although it should not be said that these places create their own advantage. More accurately, they benefit from the valorization of "quality of life" by non-local actors who can direct capital investment to certain places and not others.

These locational motivations frame software, entertainment, and tourism firms' civic modes of participation in Santa Monica, Santa Barbara, and San Luis Obispo. Although they seem to promise a new source of advantage for "nice towns" in the global economy, at this stage the political consequences are less clear. For one reason, new urban economy firms remain concerned to profit from place, even if they enact this interest in seemingly unprecedented ways. Additionally, elite workers' stories of how they chose to visit or move to the three Southern California areas reveal the workings of pre-existing lifestyle sensibilities; their understanding of how locals interpret and fight for quality of life can hardly be assumed. Finally, it is possible that the "desirability" of some places may not be entirely sustainable. Conceivably, if the quality of life in these places erodes for some reason, such as too much economic development, then they too could lose the appeal to software, entertainment, and tourism firms that made them initially competitive relative to other locations.

These sensibilities and possibilities illustrate the essentially superficial appreciation that elite workers and tourists have of place. This is perhaps to be expected in tourism, since the object of the tourist gaze gets its charge from its contrast to the tourist's home and workplace, not its innate qualities.[53] However, the tourist gaze has now extended itself to sectors where the creative milieu and the reproduction of labor have become aestheticized to a large degree.[54] As in other industrial centers with distinct urban character, such as Chicago's Wicker Park or New York's Lower East Side, local histories and qualities are appropriated by knowledge workers as "aesthetic rather than social principles."[55] In sum, economic attachments to place, for either bottom-line reasons or to accommodate elite workers, are an important correction to prevailing ideas about the rootless nature of capital. Whether they portend progressive possibilities for even "nice towns" is less assured, as the following chapters reveal.

4

Building a Site in
the New Urban Economy

A fter a software, entertainment, or tourism company (or any other kind, for that matter) selects a location, it then has to find a physical site for its business. This basic need brings it in contact with the local development sector. But are new urban economy firms' development politics substantially different than those of traditional industry or the local business community?

In this chapter, I examine the development component of local business structure to see whether these companies make a political difference in three areas. First, I look at their *site needs*. For most corporate tenants, these traditionally revolve around minimizing local operating costs, which encourage them to search and perhaps even lobby for sites with development subsidies (like tax abatements), low rents, zoning exemptions, lax environmental regulations, and a "streamlined" (read, quiescent) local planning process. This hardball development agenda legitimates the conservative politics of local developers and their urban business allies, which endorse a climate of investor prerogative in order to attract footloose capital. Second, I examine firms' *systemic relationships* with the local development sector. Depending on their site needs, clients may undertake in-depth and repeated interactions with developers whereby they can learn of shared interests, establish norms of collective behavior, and develop cooperation patterns that can lead to successful business community mobilization.[1] Slow-growth controversies can especially make clients turn to local developers, land-use lawyers, and others for their experience in planning negotiations. This in turn may furnish the local development sector with opportunities to enlist tenants in growth coalition efforts. Third, I examine *collective mobilization* within each industry around development projects. Even if companies have no special site needs or systemic relationships with the local development sector, they may still support other firms that encounter political resistance in the development process. Through material (e.g., dependence on a local supplier or customer) or sentimental (e.g., boosterism for a sector or industry) ties to other companies, their indirect stakes can galvanize an all-for-one solidarity within the local industry.[2]

WORKSPACES OF THE NEW URBAN ECONOMY

The types of workspaces occupied by the software and entertainment firms suggest that three factors in varying configurations and degrees shape their site needs. *Firm size,* as measured by the number of employees, indicates the extensiveness of a company's land use. That in turn points to the issue of local real estate market supply. Smaller firms can more easily inhabit basic small office units that are the mainstay of commercial real estate markets, whereas larger firms need bigger workspaces that are less plentiful and may need to be custom built. *Governmental obstacles,* the second factor, are those non-routine requirements that a potential tenant must satisfy before it occupies a site, based on how the relevant jurisdiction of government classifies and regulates a tenant's activities. Zoning restrictions, use permits, and environmental regulations require a company to seek prior approvals and exemptions from local planning departments and (if appeal is needed) higher governmental units; the costs and delays incurred are frequently felt as burdensome. Finally, *sectoral turbulence* refers to how the dynamism and uncertainty of specific industries influence the site needs of their firms. In sectors where corporate upheaval or project-by-project work are the norm, companies may not anticipate steady growth and expansion.

WORKSPACE AS AMENITY

As Table 4.1 shows, most software firms are small, whether in the three Southern California areas or high-tech centers like Silicon Valley. Table 4.1 reports industry firm sizes for the *counties* surrounding Santa Monica, Santa Barbara and San Luis Obispo; for a more generalizable comparison in software, the Silicon Valley county of Santa Clara is included. Regrettably, the county level of analysis exceeds the territories of the three places and especially obscures Santa Monica, but the consistency in firm size is suggestive. At least four of every five companies employ fewer than twenty people. Many are even smaller than that, as a Santa Barbara software executive explained: "Most of these companies are kind of like two guys and a dog. They're half a dozen people working in a small environment, and as is typical, I think, throughout the technology world, some small percentage of them will become long-term successes." Furthermore, very few of these companies are establishments that customers physically visit to browse, purchase, or

Table 4.1

1997 firm size: proportion of firms (number of firms)

Sector	County	1–19 employees	20–99 employees	100–499 employees	500+ employees
Software	Los Angeles	84% (2492)	11% (328)	2% (66)	0% (8)
	Santa Barbara	83% (119)	15% (22)	1% (2)	0% (0)
	San Luis Obispo	89% (63)	7% (5)	4% (3)	0% (0)
	Santa Clara	81% (1,999)	14% (351)	4% (98)	1% (21)
Entertainment	Los Angeles	91% (5,248)	7% (415)	2% (102)	0% (5)
	Santa Barbara	92% (66)	8% (6)	0% (0)	0% (0)
	San Luis Obispo	76% (16)	24% (5)	0% (0)	0% (0)
Tourism	Los Angeles	74% (11,809)	24% (3,886)	1% (225)	0% (17)
	Santa Barbara	68% (627)	31% (280)	1% (9)	0% (0)
	San Luis Obispo	73% (483)	26% (171)	1% (5)	0% (0)

SOURCE: U.S. Census, *County Business Patterns*, 1997.

consume goods and services; therefore, most do not use signage to attract shoppers from the street, nor allocate space for the general public beyond a standard lobby.

For software companies of this size, site needs pose few governmental obstacles in the development process. Unless they require substantial modifications or zoning exemptions (e.g., from manufacturing to software uses, which allows for more employees per square feet), they can expect a routine interaction with governmental planning units that, in most cases, their developer-landlords willingly make on their behalf. Environmental regulations also tend to be negligible, given the white-collar nature of most software firms' work. Parking availability was the most common land-use restriction that I heard of, but only a few firms employ enough people to face alternate transit requirements. The exceptions to routine land-use needs are found among older, defense-related R&D branches that handle regulated substances and need to occupy custom-modified buildings; notably, this group is atypical of the newer generation of "pure" software firms responsible for recent industry growth. Otherwise, most firms can reasonably avoid a complicated permitting procedure when they move in.

This overall lack of governmental obstacles, of course, assumes that local planning agencies are familiar with the nature of software activity *before* the first companies move in. Although their operations seem self-evidently white-collar and "clean" to most software companies, local governments can conclude otherwise, as pioneer migrants are most likely to discover. One described his bureaucratic hassles in San Luis Obispo after he moved a company from Los Angeles:

> Instead of waiting for the business permit application to come in the mail like you would in LA, I wanted to be Johnny Good Citizen because we were new to the community and wanted to be a part of it. I went down to the [county] government and said, 'Hey, we've rented a building and I want to get a license to do business here; I want to support the community as much as I can.' They said, 'What, you rented a building without talking to us first?' I said, 'What are you talking about?' because that's not the way it's done in big cities. They said, 'You can't rent a building.' I said, 'Why not?' and they said, 'Because you don't have a use permit.' I said, 'Okay, explain that one to me,' because I had never faced that in all the places I had been. They said, 'In our community, certain buildings are designed for certain things.' I said, 'Okay, what do you base that on?' They said federal [standard industrial classification] codes . . . So I said, 'Look us up, and see if we have any problems being in this building.' And, of course, the federal government, in their [sic] stupidity, happened to take software publishers and put them in the same category as all publishers. Well, most publishers are printers. So, because we're in a federal SIC code with printers, they tell us we can't be in that building because they don't allow anybody with that SIC code, and that's primarily because they don't want printing machines.

Just as pioneer migrants promote the local quality of life to others in their industry, their stories of "anti-business" local government can circulate quickly among colleagues and gain a currency greater than their typicality for later firms. For example, many San Luis Obispo executives frequently describe local government as "anti-business," even when they themselves did not report negative experiences moving into their buildings. Despite (or perhaps because of) such "war stories," local governments in the three Southern California places now recognize and classify software firms as white-collar operations. Following the pioneer generation, most software and entertainment companies deal with planning agencies for no more than obtaining an initial local business permit.

Since the last decade, software firms have experienced a remarkable degree of sectoral turbulence, first due to the race to establish market presence as the "Information Superhighway" was developed, and later due to the "dot-com crash" of 2000. This turbulence tends to accelerate the time-span of many companies' outlooks. High-tech buzzwords like "fast company" (a technology trade magazine), "the new new thing" (a CEO's biography), and "start up, kick butt, cash out" (a mantra for many start-up firms) evoke the planning horizons of many software firms. Especially before 2000, many have measured success less by profits than by rapid corporate growth ("scalability," in the industry jargon). One developer-landlord expressed astonishment that "these companies think they aren't hitting their target if they don't have thirty-percent quarter growth." To the dismay of some business observers, many high-tech executives openly confess plans to abandon their corporate helm once their firm has gone public or been "flipped" (i.e., acquired by a larger firm).[3] This short-term orientation makes most software firms reluctant to sink substantial costs into local real estate. "The bigger issue for a lot of these companies, unless they're a really big company, is they don't want to own their own real estate anyway," a developer observed. "That doesn't make a lot of economic sense, to be pouring your money into real estate." Most firms avoid committing to leases longer than three to five years, a remarkably short period in the development industry, and very few seek to purchase their own property.

Combined, these three factors mean that most software firms look for basic white-collar offices for their intellectual and creative work. Many companies' origins in the proverbial tinkerer's garage or bedroom illustrate how extremely modest spatial requirements can satisfy most firms with one-to-three employees, especially when their activities can be carried out on computer networks, the Internet, and research university labs.[4] This profile fits many software consultants and Internet content providers, which are often one- to two-employee operations working out of an individual's home. In industry centers like San Francisco or New York City, freelancers and very small firms especially favor apartment lofts converted into specially zoned live-work spaces, the popularity of which has gentrified whole neighborhoods into company town milieus with very local agglomerative synergies. Further away from industry centers, firms at the smallest scale occupy more conventional residential sites like apartments or single-family houses; these settings typify the pure quality-of-life migrant whose development interests turn solely on personal lifestyle, not firm-level criteria. Throughout the new industrial space, home-based operations also circumvent (and in some cases illegally skirt) the land-use restrictions imposed on commercially or industrially zoned property; live-work spaces are often exempt from residential fees like school district taxes.[5]

Up to about twenty employees, software firms rather easily obtain sites in local real estate markets. Between twenty to one hundred employees— the size of no more than fifteen percent of software firms—the supply of suitable sites grows more limited, particularly in growth-controlled quality-of-life districts. At this size, most firms look in office complexes or industrial parks where "flex-space" units allow tenants to accommodate business cycles by taking down or adding walls, and enabling a variety of cubicle arrangements. A special kind of commercial site often sought by start-up firms is the business incubator. Here, firms that meet certain criteria (usually related to age, size, and profitability) can affordably obtain a small office (e.g., two hundred to one thousand square feet), industrial-strength Internet access, at least some utilities, a landlord familiar with start-up firms' vicissitudes, and proximity to other start-up firms. More elaborate incubators provide hands-on managerial oversight by venture capitalists, consultants, and legal service providers.

In software agglomerations like Silicon Valley or New York City's Silicon Alley, the availability of "industry standard" sites and development services like incubators is just one of many external economies. However, with such benefits also come the costs of critical mass. An industrial park setting can exacerbate low morale and employee turnover, with its no-frills offices, generic cubicles, monotonous architecture, sub/exurban location, and distance from urban amenities other than convenience stores and shopping center restaurants. As one response, industrial park developers increasingly provide amenities like food courts and fitness centers. High-tech companies, a developer observed, "value those [amenities] because they realize that's employee retention." Yet, for the quality-of-life migrant who has "been there and done that" in locations where those amenities are as standard as flexible work hours and casual clothing, the prospect of working in yet another industrial park can be less than enticing.

For this reason, the site needs of many firms take account of elite workers' concerns for a quality of life superior to Silicon Valley industrial parks. To gain an architectural edge in sustaining productivity, some firms use an inspired touch to resurrect old industrial or commercial spaces, like an old kitchen supply store with a spacious open-air showroom that now provides flex-space; the second floor of a downtown department store; and a windowless warehouse space fitted for the dim lighting and mock-dungeon environs of a cutting-edge video game designer, to cite a few examples I observed. In an industry where foosball tables and fully stocked refrigerators are the norm, companies tout their uncommon amenities to employees and trade journals; one company offers a sofa for every five employees, while another designs its interior according to feng shui principles. However, such investments in architecture and interior design are often at odds with the realities of sectoral turbulence. Especially at the start-up stage, many firms do not want to sink capital into aesthetic embellishments. Also, the extent to which local developers build or modify to such specifications depends on how favorably they perceive the market's general ability to afford such premiums, the average duration of leases, and future tenants' likely demand for such settings. Nor are embellishments necessary for elite workers with only one job prospect (typical for nascent industry centers like San Luis Obispo) and/or whose residential migration alone satisfies their quality-of-life needs.[6] "The trick," one Santa Monica software executive explained, "is to balance cost-effectiveness with the right atmosphere for developing a unique start-up culture."[7]

The heavy demand for downtown offices illustrates a popular solution for firms unwilling to make special real estate investments. Downtown offices that typically house insurance companies and law firms may lack the subsidized utilities and proximity to other technology companies offered by incubators and conventional industrial parks. However, they compensate with external amenities that employees consume in lunch hours, short commutes, and from a well-placed window: village views, the specialized services and recreations that come with a thriving downtown, and even walking distance to workers' residences. Especially as firms expand to ten or more employees, they seem to increasingly value the externalized amenities that downtown locations offer. One result is clear. The demand for downtown sites frequently upgrades neighboring parcels toward the "higher and better uses" cherished by developers and other businesses: condominiums, bistros, bars, and urban amenities sought out by professional classes.[8] (In a humorous yet conspicuous nod to this new clientele, one Mexican restaurant I visited added a "software.com burrito" to its menu.)

With one hundred employees or more—a size that relatively few software companies ever attain—many firms reorganize their activities functionally and spatially, typically concentrating firm-specific activities (like administration or R&D) where the executives live and relocating those activities (like marketing or programming) that can benefit from industrial and labor-market agglomeration to larger industry centers. To accommodate growth at this size, software firms usually move to a larger local site and/or establish branches in other locations. Industrial sites that are both spacious and physically equipped for software work permeate the landscape of Silicon Valley, yet they are scarcer in the real estate markets of the three Southern California areas. Only Santa Monica has substantial space zoned for offices of this scale, a few miles outside the central business district and away from the beach. In Santa Barbara, firms must look in the crowded technology corridors of suburban Goleta and rural Carpinteria; San Luis Obispo firms have to drive ten to twenty miles away from downtown before finding such sites. Importantly, firms of this size are generally impersonal and often publicly traded operations; if the firm had entrepreneurial origins, the founder has quite often left the firm by this stage. Unless executives retain some special attachment to the location, site needs for large firms generally reflect strictly *corporate* concerns for the costs and benefits of doing local business.

LOOKING FOR THE "RIGHT ADDRESS"

In Hollywood or the quality-of-life district, only one in ten companies employs twenty or more people (see Table 4.1; San Luis Obispo departs from this profile only because four of the largest firms in this small sector are radio and television stations). Motion picture and video production companies are especially small; ninety-two percent in California have less than ten employees, and eighty-six percent have less than five.[9] Except on famous studio properties, entertainment companies do not allocate space for the general public to buy goods or visit.

Also like software, the requirements of entertainment workspaces entail few governmental obstacles. From corporate branches down to small publicity offices, most firms conduct basic white-collar work where "technology" means telephones, faxes, PCs, and entertainment consoles. Consequently, they can work in sites zoned for basic commercial use. In Santa Monica and Santa Barbara, more technology-intensive firms such as editing facilities or (in a "new media" overlap with software) studios for taping and broadcasting live Internet content may set up in light manufacturing zones; San Luis Obispo's one entertainment firm (a manufacturer of specialized technology) works out of a manufacturing zone.

Entertainment firms encounter a different kind of sectoral turbulence than software. Although anti-trust legislation has mandated "flexibility" for the film industry since 1948, this form of organization has become increasingly common and strategic in the face of corporate mergers, changing logistics of production (e.g., lower costs for on-location filming, more mobile postproduction technologies), and new niches like talent managers and digital content distributors. In this context of flux, companies work on a project-by-project basis, and exploit the advantage of a particular size: the client attention of a small production company or publicity firm, the scheduling convenience of one's own postproduction facility, the innovative specialties of a mid-sized effects house, the prestigious clientele of a large (over three hundred agents) talent agency, or the cross-marketing and risk diversification of a giant media conglomerate. Companies forecast growth in terms of increasing business activity, a growing clientele, and more projects in development, but rarely in terms of new employees and land-use intensification. Consequently, most entertainment firms do not plan for indefinite spatial expansion and can therefore seek a somewhat longer-term address than in software.

Producers, screenwriters, directors, musicians, actors, record producers, and other independent contractors do much of the important preproduction and deal-making work in entertainment. Some occupy personal or (for the more in-demand elite workers) production company offices, but most use primary and, especially in quality-of-life districts, secondary residences for making phone calls, reading or writing screenplays and proposals, rehearsing lines, composing music, and other discrete tasks. For much of this work, land-use needs involve no "industrial" infrastructure other than residential real estate and personal services (e.g., restaurants, specialty stores, mobile phone coverage). An independent producer with a primary residence in Santa Monica and an office in West Hollywood described the work she does from her weekend home in Santa Barbara: "I don't go there to do business" in the sense of keeping an office with employees and written documents, but she reads scripts and (begrudgingly) takes business calls from there.

Independent contractors' geographical distance is also possible because their links to job prospects and project approvals are sustained by talent agencies, film studios, record labels, and production companies back in Hollywood. For these entities, site needs are recognizably corporate. Small firms doing entirely white-collar, non-craft work—publicity firms, independent production companies, small management firms, and so on—choose sites primarily for proximity to the company town. Firms cluster by industry niche and status, such that the "right address" extends even to particular buildings. Most firms in these fields lease five-hundred-to five-thousand-square-foot suites in multistory buildings in Santa Monica and other edge cities like Beverly Hills, West Hollywood, Culver City, Pasadena, and Glendale. As these places are zoned for dense office buildings, entertainment firms can easily find sites without special planning constraints. "We have offices, we make phone calls," a film director explained. "When we're shooting or doing other things, *then* we deal with different agencies; we deal with the specific city government that we're trying to find locations for." One consequence is that "development politics" is not very tangible for entertainment executives and elite workers in small to medium-sized companies, since the ample real estate markets for their basic land-use needs allow them to think about real estate very rarely, if at all.

Not all firms at this size can occupy generic office settings, however. Those with specialized, capital-intensive equipment—recording studios, postproduction facilities, and digital effects houses, for example—usually need to modify their spaces substantially. Special effects houses often seek to create the same creative, "funky" environs common to video game designers and other high-tech firms (with which they often compete for employees). A Santa Monica developer-landlord observed, "These [entertainment firms] have so much money, their only concern is creating the culture they need: the environment in which their employees will be happy."[10] Given the profitability and local prestige of entertainment tenants' activities, developers often custom build these sites and/or sell them outright to suit tenants' needs.

In Santa Monica, several entertainment firms with commanding downtown locations work in the high-tech, capital-intensive area of postproduction. Perhaps because of this field's phenomenal growth, these firms often show a very conventional interest in site expansion and, related, a potential for community conflicts. For instance, the privately owned Santa Monica Studios (with eighty employees in 1997) purchased a 230,000-square-foot warehouse space to build a complex of digital soundstages, artist lofts, a restaurant, a dining commissary, and a fitness center. Designed as a "European town" environment of castle-like towers and cobblestone streets, the project generated several environmental impact analysis drafts as well as local controversy over the displacement of a resident artist colony. The firm's president declared, "I sympathize with the [artists], but I'm not going to stop the growth of my company and an $85 million expansion because they are upset."[11] He also undertook community outreach by running for the local school board (see Chapter 6) and giving money to local nonprofits (see Chapter 7), thereby revealing a savvy in growth politics not always shared by smaller and more routine kinds of entertainment firms.

With one hundred employees or more, entertainment firms usually concentrate their employees from scattered divisions into multistory and/or campus-like facilities. However, seldom do these projects entail expanding soundstage and studio lots. A *Los Angeles Times* entertainment reporter explained:

> No studio today needs to be in the real estate business. Studios today have big lots with sound stages because studio founders such as Adolph Zukor, Jack Warner, Carl Laemmle and Walt Disney built them when studios really did need them. Today, the lots run like a side business for studios. It's not a bad one, often bringing in fees to rent stages and equipment. And the sound stages provide homes for studio TV shows such as 'Friends,' 'E.R.,' and 'Frasier' . . . [Studios] need office space, which is just a cell phone call away to a commercial real estate broker. As for everything else, there's no point in buying when you can rent.[12]

More often, at this scale, entertainment corporations tend to speculate on their vast real estate properties. In the past few decades, historic studio properties in Burbank, Culver City, and Hollywood proper have changed ownership and land-use zones to great profit. A recent example of land speculation occurred when MCA/Universal, amidst two corporate acquisitions, pursued a major land-use change on its properties in Universal City (an unincorporated community of Los Angeles County) to expand its *tourism* business, the Universal Studios theme park.[13]

THE BURDENS OF LAND USE

Although firm size in tourism skews toward small employers (see Table 4.1), most companies in this industry designate the bulk of their real estate for customers, so their spatial requirements are considerably larger than comparable employers in software and entertainment. Yet even more than firm size, the land uses that local governments allot tourism companies shape their site needs. Tourism firms deal with regulated land uses over customer parking, noise levels, and alcohol sales, to name a few activities. Local politics often motivates this government regulation. Through complaints to police and planning commissions, some residents express their frustration and resentment over how tourists have "ruined" their nice town by generating noise from restaurants, nightclubs, and outdoor concerts; congesting the main streets during the summer and weekends; using up scarce public parking; and filling downtown blocks and neighborhoods with visitor centers, gift shops, hotel districts, and other visitor services. In Santa Monica, one politician said that tourism, "almost more than left or right, has been the dividing line in the community about whether you're satisfied with what has happened" since the 1990s.

Consequently, even though restaurants and hotels can find sites on the market already built for their land-use needs, they nevertheless have to obtain and, in many cases, educate themselves beforehand about permits for conditional uses, parking, and other government-regulated activities with every liquor license, sidewalk dining, and other land-use change they apply for. In a typical account, a Santa Monica restaurateur described the governmental obstacles he encountered to increase the seating allotment:

> I had to go through a conditional use permit process. It was a six-month process. It required a lot of community outreach to mitigate a lot of the concerns relative to parking, noise, traffic. So I had to interact with the city staff at the planning department and the community.

Even in years of steady industry growth, tourism encounters sectoral turbulence that derives from seasonal cycles of consumer demand.[14] In a context where land-use "headaches" mean business costs and delays, access to capital offers the best means to withstand this turbulence. With enough financing, hotel and restaurant owners can turn daily operations over to a corporate management company; growing establishments can expand; and the local development sector can be retained to navigate governmental obstacles. These uses of capital often weed out smaller entrepreneurs in favor of those with other establishments, investors, or corporate affiliations.

Generally, tourism firms profit by cutting costs and boosting revenues, which are expressed in the number of visitors per year, hotel rooms booked, meals served, and productivity per wages paid. While these all point to the intensification of land use, physically expanding an existing site is not necessarily the preferred way that tourism firms do this. Tonier restaurants and hotels may endanger their ambiance with growth over the short term (unsightly construction deters visitors) and the long (more customers dilute their "specialness"). More often, growing establishments expand by opening additional hotels or restaurants—ideally, ones that do not compete for the same market (e.g., by cuisine, location) with the original establishments. The proliferation of small bed and breakfast (B&B) establishments in Santa Barbara and San Luis Obispo also illustrates how bigger buildings are not always better when industry growth depends on the local quality of life. Still, there are diminishing returns to growth that merely increases the local supply of firms without boosting external demand (i.e., more visitors), as tourism firms are well aware. In the 1990s, fear of market saturation led Santa Monica tourism firms to successfully lobby the city for a moratorium on new restaurant licenses.

The smallest restaurants and lodging establishments typically occupy sites already zoned and developed for their respective uses. Firms of this size rarely build from scratch or (for restaurants) have developers renovate facilities that were zoned for different uses, due to the prohibitive costs and headaches of converting such a small site. By acquiring an already zoned and developed site, small entrepreneurial tourism firms minimize their business costs. Only B&Bs easily convert from non-tourism (i.e., residential) land uses, at least in localities where community sentiments favor historical preservation (as when B&Bs occupy restored Victorian houses) and city policies promote tourism. Past this size, restaurants and firms often expand incrementally by buying out and absorbing neighboring sites. The process is facilitated when firms originally set up in hotel rows, retail corridors, and other tourism zones, and can consequently avoid applying for zoning changes on adjacent parcels.

At the largest scale (over three hundred employees), tourism firms are usually large hotels or special destinations (e.g., amusement parks). In the three Southern California localities, large tourism firms spark intense controversy when they seek to develop extensive sites in areas with heavy traffic (e.g., downtowns) or cherished locations (e.g., beachfronts). Voters in Santa Monica, for instance, passed a 1990 ballot measure prohibiting hotel development on the beachfront after a local entrepreneur received the city council's approval to develop a large hotel on state-owned land. This did not halt two other major hotel projects that were slated for construction across the street from the beachfront, which still ranks among the Los Angeles region's top hotel markets.

Because government and political obstacles loom so large at this scale, firms often turn to local business leaders like land-use lawyers or architects for the political acumen needed to advance a large hotel project. Or large tourism companies may use their resources to present their case to locals themselves; one Santa Barbara hotelier sought to circumvent city hall with a 1998 ballot initiative to approve expansion up to 225 rooms—seventy-five more than permitted under local zoning laws. Additionally, by encouraging the establishment of quasi-public agencies to oversee land-use authority on tourist zones, tourism firms can hope to get a "fairer" (i.e., once-removed from public) hearing. Although its scale is not really applicable to the three Southern California localities, the case of Walt Disney World suggests yet another strategy by which a deep-pocketed tourism firm can control the political and regulatory environments for its massive development: establishing its own private government and land-use authority.[15]

RELATIONSHIPS WITH DEVELOPERS

Describing his fortunes in the new urban economy, one developer voiced a sentiment shared by others in Santa Monica, Santa Barbara, and San Luis Obispo: "Thank goodness Hollywood, Internets, and other things all came along" to offset the decline of Cold War–era defense R&D firms. Office rents have increased dramatically in the three places, Santa Monica's being the highest (for the Los Angeles metropolitan region as well) at $3.00–4.35 per square foot for beachfront properties and one or two dollars more for the city's Class A office space.[16] In the same year (2000), a developer with high-tech properties in both Santa Barbara and San Luis Obispo told me average rents climbed to $1.30–1.70 per square foot in the former area, and somewhat less in the latter. At least before the dot-com crash, developers regarded software and entertainment firms as prestige clients able to pay the highest rents for the best spaces. In smaller markets like San Luis Obispo, software and entertainment firms are "the minority of what's going on now," one developer reported, "but they are so high profile that they take on maybe more visibility and maybe more relative importance because if these guys hit the big time, it's kind of like the lottery." Tourism firms are less lucrative tenants for the development industry, but, in their favor, they help anchor downtown and beachfront real estate values. Developers also see tourism firms as proof that "people want to be here," reinforcing the idea that the other two sectors have local potential as well.

Yet profits aside, does the new urban economy create systemic relationships between firms in the three sectors and developers? Qualitatively different than "arm's-length" transactions, systemic relationships here involve repeated face-to-face interactions between developer and client, ideally at the executive levels for both parties. With such privileged access, developers and their allies can potentially mobilize their clients to aid their pro-development agenda.

However, systemic relationships do not appear to be the norm in software and entertainment. Since most firms in these sectors are small and have no special land-use requirements, they comprise *routine tenants* that most likely maintain only arm's-length dealings with developers. Although their prestige and ability to pay high rents make developers willing to help them move in "from start to finish," their site needs necessitate only a very simple interaction. This starts with their initial site search, which developers describe as remarkably informal. Most firms simply retain a real estate broker to show them potential sites and then contact the chosen site's developer-landlord to negotiate a lease; in some cases, they skip the broker and contact the developer themselves. This casual site search helps keep these firms off the radar of the older business community. As a developer observed, "A lot of the times, you don't even know the software companies exist. They're quiet." Also, their basic site needs tend to insulate them from the construction and zoning process. They occupy a building *after* the developer has obtained land-use and building approvals and, in growth-conscious municipalities, after local growth battles have been waged. If that process makes occupying a building more expensive, developers incorporate the costs into the rents they charge, which do not appear to deter software and entertainment companies from paying them. Consequently, developers have little opportunity to expose routine tenants to conservative sentiments by depicting local government and community activists as "anti-business" adversaries.

Custom tenants, a minority in software and entertainment, includes firms that cannot usually satisfy their site needs on the existing real estate market and are therefore more likely to purchase or "build to suit" their sites. This group consists mostly of mid- to large-sized firms that are financially willing and able to invest substantially in real estate. To find and build a suitable space, this group is more likely to approach the traditional civic network proactively, for example, by contacting local chambers of commerce beforehand about local site prospects.[17] Developers may even court the largest firms as anchor tenants to help secure financing for big office or industrial park projects. These activities entail repeated interactions with developers and related businesses that lay the basis for systemic relationships, in contrast to routine tenants.

Importantly, large software and entertainment firms usually have real estate divisions that mediate these systemic relationships. Whether they serve to amplify or reduce the developer's influence appears to hinge on the availability of suitable sites. In an example of the former, a film studio moved into a sizable Santa Monica office park after its spatial requirements for class A space on the Westside to house hundreds of employees left it only one alternate site, in the "more congested" Century City. An executive from this studio told me he personally knew the developer-landlord (one of the region's largest), backed the same electoral candidates as the developer (see also Chapter 5), and endorsed the developer's pending Playa Vista project (discussed below).

Yet corporate real estate divisions can also reduce the client-developer relationship to a merely pecuniary one. For instance, one of Santa Monica's largest software firms has moved four times for cost considerations after each lease expired: "We've kind of been in this area [for twenty years], but we really have not paid attention to whether it's been Marina Del Rey, or Westwood, or the other place on Sawtelle, or Santa Monica." While this was the only firm that I encountered to employ such an economizing strategy, its incidence is no doubt more common where large firms have greater choice of suitable sites, like in Silicon Valley.

Software deserves special mention, since Silicon Valley and other software districts have introduced real estate innovations that effectively thicken firms' relationships to developers. In the business incubator, where developer-landlords appreciate the unique hurdles that start-ups face, tenants can obtain shorter lease terms and other special considerations. More generally, developers may also discount rents in exchange for options and other rights to company profits.[18] While this kind of rent-for-profit agreement "goes on every day in Silicon Valley, if you read the trade magazines," it seems less common in smaller markets where local developers are unfamiliar with how the software industry works and do not view developing amenity-laden workspaces as worth their efforts for such a small fraction of their clients. "You need a certain breed of partners for such an arrangement," a Santa Barbara developer told me, "and most of our partners aren't interested in using their real estate funds to go into the high-tech business." Nor is it certain to become widespread outside of Silicon Valley, since landlords have lost substantial sums from bankrupt companies after the dot-com crash of 2000. "Landlords are going to stop doing business with start-up companies," warned a New York City realtor. "It's not worth having to go through this."[19] Although these innovations make systemic relationships possible, they require a certain level of specialized expertise that developers often lack outside of the most important industry centers.

Of the new urban economy sectors, tourism firms are most prone to systemic relationships with the local development sector. No matter how basic their site needs might be, local regulation of their business makes them likely to seek out developers and other businesses with expertise in planning and land-use matters. Again, an important intervening factor is the degree to which tourism firms can obtain financing. Entrepreneurial firms are often "small potatoes" for developers because they cannot always afford extensive conversions or expand as much as they hope. To circumvent governmental obstacles, they often do the work themselves and gain hands-on expertise. As the following chapters illustrate, small tourism entrepreneurs tend to be especially active in local business organizations, electoral campaigns, and other community affairs, in large part because these activities offer informal opportunities to meet local development representatives and acquire political expertise and information about potential land-use headaches.

By contrast, corporate and larger tourism firms can regularly afford to retain the local development industry for such expertise. This appears to be standard procedure for corporate hotels, since managers are usually nonlocal and are rotated every few years, thereby depriving their companies of any local knowledge they acquire during their tenure. A land-use lawyer observed that corporate hotels "sometimes have a healthy level of sophistication, but usually they're distanced from the community, which makes my job more complicated." The largest corporate chains usually have real estate divisions to mitigate these systemic relationships. Occasionally, they are willing to aid developers *quid pro quo* on certain urban business community efforts, but unlike entrepreneurial firms they rarely sink costs in either money or energy beyond what is required for their immediate benefit.

BIG PROJECTS, LITTLE SOLIDARITY

Even if most companies have no potentially problematic site needs, do they support the projects of others in their industry that do encounter political resistance? Vested interests in local industry growth or certain companies' success are two factors of local business structure that might rally firms or business leaders when one of their own faces development controversies.

Three of the biggest software, entertainment, and tourism projects around the three Southern California localities reveal the reasons why and extent to which these industries collectively mobilize around development politics.

THE SIGNATURE R&D CAMPUS

Even a brief drive along Silicon Valley's freeways might lead the casual observer to suspect that the chief way a software company "arrives" in the industry is by building its own corporate campus. Generic corporate suburbs, satellite platforms, and one-company towns reveal the same icon: an extensive tract surrounded by greenbelts and parking lots, one or maybe more centralized buildings, architectural flourishes (like giant windows, unconventional angles, and curved corners) to embellish an otherwise rectangular edifice, and prominent signage featuring the corporate logo. Although firms past a certain size can derive great functional value from a campus setting, less bottom-line factors seem to be operative as well, like a semiotic claim to industry status and a signature "footprint" upon the landscape that the company inhabits.

At least that is the impression neighbors might get in places like Santa Barbara, where corporate campuses with commanding locations are less common among the new generation of software firms. An R&D campus proposed by Carpinteria-based QAD illustrates the local controversies and behind-the-scenes dealings that such projects can engender. Often described as "exactly the kind of firm you want here," QAD is the biggest software company in the Santa Barbara region, with 550 employees in five local branches plus more at international branches. To accommodate the firm's rapid growth, the CEO (one of *Forbes'* 400 richest people) and her husband *personally* bought a thirty-two-acre lemon grove in unincorporated county land, upon which they proposed to build an R&D campus. At roughly 400,000 square feet, this would be the largest software project ever proposed in the area, as well as a rare case in which a software firm opted to purchase real estate. To this end, QAD requested that the city of Carpinteria annex and rezone the land from agricultural to industrial use. The zoning variance would extend Carpinteria's industrial corridor, already highly in demand by high-tech firms for its ocean views, into the adjacent agricultural areas and save the company millions of dollars by effectively obtaining industrial land at far cheaper agricultural prices.

Immediately after QAD's proposal, locals dug in for another of Santa Barbara's many growth battles. Two agricultural preservation groups charged that QAD's rezoning request would set a dangerous precedent for the industrialization of agricultural land and the erosion of Carpinteria's urban limits. In perhaps a more diplomatic tone, many Carpinteria residents listened to but remained unswayed by arguments that as a significant employer, taxpayer, and corporate neighbor, QAD merited special consideration, or that its campus would enhance the county's growing software industry. Perhaps less predictably, Santa Barbara's more prominent environmental organizations greeted QAD's proposal with criticism but not absolute opposition. As one environmental organizer explained,

> [QAD's project] was clearly a land use no-no: "What's that project doing in the middle of the Carpinteria Valley?" But I think a lot of the reason there wasn't a lot of opposition was [because] the environmental community had spoken up for [high-tech] kinds of jobs [in previous opposition to other potential industrial uses like offshore drilling and commercial sprawl], they didn't want to slam the first big one that came around, and they didn't have a better response . . . [T]he environmental community is now faced with the good problem of saying, "High-tech growth does seem to be growing here, now how do we get behind it?" Because no one wants to be seen as saying no to everything.

While QAD's application was pending, Santa Barbara's software trade associations funded a study of QAD's economic contributions to Carpinteria and facilitated meetings between the firm and city planners. However, behind this apparently united industry front lay greater ambivalence among local software executives and business leaders. Some supported the project on booster principles:

> Well, I think the ability for QAD to grow does have indirect impact on us, just in that having more visible high technology companies in this area is good for all of us . . . So to the extent that they can't grow, it's a shame. I think it will have an impact on their business, and I think it does have an impact on perpetuating [the idea] that this area is business-unfriendly.

Others criticized the project for its highly unusual procedural basis and its potential environmental consequences; one software executive proudly told me that several of his employees were active in the agricultural preservationist groups opposing the project.

These contrasting opinions reveal three features of software's local business structure. First, QAD's atypically large size means most firms did not share its structural interest in real estate development. As a local software executive told me,

> Quite frankly, there's not a lot of software companies that will get to the size that QAD is. So I don't think it's an issue in most of these people's minds. In most of these people's minds is, "Can I get my company to a level where it's a profitable company with a supported infrastructure and be a reasonable growth company?" not "Can I build a several-hundred-million-dollar company?"

Second, most firms locate in Santa Barbara for the quality of life, not proximity to other local firms:

Do I think it's good to have other companies in this high-tech space? Yeah. But other companies that do what we do? It's not important.

As this suggests, the locational value of Santa Barbara means that almost no other local software firm had a direct stake in QAD's prosperity. Any motivations to support the "home team" were largely non-economic and discretionary.

Third, QAD's lack of systemic relationships with the local development sector and the traditional urban business community did not help its case. From an environmental organizer with ties to the business community:

A couple of developers were *pissed,* they were *angered* . . . that QAD might actually get [their zoning request approved]. Their response was, "I've been here twenty years. I've learned how to play by the rules. I learned how to do my projects so that the decision-makers like them. Goddammit, who are those people who think they can just come in here and be the eight-hundred-pound gorilla and flip the board? It's not fair."

During negotiations several sympathetic older business leaders requested personal meetings with company executives, to no avail. Those who defended the company against charges of "arrogance" shed further light on its social distance within local business circles: "QAD is such a rapidly growing and outwardly focused company that it was very difficult for [the firm's co-founders] . . . to focus themselves on the community and the interaction with the community. That got delegated down in the organization and, as a result, quite often didn't get very effectively done." Accurate or not, this statement underscores how QAD's interest in growth did not suffice to mobilize potentially sympathetic developers and their allies in the older business community.

Three years after filing its request, QAD indefinitely shelved its R&D campus proposal and focused on its initial public offering and other company affairs. To the relief of many, QAD has not left the Santa Barbara area but instead shifted internal growth to non-local branches. In hindsight, many believe QAD's proposal illustrated two lessons. First, it showed many local software firms and their trade associations how to "play the game" in growth-conscious places like Santa Barbara. As a local businessperson involved in the negotiations told me, QAD need only have "taken the approach that the environmental community has legitimate political power in this community. And if you throw them a few bones—especially when they're coming to you and saying, 'We want to support you; here's what you can do'—I think they could have made this thing happen." Perhaps acknowledging this advice, a QAD executive later accepted an offer to join the board of Santa Barbara's most prominent environmental organization.[20]

Second, the failure of this giant (for Santa Barbara, at least) project has altered the thinking of software leaders about what forms of industry growth are preferable in the quality-of-life district. Many now urge local business leaders to seek out "boutique" software firms, R&D branches, and other typically small high-tech operations. As a civically active software executive observed,

> I think [QAD's proposal] helped us determine who's the target we're trying to go for [in regional marketing efforts]. Are we trying to attract one-thousand-person companies or not? We decided we're not. One-thousand-person companies need more resources, more square footage, more housing than we have to offer here. I think the twenty- to two-hundred-person company is more the size that all of the infrastructure here can support: transportation, the housing, the facilities where you can live or work.

THE NEW URBANIST STUDIO

As filming and recording become feasible just about anywhere, Hollywood ponders how best to use the vast soundstages and studio lots built for the past era. The case of Universal Studios described earlier illustrates one strategy: turn these properties into tourist destinations. Others studios may still want to create large centralized sites for content production, thanks to the increasing roles of special effects, animation, new media, and other high-tech fields with their attendant forms of flexible organization and agglomerative synergy. Crystallizing the latter vision is an entertainment-related project that could be Los Angeles's largest single development ever: Playa Vista, located five miles south of Santa Monica in the Los Angeles neighborhood of Marina Del Rey. At its onset, developers anticipated that this project would mix 13,200 residential units, 600,000 square feet of retail stores, schools, libraries, and a five-million-square-foot "entertainment and technology campus" with the first owner-occupied studio soundstage built since the 1930s. Los Angeles boosters have shown their usual support for Playa Vista's economic potential, as have architectural and urban planning advocates of the "New Urbanism" (architectural principles for community design using mixed residential/business zoning and public spaces for informal neighborly interaction) for the project's "community scale" and environmental mitigations.[21]

However, controversy has dogged Playa Vista from inception to its latest blueprints, chiefly centered around its setting: Los Angeles's last remaining wetlands, Ballona Creek. Acquired in the 1930s by tycoon Howard Hughes, the Ballona Creek area was preserved from the surrounding urbanization until the Summa Corporation (a Hughes subsidiary) announced plans in the 1970s to develop all but 172 acres of the remaining open space. This first development proposal received local and state approvals until the "Friends of the Ballona Wetlands" coalition brought forth an environmental lawsuit against the project. Maguire Thomas Partners, one of the region's largest development firms, subsequently obtained the project and settled the lawsuit in 1990 by devising several wetlands remediation projects.[22] Subsequently, the Friends of the Ballona Wetlands coalition endorsed the project, although other environmental groups continue to oppose it. In 1995, Maguire Thomas Partners unveiled Playa Vista's current blueprints and announced high-tech anchor tenants like IBM, GTE, Silicon Graphics, the special effects house Digital Domain, and—the most anticipated of all—the newly formed DreamWorks SKG entertainment corporation, which was to build "the digital studio of the future" on the site. Raising expectations further, the city of Los Angeles granted DreamWorks a favorable new tax category for multimedia businesses, a five-year "jobs creation" tax credit, and over $35 million in other fiscal incentives to keep the studio from fleeing to metropolitan edge cities.[23]

Almost unanimously, entertainment movers and shakers have supported DreamWorks's studio proposal and the larger Playa Vista project, although many admit that "I haven't really talked to anybody about it" in the industry. Most concur with DreamWorks's claim that modern entertainment production entails new infrastructure requirements (e.g., access to trucks for mobile production, close proximity to Los Angeles Airport) which a new studio at Playa Vista could satisfy far better than existing soundstages or alternate locations. Many also think that the area's quality-of-life advantages would nicely complement its geographical centrality within the larger entertainment district:

> I think that everybody would rather go somewhere by the beach, where there's fewer people, than driving into the middle of Burbank on a hot day. I mean, you can't even see the air [in Burbank]. I'd rather move into the Westside and live on the Westside [as DreamWorks principals would be able to do] than have to go into the Valley . . . because it's just cooler and nicer.

As a New Urbanist development, Playa Vista (some believe) would especially enhance the quality-of-life amenities of the area. The industry also seems largely unmoved by persistent, if increasingly isolated, environmental protests. A self-proclaimed "liberal" executive (whose company occupies a Maguire Thomas–developed complex in Santa Monica) declared, "The property may be considered wetlands, but it's really marginal and unappealing territory as it currently is."

However, very few industry representatives regard Playa Vista's fate as a bellwether for the entertainment industry's local growth, in contrast to what many Los Angeles business advocates have argued, for two reasons. First, "DreamWorks will not be any less productive" if Playa Vista fell through, as a talent agent explained. "The amount of product that television, motion picture, music, video games, or whatever other production they are involved in [generates] will not be curtailed in any way." Although a DreamWorks studio at Playa Vista might more tightly concentrate the studio's production networks, these would not dissolve in its absence. More certainly, Playa Vista would benefit *non-entertainment* groups by intensifying and upgrading local real estate with entertainment and new media activity. As a music industry executive told me, "Certainly, property owners are probably happy to have all that influx of new business. It's probably going, I would think, to raise property values for all the employees who want to be housed closer to their work."

Second, those firms most likely to share DreamWorks's concern for a pro-development agenda, the major film studios, have no significant tradition of collective solidarity regarding local land-use issues. From the same talent agent:

> I'm not aware that . . . studios have coalesced on this one issue and fought on each other's behalf. It tends to be more, Fox has its problems [in Culver City], Warner Brothers has its problems [in Burbank], Universal/MCA owns a great deal of lands [in Universal City] and seems to have fewer problems, Paramount is pretty well established [in Hollywood] and doesn't seem to be interested in expanding.

One explanation for studios' lack of collective solidarity is suggested by the Hollywood politics of labor. Echoing DreamWorks's isolation around its Playa Vista project, studios and other key firms failed to articulate a collective employer stance when actor guilds prepared to strike in the summer of 2000. The "days are gone when a towering figure like Lew Wasserman," the former MCA studio chief and once-powerful agent, could personally maintain labor peace, the *Los Angeles Times* reports:

> Wasserman forged deals behind the scenes with the understanding that he was speaking for all of the studios. Today, studios are owned by conglomerates with divergent priorities and agendas . . . These companies are so large that they could withstand a lengthy strike. In addition, the executives in these companies who would most directly be affected by a strike—studio chiefs, network bosses and producers—run proportionally smaller and smaller pieces of their parent company operations. No executive, not Disney's Michael Eisner nor News Corp.'s Rupert Murdoch, has stepped forward to fill the vacuum left by Wasserman's retirement.[24]

Notably, at the time of DreamWorks's studio proposal, principal Jeffrey Katzenberg was pursuing a highly visible breach of contract lawsuit against his former employer, the Disney Corporation, which was eventually settled for about $250 million in his favor. Thus, in an industry where most firms and elite workers are bound together by extra-corporate relationships and specific projects, it is perhaps logical that entertainment insiders usually "haven't really talked to anybody" about the controversy surrounding

DreamWorks's project. As an independent producer explained, "I think that's between DreamWorks and Playa Del Rey, and that's nobody's business, and I think nobody has taken a position."

Only a few months after it purchased land in the project for the studio, DreamWorks's role in Playa Vista came to a close in July 1999. Amidst disappointing box office sales in its first five years and the Disney-Katzenberg settlement, the studio announced that it was abandoning Playa Vista in order to cut costs. True to insiders' predictions, DreamWorks's production schedule has not suffered since its stake in Playa Vista fell through, as the studio has shifted production to contract facilities elsewhere within and outside the Hollywood region. As of this writing, the developer continues to break ground on Playa Vista, now master-planned (as it was originally) without a major entertainment studio.

THE DESTINATION RESORT

Although proposals for very large hotels galvanize heated opposition in all three Southern California places, the industry's collective stakes in any one project are arguably minor in Santa Monica and Santa Barbara, where the amenity infrastructures for a variety of tourist markets are already established. Consequently, the fortunes of the local tourism industry rarely stand or fall with any one hotel in these places. In San Luis Obispo, by contrast, where the market lacks upscale visitors, many tourism boosters have long sought a "destination resort" that could upgrade the area's amenity infrastructure and thus its profit potentials. A project proposed by the Hearst Corporation, the privately owned newspaper conglomerate, illustrates the prospects and controversies of such a resort.

In 1919, publisher William Randolph Hearst built his Hearst's Castle on a sprawling 83,000-acre estate in the coastal hills of San Simeon, an unincorporated town then populated largely by Swiss dairy farmers some twenty miles north of San Luis Obispo. The Hearst Corporation donated the famous mansion to the state of California in 1958 and retained the rest of the estate; soon Hearst's Castle became a favorite attraction on coastal State Highway 1. In 1997, the corporation announced plans to build a 650-room Hearst Ranch Resort and golf course on the rest of its estate and retained a local architecture firm to promote the project. Environmental groups and many residents heatedly opposed the project for its mammoth scale, impact on limited local resources like water, and potential domino effect on related coastal development (including a proposed 265-home subdivision nearby that was also allowed in the regional plan update assembled by the county for the Hearst project). To their dismay, the county board of supervisors approved the proposal and advanced it to the state's Coastal Commission for further approval.

As Hearst energetically lobbied local, county, and state officials, the Hearst Ranch Resort project quickly became the big issue in San Luis

Obispo politics, triggering widespread protest at county and state hearings, and dividing voters for and against supportive candidates in local elections. The project split the traditional urban business community, which was shocked when the local newspaper withdrew its sponsorship of a local economic development organization after the latter endorsed the project. One hotelier recalled a Lions Club meeting in a neighboring tourist hamlet (Cayucos), where Hearst's local development representatives presented the project to the local business community:

> [P]eople were so rude and obnoxious to them, it was embarrassing: "Why don't you go back where you came from? We don't want that up there! You're going to ruin it!" People were interrupting and screaming at the Hearst representative while he was making a speech. Hearst made [another] presentation to the San Luis Obispo chamber that was politely received, but I don't think they swayed anybody there.

Sentiments for and against the Hearst Ranch Resort revealed the tensions of a growing tourism industry based chiefly on environmental amenities. A few tourism leaders espoused a conservative stance against governmental regulation of and interest group intervention in matters of private property. However, most proponents endorsed the project as a way to upgrade the region's profile to a luxury resort–golf course destination on par with nearby coastal towns like Santa Barbara, Carmel, and Pebble Beach, and to generate bed taxes (a.k.a. transient occupancy taxes) of $1 million a year, thanks to the resort's higher rates.

Other hotels and other tourism firms opposed the resort project for a variety of business reasons. Many questioned whether a market for "that five-diamond, Ritz Carlton-level destination" (in the words of one hotelier) could realistically materialize in the area. Others, especially in adjacent coastal towns like Morro Bay and Pismo Beach, feared the resort as a Goliath-sized competitor. However, perhaps the most common complaint decried the project's location on a relatively undeveloped coastal route through which many visitors enter the San Luis Obispo area. As one hotelier stated, "Ecologically, I'm not so sure I like the project. That's where my problem is, not from a competitive standpoint." Many in the tourism industry wanted to protect this uniquely "natural" route from development that literally frames the place that visitors consume. For this reason, hotel expansions away from the coast have not generated such widespread opposition, as tourism insiders have noted. As a San Luis Obispo hotel and restaurant owner argued:

> Just because the same party has owned the land on the ocean for years doesn't mean they have a right to develop that land. It's not a property rights issue. I don't think [the Hearst Ranch Resort] should be developed in a way that

would jeopardize the pristine experience people have on the coast, which apparently the Hearsts say it won't.

In 1998 the state Coastal Commission rejected the county's regional plan update and ordered Hearst representatives to address 137 new conditions, including the rejection of the proposed golf course and a recommendation that the number of rooms be scaled back by nearly half. As of this writing, the Hearst Corporation was pursuing the development of "visitor-serving business" on 258 acres of its estate and selling agricultural conservation easements to the Nature Conservancy and other conservation organizations for the remaining property.

DEVELOPMENT POLITICS WITHOUT DEVELOPERS

As these cases demonstrate, firms that promise the benefits of the new urban economy can have extensive site needs and stir as much opposition to their ecological impacts and hardball political tactics as any "old economy" firms. However, the visibility of these examples may overshadow their generalizability. Furthermore, the ways in which these new urban economy projects have arrived at mixed results—shelved proposal, withdrawal, and scaled-down approval—illustrate important breaks with conventional forms of development politics.

For software and entertainment, there are two important issues. First, most firms have little need to sink costs into local real estate. They depend on particular localities, as the last two chapters showed, but not on a scarce number of particular *sites* (i.e., that are zoned and available for large industry) within those localities. The amenities they demand are increasingly built into facilities (e.g., industrial parks) or surrounding neighborhoods (e.g., downtowns). Most software and entertainment firms do not have to strategize how to obtain their sites through the political process. Simple arm's-length transactions for these sites tend to reduce their exposure to developers' "pro-business" land-use agenda. Only larger firms and/or those with specialized equipment depend on particular sites, need to engage in the governmental planning process directly, and work with developers systematically. At the largest scale (e.g., entertainment studios with vast real estate holdings), this group can even profit handsomely by speculating on land-use changes. This exception to the development politics of most software and entertainment firms is important; as subsequent chapters will show, these firms intervene in community affairs in very conventional ways.

Second, in places where software and entertainment firms locate to satisfy elite workers' lifestyle demands, not to do business with other local firms, corporate profitability does not turn on the synergies of collective growth, as it might in the flexible district, or the specific distribution of growth within the locality, as it does for a territorially based business community.[25] Even in the flexible district, companies' interests in their collective growth does not necessarily mean much more, as entertainment's response to the proposed DreamWorks studio suggests. Although elites supported this project, recent failures by studios and other lead firms to mobilize around real estate and labor politics show how the industry is currently unable to cooperate and therefore produce effective social power around this and other important local issues.

Tourism firms show a stronger proclivity toward development "business as usual." Because they profit by intensifying their land use, they usually have a concrete interest in physical expansion. Because at any scale they usually face "headaches" over permitting, licensing, zoning, and other issues regulated by local governments, they can more easily see the value of a "pro-business" land-use agenda. Local developers may systematically influence their politics toward this end, depending on whether tourism companies can afford their expertise. However, this industry also faces counterpressures to its otherwise conventional development politics. First, without growth in visitor demand, an expanding supply of local tourism activities more likely promises diminishing returns than agglomerative synergy. Second, given how quality of life is constructed in the three Southern California locations, most tourism firms have much to lose if growth threatens the local distinctiveness that draws visitors. These two factors give tourism firms a material interest in at least moderating the pace and shape of local development.

Overall, most firms in the new urban economy sectors never have projects that necessitate an agenda of complete investor prerogative, nor need to support other firms' projects of this nature. When they have extensive site needs, they are likely to advance them without the systematic influence of local developers; perhaps for this reason, environmental organizations and other outsider institutions are just as likely to set the tone of development. To be sure, local developers create the real estate supply that software, entertainment, and tourism firms inhabit. However, by rarely having more than an arm's-length role in their new clients' business, developers and the older business community have less opportunity to make their "pro-business" agenda a new urban economy concern.

5

Doing Local Business in a Global Industry

After a company has obtained a physical site, it is time to do business. By working out of a particular locality, a firm may encounter central institutions in the traditional civic network. First, the *chamber of commerce* lets firms from many local sectors share information and promote their businesses with one another. By centralizing networks of business members, chambers can coordinate and advocate the local business consensus, as well as widen the business community's scan over issues like investment prospects, public subsidies, and government regulations.[1] Second, *local banks* provide financing for local companies, which is particularly crucial during corporate formation and expansion. Through their control over capital flows and representation on corporate boards, banks have the fiscal and social means to connect and promote consensus among their clients, particularly those in urban business communities.[2] Finally, local trade associations, networking forums, and other *local sector-specific associations* offer services tailored to particular industries. By providing more exclusive settings and pursuing narrower goals than chambers, these organizations can perhaps better coordinate firms' resources and advocate their local interests.[3]

As these features suggest, how software, entertainment, and tourism firms use these three local business institutions has important consequences for urban politics. Manufacturers and other big businesses often use them to mobilize local companies behind their corporate agenda. However, power can move the other way as well in subtle yet important ways, as urban regime theory has shown. Through repeated use, these institutions' organizational capacities are trained to certain ends (usually, pro-growth activities like regional marketing and governmental monitoring) and not others. These capacities enhance the "doability" of some collective efforts and frustrate others—a major reason why local business institutions become such regular pro-growth vehicles. By joining local business groups and working with local banks, members and clients reinforce these institutions' political thrust, even if they do not share the same political interests.[4] If push comes to shove, local business groups and banks can even punish dissent among their members and clients via business ostracism or capital strikes, respectively. Therefore, how and why software, entertainment, and tourism firms participate in local business institutions reveals whether the new urban economy sustains the institutional strongholds of the traditional urban business community.

USING THE CHAMBER OF COMMERCE

Although their older members sometimes voice resentment about the attention they have lost, most chambers of commerce perceive the new urban economy firms and industries with optimism. Chambers regard the growth of software, entertainment, and tourism as a sign of local prosperity amidst economic changes. The ones in Santa Monica, Santa Barbara, and San Luis Obispo do not actively recruit outside companies to their localities, unlike many chambers elsewhere;[5] nevertheless, they vigorously advocate the growth of software, entertainment, and tourism firms. In Santa Monica, one of the local chamber's five goals has been "proactively establish[ing] positive relationships with new media companies by creating value for them." In Santa Barbara, the chamber's "number one priority" has been to support the efforts of a local high-tech association by sharing contacts, office space, and other resources. In San Luis Obispo, the local chamber co-authored white paper reports endorsing a proposed high-tech industrial park and criticizing a federal offshore oil drilling study, in large part to defend "the lucrative tourism industry."[6]

MEMBERSHIP DRIVES

To "create value" for software, entertainment, and tourism firms and entice them into joining, all three chambers have subcommittees like the "Business, Technology and the Future Committee" and the "Emerging Technologies Committee," as well as the more blandly named "Entertainment Committee" and the "Hospitality Federation." In these, chamber organizers invite the new businesses and their executives to various functions and networking events, where they hope to pass on important social contacts, news and views on the political environment for local business, and other services and information of presumed value. Finding new chamber members and business opportunities for themselves are not far from their main objectives, either.

However, companies courted by chambers seem reluctant to return the outreach, as indicated by the proportion of local software, entertainment, and tourism firms that become chamber members. In Table 5.1, on page 107, I use banks as a comparative baseline of significance; by reading across each row, the

Table 5.1

Membership in local chambers of commerce: proportion of local firms (number of members)

Locality	Software	Entertainment	Tourism	Banks
Santa Monica	0.25 (27)	0.09 (24)	0.28 **(123)**	**0.67** (22)
Santa Barbara	0.29 (41)	0.02 (2)	0.32 **(210)**	**0.73** (37)
San Luis Obispo	**0.52** (29)	0.00 (0)	0.29 **(161)**	**0.52** (14)

SOURCE: 1997/98 Santa Monica Chamber of Commerce Business Profile & Membership Guide; 1998 Santa Barbara Chamber of Commerce Membership Directory; 1998 San Luis Obispo Chamber of Commerce Membership Directory & Buyer's Guide.

reader can see which sector ranked highest in membership rate (and in absolute number of members, shown in parentheses), as reported in bold text.

All three sectors, especially entertainment, are less likely than local banks to join the chamber. The only exception is San Luis Obispo, where software firms join equally to banks. Additionally, software and entertainment firms each count for no more than three percent of members in any chamber. Only tourism makes up a substantial bloc, representing twelve to fifteen percent of all members, despite its relatively low sectoral membership rate.

Why do software, entertainment, and tourism firms join or abstain from their local chambers? In contrast to what many local business leaders expect, the critical factor is not where the company is located, but rather where they find markets for their goods and services. As discussed earlier, some firms primarily serve markets outside the locality—indeed, in the new industrial space, they may effectively have global markets, constituting what I call *core firms*. By contrast, others primarily serve local markets; accordingly, I call this group *peripheral firms*. The distinction entails vastly different scales of business activity and profit, and core and peripheral firms often correspond to the "stars" and "bit players," respectively, of local economies.

A handful of core software and entertainment firms belong to the local chambers. The Santa Monica chamber's members, for example, include a major film studio, a cable network, a major record label, a national music industry organization, a postproduction film facility, and at least three multinational software firms (one of which was headquartered locally). Yet relative to peripheral firms, core software and entertainment firms compose a very small minority of chamber members, and their prominence obscures the small size and local market orientation typical of most software and entertainment members. From software, most chamber members are local Internet service providers, web designers, systems consultants, training providers, Internet businesses providing on-line real estate listings, and the like. A Santa Monica chamber leader described them as fitting "a conventional mom-and-pop [store] definition. They may be aware that the Internet is global, but they're not thinking in those terms." Similarly, most chamber members from entertainment are minor video production companies and studio facilities, and it is unclear whether they belong to the most important production networks. By contrast, chamber members from tourism regularly include the largest hotels, restaurants, and destinations. Importantly, they all rely substantially to nearly exclusively on regional markets and can in this sense be regarded as peripheral firms. In short, peripheral firms overwhelmingly characterize the chamber's new urban economy members.

For software, entertainment, and tourism firms that join, certain interests are evident. First, by design, the chamber promotes local business to other local businesses, a service of obvious value to peripheral software and entertainment firms: "Those people in the chamber . . . are looking for a group and some people where they can hang out, meet new people, and try to pick up clients." In the same way, *all* tourism members benefit when the local chambers promote the localities, for instance, by subsidizing visitor information centers. Second, certain members find particular value in the local scan on the political environment that business networking across local industries makes possible. As the last chapter suggested, large companies (e.g., film studios) and those that generate environmentally regulated emissions (e.g., defense-related R&D firms atypical of the newer generation of technology companies) might especially be interested in inside news on land-use policy. "Let's be honest," a film studio representative announced at a chamber subcommittee meeting; the studio belongs to the chamber in large part "to meet [local] people with influence in case we ever need them." Third, in software and entertainment, larger core firms use the chamber to conduct local public relations:

> The bigger companies, they have civic obligations. So Microsoft will join just because they're here, and they're savvy enough to know they have a civic obligation. It's good PR for them to be a member of the chamber, but you'll never see them, except if they want to come in and do a program. Then they'll call and say, "We want to do a program" . . . So [bigger software and entertainment chamber members have] a cordial interaction with the banks and more conventional businesses [in the chamber]. It's not close, just cordial.

"Civic obligations" apparently have limits, however, since several large software and entertainment firms failed to renew their membership in recent years.

As for the majority of local software and entertainment firms that do *not* join the chamber, there are several reasons why, chief of which is the lack of benefits that chambers offer core firms: "The chamber of commerce caters to local bars and grocery stores. They're not there for high-tech companies." In part because local growth in software and entertainment industries is relatively new to the three Southern California places, lawyers, accountants, and other mainstays of the chamber have not usually developed the special experience or expertise that their potential new clients would want. Consequently, networking at the chamber offers little for these companies, as a software CEO explained:

> Information about [hiring new software] employees is important, but we
> probably know more about how to steal local employees than anyone could
> tell us from a local [business organization]. Perhaps a trade association deep
> enough to engage [developers specializing in high-tech projects] could help.
> But that community generally isn't accessible through local organizations;
> the chamber of commerce wouldn't know much about that.

Although this lack of specialized services for and "understanding" of the software and entertainment industries has an obvious basis in quality-of-life districts, where the absence of prior industrialization is an important locational asset, conceivably it might not hold true for chambers in larger industry centers. However, chambers throughout Silicon Valley and Hollywood have not fared much better, despite being close to the action in high-tech and entertainment, respectively.[7]

Some software insiders acknowledge that social distance between their industry and the traditional urban business community may mean losing potential customers. In a Southern California trade journal, one Internet business leader argued that "bricks and mortar" companies typical of the chamber:

> . . . are the people we need to be meeting while networking. They don't know
> how to find the best and the brightest in our industry. We are a forbidding
> crowd to them. They do not understand what all this fuss is about, and they
> can't even pick up the trusty phone and call many of the companies that they
> read about in the newspaper . . . And many companies that have graced the
> pages of the top business publications are no longer going by the same names.
> What's a self-made millionaire tool-and-dye maker to do? With a dog-eared
> copy of his favorite business journal on his desk, he is trying to find that company,
> the one that can turn his business into a modern e-commerce miracle.
> They're not listed in information. All they have is a dot-com address. He's
> been intending to learn about this Internet thing. Got the kids a computer
> last Christmas. Is this yet another task for little Nancy?[8]

However, it is uncertain that many in the industry have heeded such sentiments.

One reason may be that information-industry practices and cultures widen the distance from the traditional urban business community and frustrate chambers' recruitment efforts. Many entertainment insiders acknowledge that Hollywood has been "insular" vis-à-vis the metropolitan business community.[9] In a sprawling metropolis like Los Angeles, people seldom live and work in the same community, so they may feel less civic attachment to a particular community, or they might simply choose not to lengthen their workday by attending chamber functions in the evening. A chamber organizer believed that for software workers,

> There are so many different things going on, and they have different ways of socializing, getting together, and all that kind of thing . . . [I]t doesn't seem like too many people in those industries are involved in the same kind of, quote unquote, booster activities like the chamber . . . I think it's hard to draw them into doing things like this, coming down to [the chamber] to hear somebody talk. It's ridiculous thinking that someone who's working at [a local special effects firm] eighteen hours a day as a hacker is going to be interested in going to some chamber activity, you know?

Without a compelling need to join the chamber, core software and entertainment firms view chamber participation as a discretionary act of "civic" involvement, akin to local philanthropy.[10] As a software CEO explained, using the chamber "is a matter of, 'do you have time for general civic affairs?' We haven't had much."

Some chamber officials are content just to attract a few industry leaders to their boards of directors. Compared to the representation from local banks, however, their efforts have been less than completely successful, as Table 5.2 shows.

As with membership, directors are less likely to come from the three sectors than local banks; again, only San Luis Obispo departs from this pattern. Furthermore, software-based directors predominantly come from peripheral firms, such as Internet service providers or consulting firms. With two directors from a motion picture studio and major record label, the Santa Monica chamber appears to depart from the peripheral orientation of its entertainment directors. However, they do not necessarily represent upper

Table 5.2

Directorates of local chambers of commerce: proportion of local firms (number of directors)

Locality	Software	Entertainment	Tourism	Banks
Santa Monica	0.01 (1)	0.01 **(3)**	0.00 (1)	**0.09 (3)**
Santa Barbara	0.01 (2)	0.00 (0)	0.00 (1)	**0.06 (3)**
San Luis Obispo	**0.05 (3)**	0.00 (0)	0.00 (2)	0.04 (1)

SOURCE: 1997/98 Santa Monica Chamber of Commerce Business Profile & Membership Guide; 1998 Santa Barbara Chamber of Commerce Membership Directory; 1998 San Luis Obispo Chamber of Commerce Membership Directory & Buyer's Guide.

executive-level involvement from their firms; as one chamber executive told me, "the larger companies are represented by mid-level people or maybe a little higher [in the firm], not CEOs."

SUBCOMMITTEE EFFORTS

Without many employees and executives from core firms, the chamber's software and entertainment members tend to consist of local web designers, small Internet service providers, would-be Internet entrepreneurs, struggling actors, and other entertainment talent looking to do business with core software and entertainment firms. This is most evident in the chamber subcommittees that specifically promote local software and entertainment sectors, where peripheral software and entertainment workers and entrepreneurs work alongside real estate agents, business service providers, restaurateurs, and other members trying to profit from these sectors.[11] Subcommittees' inability to attract or even successfully find a contact with core firms, business leaders, or industry-specific organizations means that chambers often remain unaware about new development proposals or other opportunities where they could ostensibly create value for entertainment and software firms (for example, by opening doors to local decision-makers and opinion-setters). A Catch-22 can emerge whereby chambers cannot increase software and entertainment involvement without a prior track record of such involvement.

The quality of participation and subcommittee efforts is altogether different for tourism, since members usually include the most prominent local tourism firms. The local circulation of visitor dollars makes tourism central to the fortunes of the locality and many non-tourism members. Combined with extensive local government taxation and regulation of this industry, this sustains a higher level of tourism firm participation in the chamber and, by extension, the traditional urban business community as well. Through the chamber, tourism members share information and hone collective efforts regarding the local business climate far more effectively than peripheral software and entertainment members. This is illustrated, for example, by San Luis Obispo hoteliers' resistance when the city proposed to audit their bed tax payments:

> The tourism council passed the audit idea on to the chamber board, and I was the lone dissenter against the idea. I started calling up some of my friends in the hotel business to tell them what it was all about. They circulated a petition in opposition to it and brought it to the chamber board. The chamber board was incensed and sent a letter of opposition to the mayor and city council. The end result was that the number of hotels to be audited got reduced to fifteen properties each year for three years, which I still don't like, but I think it's better.

Chambers' successful track record on behalf of tourism, of course, does not prevent individual tourism firms from free-riding on the actions of other chamber members.[12] Indeed, it probably encourages free-riders, which may explain why more than two-thirds of all local tourism firms do not join the chamber. Nevertheless, the industry's regular reliance on chamber capacities like monitoring local government means that the chamber creates value for tourism firms worth free-riding on, a sharp contrast to its inability to promote the business of core software and entertainment firms.

As software, entertainment, and tourism increasingly drive the local economies in the three Southern California localities, at least the first two sectors have failed to keep local chambers of commerce representative of these changes. To be sure, this does not preclude chambers from endorsing the local interests of several software and entertainment firms. For example, chambers are stalwart allies in prominent software and entertainment companies' public relations campaigns to get their development projects built. However, chamber advocacy is not the same as mutual engagement. In the latter regard, much like with local developers, tourism firms do so in quantity and quality far more than software and entertainment firms. Overall, the relationship between local chambers and core software and entertainment firms is "like oil and water," as a software entrepreneur and chamber organizer opined. "They're living in two different worlds, from my perspective."

FINANCING THE NEW URBAN ECONOMY

Do software, entertainment, and tourism firms obtain local financing in a way that ties them to the traditional urban business community? Again, the answer varies by sector. Local banks primarily serve the financial needs of locally owned businesses, which include small or entrepreneurial tourism firms. Importantly, these are the kinds of tourism companies most likely not to join the chamber of commerce or retain developer services extensively. Few tourism companies, then, escape the gravitational pull of at least one node in the traditional civic network.

However, most software and entertainment firms appear to remain outside the sphere of local banks. A software executive in San Luis Obispo observed, "One thing we're completely missing [here] is the financial side to technology. The center of [banks'] interest, the focus, is all real estate here." His statement touches on how the business of software and entertainment, on the one hand, and banks, on the other, is not mutually oriented. Part of the reason may be the respective clash of global and local business concerns; more than one software executive complained to me of parochial bank executives who "wouldn't know what to do with a $100 million company," especially in less-populated quality-of-life districts. However, there are also systemic reasons for banks' failure to make clients of most software and entertainment companies. Many software executives noted that local banks "just want your checkbook; they don't care about your business." As this comment suggests, most local banks do not accommodate the special capital needs of software and entertainment firms.

For software firms at the start-up stage, initial "seed" capital usually comes from the assets of employees, friends, families, colleagues, and private investors.[13] Once depleted, start-up firms have to turn to other sources, which conceivably can include local banks. However, local banks frequently evaluate start-up firms as too risky and lend them less (if any) money than entrepreneurs need.[14] Many start-up firms' frustrations stem from their lack of credit history, unconventional capital needs, special risk, and "virtual" forms of collateral. A software executive described how conventional loan officers view these as obstacles:

> "Well, what, you want to buy a computer? Well, we don't count that [as assets
> for collateral, so] we won't let you have a loan. You want to buy software?
> What's software, a bunch of things on a disk? You want to pay $10,000 for it?
> No, we won't participate; we don't count those as assets." [Local banks are]
> extremely low-risk oriented. They're very tradition oriented . . . "Oh, you're
> buying a milling machine?" That would be a different story. Doors would open,
> but try to do something with technology, and the banking doors are closed.

In Silicon Valley, several local and regional banks have developed such expertise to become important financiers of software firms, even outpacing the more notable financiers in neighboring San Francisco.[15] However, in places with less history of technology sector growth, local banks appear to serve local firms' capital needs far less effectively.

Another source of local capital that deserves mention is local economic development organizations. Formed specifically to promote economic growth, local economic development organizations are well known for promoting "pro-business" agendas.[16] Participation in their capital programs thus offers another way to link firms to the traditional civic network. My evidence here is modest, since only one of the three places has such an organization, but the pattern is telling. San Luis Obispo's local economic development organization targets three sectors—high-tech, destination tourism, and value-added agriculture—deemed the best prospects for economic development by its directors, all but one of whom represent government and industries other than high-tech, tourism, and agriculture. However, its highly restrictive loan criteria and extra conditions (for instance, requiring borrowers to enroll in counseling at the community college's small business assistance center) offer little relief for most software firms. As one software executive related: "Like a bank, they don't look at your actual business or understand how high-technology companies work." One of the local economic development organization's directors confirmed that it has loaned very little money to new and expanding businesses to date.

Given these local constraints, most software companies must look elsewhere for capital. Frequently, they turn to other companies. In the three localities, several software and entertainment firms have obtained capital through mergers, investment, licensing, or other intercorporate mechanisms. The price for intercorporate financing is usually the loss of corporate autonomy, although this is frequently a goal that short-term focused entrepreneurs build into their business plans. Executives and other elite workers appear to tolerate this price as well, given their disposition to hop between companies.

Venture capital is yet another option. In contrast to local banks and local economic development organizations, venture capital firms usually have an expertise in software and other technology sectors—indeed, they increasingly provide important managerial and consulting services for start-ups—since most of them are headed by former technology executives.[17] In the mid-1990s, software executives expressed disappointment about the regional availability of venture capital. At that time, Southern California held no special attraction for venture capitalists, most of whom are based in Silicon Valley and are geographically insular, even "incestuous," about which business proposals they consider. This threatened a vicious circle of local venture capital drought. As the founder of one of Santa Monica's largest software firms observed, perhaps in overstatement,

> The reason people don't start companies here is because, fundamentally, venture capitalists and investors don't invest in companies here. They would rather invest in Silicon Valley. And I guess the reason they don't invest here is because people don't start companies here!

The prospects of attracting venture capital appeared even dimmer in Santa Barbara, while "San Luis Obispo County isn't even a blip on venture capital firms' radar screen."[18] Perhaps unsurprisingly, many local trade associations schedule (or at least promise) events where local entrepreneurs can circulate business plans among Silicon Valley venture capitalists.

When and how the vicious circle turned virtuous is beyond the scope of this book,[19] but by the end of the 1990s and even past the dot-com crash of 2000, software firms have begun to obtain non-local venture capital. The executive director of a Santa Barbara business incubator described the process:

> If you have one or two successes—and we're starting to have some now—then you'll see [venture capitalists] coming in like gangbusters. We've got one company in this building that's got $6 million in venture funding from Palo Alto. That's new for Santa Barbara. What that means now is that [we're seeing] ancillary groups that follow venture capitalists and team with them. Like, a small, very aggressive bank out of the Bay Area, they're the bank for this com-

pany. Now, as a result of banking with this company, I've met these guys, and we're now introducing them to two other companies in the building. They're coming here next week to meet with those companies and talk about banking for them. They, in turn, will turn around and help them get venture funding. So it's a geometric progression, we hope, and it's got to get started someplace.

These external capital flows have important ramifications for local banks. As local software firms tap "insular" flows of venture capital and bring others like them to venture capitalists' attention, local banks face the prospect of being squeezed out of the software industry. Of late, some banks and others in the traditional urban business community have been "getting the message" and "educating" themselves on how to better serve these firms' financial needs. In Santa Barbara, a few banks have backed a new business incubator formed by entrepreneurs who made quality-of-life migrations to the area. In Los Angeles, the corporate parent of the *Los Angeles Times* has formed the largest investment fund for the region. However, it remains an open question whether this strategic shift comes in time, since most local firms systematically look outside the locality for financing.

In entertainment, intercorporate financing is the primary source of funding; production companies and other contractor firms usually grow based on investment in the projects they work on, not the companies themselves.[20] Companies that are more technology-intensive (e.g., postproduction facilities) and blur into more conventional high-tech fields (e.g., new media companies) often depend more on venture capital or, when their risk and track records can be conventionally "proven," sometimes local banks. At least in Santa Monica, local banks appear to have a slightly bigger foothold into entertainment than software. However, with the industry's rapid growth, even this foothold may be fleeting. As a Santa Monica banker said of the city's entertainment firms, "So many of them expand so rapidly, they quickly outgrow this bank."

ORGANIZING FROM WITHIN

To different degrees, software, entertainment, and tourism firms generally do not find time for local business institutions, like the chamber or local capital, that build networks to the traditional urban business community. However, this does not preclude the three sectors from organizing themselves locally. Local trade associations, networking forums, and other sector-specific associations can take up the cause of their industry's firms without the distraction of other industries' agendas. None of the ones I studied are explicitly "political," i.e., seek to influence local elections, which is prohibited by their nonprofit status. Yet by bringing together and giving voice to similar companies, they can establish processes and channels for local industry mobilization that can have political consequences, if not already deployed toward explicitly political ends.

SOFTWARE-SPECIFIC ASSOCIATIONS

One of the more visible signs of software's growth in Southern California is the many local software associations that, in the words of one executive, seem to "spring up like weeds." While none has become as central in local politics as the trade associations of Silicon Valley,[21] core software firms nevertheless appear more likely to participate in at least one of them than in the local chamber. In the late 1990s, a variety of industry associations proliferated; some have left the scene, while others have entered, since that time. Although they have vastly different goals and capacities in, say, software-heavy Santa Monica versus software-nascent San Luis Obispo, there are essentially three organizational types: boosters, fixers, and networking forums.

Boosters gather industry and non-industry representatives specifically to advocate the growth of their targeted industries. Through public events (dinners, lectures, etc.) and private committee meetings, they support networking between software executives and interested government, business, and community representatives; they market the localities and their local software industries to potential newcomers; and they articulate participants' concerns into more or less formal policy positions and initiatives. Santa Monica's boosters are actually regionally focused, the most notable being the Digital Coast Roundtable, which promotes Los Angeles's Internet, new media, and affiliated software firms with strong municipal and private support. Santa Barbara's booster (the Santa Barbara Region Economic Community Project) is an influential advocate for local high-tech growth and the business organization with which most government and community leaders choose to deal. San Luis Obispo's booster (the Central Coast Software and Technology Association, a.k.a. "Softec") has also gained the attention of city officials, university administrators and faculty, local businesses, and other industry outsiders, although unlike its Santa Monica and Santa Barbara counterparts, it has yet to espouse local policies.

In all three localities, software firms face infrastructure shortages that the market does not solve, like industrial-strength Internet access and affordable industrial space for start-up firms. A handful of *fixers* seeks to address such local shortcomings.[22] In Santa Monica, one fixer serves a "hacker" constituency by providing multimedia and telecommunications technology designers with experimental environments for "co-creation and collaboration in real-time networked environments" via a monthly virtual reality users group and individual demonstrations. A Santa Barbara fixer promotes industry development more directly by offering high-speed Internet access and sponsoring a business incubator for start-up firms.

To the extent that boosters and fixers gather software workers in a common physical and/or virtual space, they enable interfirm and employee networking. However, several *networking forums* focus solely on fostering entrepreneurial and creative networking. The most informal and mercurial of the three types of industry associations, networking forums particularly appeal to (and are often organized by) mid- and lower-level high-tech employees, young entrepreneurs, and others left out of more elite-constituted groups. One networking forum based in Santa Monica (the Los Angeles New Media Roundtable, or LAwNMoweR) encompasses Los Angeles and, increasingly, Southern California; important initiatives and associations have sprung from its meetings. Santa Barbara has several networking forums of varying formality for technology-related discussion, ranging from one that hosts free monthly lectures on technology issues to a weekly mixer at a downtown Santa Barbara bar that seeks to stimulate the informal schmoozing ubiquitous to Silicon Valley's creative milieu. The software sector's relatively small size in San Luis Obispo means that most mid- to high-level software executives network at the dinner meetings of Softec, the local booster; lower-level employees, engineering students, and other local software talent seem to use informal computer-users groups for networking.

In Silicon Valley, local industry-specific associations such as the Silicon Valley Manufacturers' Association have historically allowed members to articulate business and political interests that differ from and even conflict with those espoused by the traditional urban business community.[23] In the three Southern California communities, however, software associations reveal significant involvement by the traditional urban business community. Notably, software executives do not comprise a majority on the boards of any of the most important boosters; bankers, lawyers, accountants, financiers, publicists, and other providers of business services rank second or (in Santa Barbara's case) first in representation. Moreover, none of the latter particularly specializes in high-tech industry. Instead, their primary markets are growth-dependent local businesses, which they themselves are, too.

In fact, the "enlightened self-interest" of growth-dependent businesses has played a significant, if not driving, role in boosters' origins. Los Angeles's Digital Coast Roundtable originated out of LAwNMoweR, a networking forum founded by a high-tech industry publicist who sought to compile a client mailing list. As the latter's attendance grew, it attracted the attention of other public and private representatives and eventually spun off the Digital Coast Roundtable with the encouragement of former Los Angeles mayor Richard Riordan. Similarly, a traditional business community push led to the Santa Barbara Region Economic Community Project. Its original founders consisted of three high-tech executives (one of whom later became a venture capitalist), a local lawyer, two or three local bankers, and a university administrator—a dual high-tech/local business services profile it still maintains.[24] As one of the founders recalled, "A bunch of us got together, and it was kind of what I would call, not the financial barons in town, [but] working turks, the guys and women who were making things happen . . . We all sat down and said, 'Look, what are we going to do to make things happen?' " In the case of San Luis Obispo's Softec, a local venture capitalist brought together a handful of local acquaintances from software firms, a local accounting firm, a local lawyer, and a university administrator; the founding lawyer and accountant specialize in technology-specific business services but work for firms that serve a variety of local businesses. This pattern of traditional urban business community involvement in software associations also appears outside of Southern California. For instance, the New York Information Technology Center, a fixer organization for new media firms from the city's Silicon Alley district, has also benefited from leadership by a telephone company, power utility, and others in the traditional urban business community.[25]

Thus, at least the most important local software-specific associations link core firms to the traditional urban business community more so than any other node in the traditional civic network. Here is where the older business community meets the software firms and leaders that otherwise avoid local business institutions. However, what is the *quality* of the relationships forged by these organizations? A closer look at the values derived by software firms and the traditional urban business community suggests that the latter's influence over the agenda of local software firms should not be exaggerated.

To begin with, paying dues does not mean active participation by software firms. A local developer and traditional business leader claimed that at meetings of the Santa Barbara Region Economic Community Project, software and other high-tech companies "barely show up . . . They're not there in droves trying to protect their own interests. They're busy doing their own software or manufacturing, and they leave it to us to protect their interests." Most software executives confirmed their frequent lack of participation in the local associations they joined, saying, "When you keep your eye on the global ball, you really can't set aside time for the local community."

For software companies that do make time, what kinds of "interests" can they pursue in these associations? As numerous trade journals and management books attest, for core technology firms competing in a global market, the primary benefit of trade associations is access to new ideas and human talent.[26] However, such access may be better facilitated by *non-local* organizations, conferences, and trade shows, where software firms can find workers and clients in a broader range of software fields as well as the narrow product niche they compete in. In these non-local settings, as one software CEO described, "you go to meet your customers, your competition, [and do] what I like to call 'cooperatition'. The people you compete and cooperate with are at trade shows and conferences." Business networking also proliferates within demographically distinct groups (like Women In New Technology and The Indus Entrepreneurs) and diffuses into the creative milieu itself (for instance, informal "digital dinners" held at colleagues' homes).

Local software associations with a smaller number of potential members, by contrast, cannot offer comparably extensive networking. Core firm executives generally find that the geographically narrower an industry organization is, the less valuable it is for access to ideas and talent. For instance, by my count, more firms from the three Southern California areas attended the Association of Computer Machinery's 1997 "Siggraph" convention (eponymously named for the national organization's computer graphics section) held in Los Angeles than belonged to its regional chapters. Software associations outside of industry centers are especially disadvantaged in this regard, as Santa Barbara and San Luis Obispo illustrate. Many executives find local boosters and networking forums best suited for after-work entertainment and for lower-level employees to exchange news about local employment opportunities; this is one reason why several firm executives *discourage* their employees from attending networking forums. Only in Los Angeles, the largest industry location in Southern California, do executives and talent regularly find value in a local industry association. Perhaps for this reason, Los Angeles's industry-specific networking forums publicize the attendance of important executives in their promotional materials.

Industrial infrastructure is a second area where local software associations do create value for global-minded firms. If their infrastructure needs are basic (e.g., more airline connections to Silicon Valley), then core software firms find worth in the work of local software associations, provided that infrastructure shortcomings did not deter core firms from locating there in the first place. Similarly, software firms also value fixers that serve more specialized needs, like industrial-strength Internet access or business incubator services. Busy software executives appear to prefer fixers that have lean organizational structures. For example, Santa Barbara's fixer attracts more software firm members than other local associations in part because it requires fees but not much time from its members. Its executive director described the fixer as a "guerrilla network" that carries out its goals with minimal participation from members, in contrast to software boosters:

> [Boosters] tend to be organizations that, the moment you take your eye off it [sic], they stop functioning. It takes a level of commitment from individuals to run those kinds of things that is enormous, because they're very meeting-oriented. There's a tremendous amount of meetings, a tremendous amount of studies that are done, and a lot of collaboration that goes on.

The executive of Santa Barbara's software booster, the Economic Community Project, confirmed this pattern:

> A lot of high-tech executives aren't giving us much time. They say up front they are running their business and so they can only contribute $2500 a year, some

> staff to help, and appear in the [promotional] video . . . You have to show high-tech executives why it's in their interest, and still they don't have time.

As is probably true in many other industries, core software firms appear more willing to commit money than executives' time to a local industry organization, which again diminishes the quality of the relationships between the old and new business communities.

Marketing the region is another strength of local software associations. The Santa Barbara Region Economic Community Project, for example, spent $60,000 in a 1997 marketing campaign entitled, "Santa Barbara: The New Environment for California Technology." However, most software executives keenly recognize that such marketing benefits their companies less than it does the traditional urban business community. The reasons why depend on the location, although the result is the same. In industry centers like Silicon Valley, the agglomerative pull on workers, firms, and customers makes advertising and promotion largely redundant. In quality-of-life districts, few firms locate to do business with other local firms. In either case, many members question the value they get from a heavy emphasis on marketing the region to software firms across the world. They might benefit from the larger and more competitive labor pool that accompanies local software growth, but especially in quality-of-life districts, they weigh this potential gain against the employee turnover and environmental strain that typically accompany critical mass.

As for what the traditional urban business community gains from marketing efforts, many software executives express indifference. A CEO recalled the county task force that greeted his firm after it relocated to Santa Barbara:

> The people they had involved were real estate brokers, insurance agents, people who were looking to develop their own business. They weren't really here to help us. They were here to try and get business from the individuals here if we moved here. To me, that's mind-boggling, that the county doesn't take seriously enough this kind of activity and staff it properly with people who don't have a conflict of interest. It's a conflict of interest to send somebody out to show me places that I might be willing to move my company to, and at the same time they're saying, "Oh, by the way, I can help you buy your house, too." That's a conflict of interest, and that's what happened.

Although most of his local counterparts did not express his level of disdain, they nevertheless value software associations' marketing campaigns less than the traditional urban business community does.

Perhaps the primary issue where the traditional urban business community's expertise best fit core firms' business needs is land-use policy. Local software associations generally take the lead in policy efforts to shape relevant zoning laws and expand the supply of land available for relocating and expanding firms. Still, this coincidence of interests is narrow, applying mostly to the few larger or locally expanding firms. The result is that, while some traditional urban business leaders help govern software *associations,* their influence does not extend to make their agenda a widespread concern for most software *executives.*

ENTERTAINMENT-SPECIFIC ASSOCIATIONS

Entertainment's regional concentration in Los Angeles and New York is the geographical setting in which its business leaders adopt a fundamentally global outlook.[27] Perhaps for this reason, I found no "local" entertainment-specific associations in which entertainment firms and talent participate. Instead, the industry is organized chiefly through collective entities that, although regionally dominated, are *national* associations.

For instance, all major film studios belong to the Motion Picture Association of America, a national booster that represents the industry before international governments and the private sector on issues like intellectual property rights, broadcast media regulation, and motion picture ratings (which the Association also assigns to individual films). The Academy of Motion Picture Arts and Sciences is an exclusive booster association that, over the years, has focused its once-broad array of activities around organizing the annual Academy Awards, perhaps the premiere certifier of film industry status. The Academy's membership comprises the most elite film professionals, who either have accrued a certain amount of screen credits (for actors, directors, writers and other talent) or are nominated into non-voting status (for non-creative executives and talent agents).[28] Whereas elite workers typically have only short-term affiliations with any one project or company, their talent guilds structure their careers over the long term. The Directors Guild of America, for example, negotiates standard contracts for its members that determine salaries, benefits, and residuals (i.e., royalties) in individual film projects, provide them with health insurance and pension plans, and represent them collectively in labor disputes. Comparable talent guilds exist for film actors (Screen Actors Guild), television actors (American Federation of Television and Radio Artists), screenwriters (Writers Guild of America), "below-the-line" crew members (International Alliance of Theatrical and Stage Employees), musicians (American Guild of Musical Artists), and so on.[29] Technical and craft workers use their restrictive labor unions to centralize and obtain job opportunities.[30] Special effects houses, if they belong to any organizations at all, tend to join high-tech organizations, like the computer graphics section of the Association of Computing Machinery, in order to keep abreast of the latest innovations.

In the popular music industry, record labels belong to the Recording Industry Association of America, a national booster similar to the Motion Picture Association of America, which represents the industry on issues like royalty remuneration, copyright protection, and broadcast regulation. If nominated, recording producers, engineers, and musicians can join the National Academy of Recording Arts and Sciences, another national booster that represents members and sponsors at seminars on issues like music piracy, archiving, and intellectual property rights in addition to sponsoring the annual Grammy music awards and pursuing music-related philanthropy. Record labels also join more narrowly focused associations like the California Copyright Conference to stay on top of legal changes. In specific fields, music-related marketers, tour managers, artist managers, and A&R (artist and repertory) representatives might attend specialized conferences to keep abreast of the latest industry developments.

Since filming and recording can increasingly take place anywhere, Hollywood has become essentially a talent-intensive hiring hall of deal-making, relationship maintenance, and job searches. Industry-specific associations like these provide much of the formal context for these activities. For example, a talent agent observed that "it's easier for agents if they represent members or people who have been nominated for an Academy Award"; for this reason, she would "love to become a member" of the Academy of Motion Picture Arts and Sciences. Occasionally, the hiring hall travels outside the region for special activities and events, like the Sundance Film Festival (in Sundance, Utah) or the South By Southwest Conference (in Austin, Texas) for the music industry. Although outsiders to the industry can take part in these, they have little influence over the industry deal-making, relationship maintenance, and job searches that go on there. Remarkably, the same is true back in Hollywood. Although entertainment shares with software a primary reliance on ideas and talent, its industry associations create an even more socially exclusive milieu that allows almost no room for the traditional urban business community or its agenda. Alongside other factors that encourage industry insularity, entertainment's industry-specific associations make the industry nearly impenetrable to the traditional urban business community.

An important consequence is that the traditional urban business community has no forum to expose entertainment firms and talent to their concerns, most of which revolve around entertainment investment in local real estate and production. These issues have become increasingly contentious as Hollywood shifts away from capital-intensive production (e.g., in studio lots) that filters through local economies and brings inward investment. The comments of an executive from one of the few core entertainment firms to join a local chamber (in Hollywood proper) reveal the agenda mismatch between the traditional urban business community and Hollywood. His record company participates in local business advisory groups and economic studies "only through the chamber."

But separate and apart, no, we're not about trying to influence investment in Hollywood; that's not one of our goals . . . We might [benefit from more entertainment companies], but that's not what we're focused on. Our only community goal, which is inchoate, is to make the surrounding area as clean and friendly as possible.

Executives uniformly express pride in entertainment's importance in the regional economy, yet none of them, nor any executive-level industry group I observed, has taken action to halt the flight of film production to Canada and other places outside Southern California, much less to increase local investment in entertainment production. Consequently, these efforts are left to increasingly anxious talent guilds, labor unions, and industry outsiders like local politicians, developers, and the metropolitan newspaper.[31] The difference in attitudes reflects how entertainment executives and the older business community understand the industry's local essence as social versus economic capital, respectively. Although Santa Monica and the greater Los Angeles region retain quite substantial investment in entertainment production, the traditional urban business community appears relatively powerless to influence its form.

TOURISM-SPECIFIC ASSOCIATIONS

In contrast to software and entertainment, the industry-specific associations that tourism firms join have strong and multiple connections to both the traditional urban business community and municipal government. The local visitors and conventions bureau illustrates the external networks that permeate tourism industry associations. Whether formed as a chamber of commerce offshoot or a city-initiated economic development strategy, visitors and conventions bureaus promote local tourism by advertising in newspapers and other publications, scheduling conferences, and coordinating visitor flows among visitor-serving businesses during special events, among other things. Typically, membership dues and government revenues fund visitors and conventions bureaus, and boards of directors usually include both private- and public-sector representatives. Members come from a variety of sectors that mutually benefit from the region's promotion to visitors, from hotels and restaurants to real estate agents and (to my surprise) even local Internet service providers. An executive at San Luis Obispo's largest local Internet service provider explained to me, "We're basically involved in anything where business customers are, because that's where our revenues come from."

Tourism firms use their local associations to a relatively high degree due to their dependence on local public-sector funding and the government scan that their associations can provide. Since government funds for visitors and conventions bureaus come largely from bed taxes levied on all lodging establishments, hotels that seek representation for their taxation have an increased incentive to join these associations. In the three Southern California destinations, municipal governments levy a tax of around ten percent on each hotel room, which generates substantial revenue streams.[32] As in chamber subcommittees, hoteliers make sure that government collections of bed taxes support tourism promotion and not other government expenditures. Also, tourism firms have an interest in ensuring that promotion does not single out particular tourism firms, projects, or destinations. In addition to these potential divisions from within the tourism industry, visitors and conventions bureaus occasionally take the brunt of criticism from residents for appearing to promote projects or even an entire industry that locals oppose. For these reasons, visitors and conventions bureau staff frequently avoid "political" issues well beyond their nonprofit prohibition on endorsing political candidates. They typically refrain from faintly endorsing any project without the consensus of all members; since few projects cannot avoid increasing competition with existing tourism firms (as the Hearst Ranch Resort illustrates), visitors and conventions bureaus usually remain silent on this front.

Specific sets of tourism firms take part in more narrowly focused associations. For example, special assessment district corporations in popular destinations (like shopping districts and piers) receive funds from tourism firms and other tenants, and represent tenants before redevelopment agencies and other local authorities. Hotel and restaurant managers and owners participate in local lodging and restaurant associations, respectively, as well as their regional or state counterparts. In contrast to how visitors and conventions bureaus avoid political controversy, these other industry-specific associations frequently organize industry protests before government and public forums on issues such as cigarette-smoking bans and offshore oil drilling.

Tourism-specific associations, then, provide widespread, binding, and substantial connections to the traditional urban business community. Their many ties to other businesses, executives, and organizations bring tourism executives and the traditional urban business community into routine contact. Embedded in these networks, they may advocate "pro-business" issues that, more than software or entertainment, reflect the growth dependence of the traditional urban business community. However, tourism issues occasionally include "anti-business" concerns like opposing certain kinds of development and industrialization that might deter visitors. In this case, tourism-specific associations can deploy their very conventional capacities for business mobilization to advocate stances that go against the thrust of the "pro-business" agenda.

HOLLOWING OUT LOCAL BUSINESS INSTITUTIONS

Although the local chambers, banks, and even industry-specific associations often promote the new urban economy's growth, their capacities do not "create value" that overwhelmingly benefits software, entertainment, and (to a lesser degree) tourism firms. This is significant. Merely by virtue of the ways they do business, new urban economy firms diminish the representativeness, centrality, and horizons of the traditional civic network.

In industry centers like Silicon Valley, local business organizations, banks, business services, and many others in the traditional urban business community have adapted to the needs of technology firms. Elsewhere, however, most software firms do not use local chambers or capital. When core firms do join local business groups, their participation is typically so modest and narrow (usually around land-use policies) that traditional business leaders have relatively few opportunities to develop systemic relationships and exert influence over the new urban economy. The situation for entertainment is even starker. Most entertainment firms rely on specialized production networks, national associations, and deal-making relationships in which the traditional urban business community plays almost no role. In both software and entertainment, only peripheral firms rely on the capacities of the local chamber and capital. Tourism firms, by contrast, are strongly integrated into all these institutions. Whatever independence from the traditional urban business community they have derives mostly from a substantial rate of organizational free-riding and, within business organizations, their normative support for preserving the quality of life.

These patterns raise doubts about traditional business leaders' claims that they "protect the interests" of new urban economy firms. Of course, globally minded firms need not actively participate in local business networks to convey conventional "pro-business" interests; these are effectively transmitted by the interurban competition for capital investment that sustains the "old" urban economy.[33] However, new urban economy firms' interests are different, and may no longer be accounted for by traditional "pro-business" institutions. In the quality-of-life district, the pro-growth thrust of traditional business leaders' efforts can even grate against the lifeboat syndrome of many new urban economy executives, although the latter have deprived themselves of an organizational venue to express their concerns. In short, software, entertainment, and tourism firms' weak integration into the traditional civic network, especially in the quality-of-life district, implies another important break with business as usual.

6

Corporate Interventions into Local Government

T o this point, I have examined how software, entertainment, and tourism firms select locations and do business in the new industrial space. Because these follow straight out of the competitive imperatives of capitalism, few companies view the issues they raise as necessarily political. In many business discourses, "politics" is contrasted with "business" to describe discretionary activities that run the risk of distracting businesspeople from work, corrupting their bottom line focus with irrational value judgments, drawing the unwanted attention of vindictive politicians and agencies, poisoning the workplace, and alienating consumers. Yet, despite this supposed antithesis, government necessarily shapes the business environment, and not always for ill. Business efforts to influence policy or office-holders reveal how government can order or destabilize this environment by regulating economic activities and actors. Companies may individually seek governmental access and benefit out of immediate self-interest. Collectively, companies, industries, and business leaders tend to demand at least a predictable, if not favorable, playing field for business.[1]

To their credit, most of the software, entertainment, and tourism executives I interviewed were a little more up front in acknowledging how their business can "get political," but their examples tended to revolve around tax rates, trade policy, intellectual property rights enforcement, worker immigration, and others that pertain to national or, at the smallest scale, state government. Several seemed dubious that *local* politics matters for their business at all. The question I take up in this chapter is: How and why do companies and elites in software, entertainment, and tourism seek to influence local government?

HOW BUSINESS SETS CITY HALL'S AGENDA

Comparable research on the traditional urban business community has long demonstrated that the traditional urban business community has very real incentives to monitor, engage, and influence the composition and policies of city hall. Local government can stimulate urban growth and corporate prosperity positively (by subsidizing local developments and firms, soliciting federal and state grants and infrastructure, etc.), as well as negatively by imposing constraints, for which it is perhaps better known (by enforcing land-use zoning, imposing local taxes and fees, etc.). Thus, the traditional urban business community has an interest in ensuring a "pro-business"—that is, fiscally conservative, pro-growth, and anti-regulatory—agenda in city hall.[2]

To this end, business leaders may themselves run for elected office, although more often they make campaign contributions to local candidates for mayor, city council, and other elected offices. Thanks to low American voter interest in local elections, contributors can easily obtain personal access to local candidates because the latter can win with relatively small advantages in campaign chests.[3] If the elected official has not already been favorably swayed, contributors can at least use their access to lobby the official and thereby shape city hall's agenda. Contributors frequently hedge their bets by contributing to rival electoral candidates in order to ensure future access to decision-makers.[4]

Traditionally, business leaders support "pro-business" candidates who are not necessarily businesspeople themselves but hold leadership positions in civic organizations (e.g., chambers of commerce, local charities, museums) and lesser municipal offices (e.g., school boards, parks commissions). By ascending through the traditional civic network, local candidates can learn of the traditional urban business community's interests and norms.[5] A restaurateur described how this works: "You were president of the Boys Club, then you were president of the chamber, and then you got on the city council, and you did all the favors for all your buddies that you knew." The reward for their business advocacy is further financial support for election campaigns, since sympathetic business leaders and industries can open doors to other potential supporters.[6]

Although the traditional urban business community shares a collective interest in who presides over city hall, the bulk of business contributions usually comes from real estate interests, since they specifically need to curry the favor of politicians reviewing their projects.[7] Other local industries usually give fewer campaign contributions because their stake in electing probusiness candidates is less direct and more normative. Among these local businesses, campaign contributions tend to reflect the degree that contributors see themselves as business leaders with a duty to set the tone for local politics. Local banks are a case in point. In absolute dollars, they tend not to give as much as real estate interests, but they typically follow behind (often in second place) as financial contributors.[8] Overall, campaign contributions are a primary indicator of the traditional urban business community's systemic power, since citizens and other interest groups that do not make campaign contributions do not always get such privileged reception in local government.[9]

However, this is less the case in Santa Monica, Santa Barbara, and San Luis Obispo, where "anti-business" community movements have seriously undermined, if not completely overturned, business hegemony in city hall since the 1970s. In bitterly opposed reversals of business as usual, activists ran successful initiative campaigns that established local growth limits (in Santa Barbara in 1977 and 1989) and rent control (in Santa Monica in 1979). Also, community activists regularly field their own electoral candidates with perspectives independent of the traditional urban business community's influence. Santa Monica's rent control activists have gone the furthest by creating a local party, Santa Monicans for Renters Rights (SMRR), to institutionalize their endorsement and campaign support activities. One sign that community activists have effectively changed the traditional electoral game is that, since their political ascendancy, local campaign contributions have dramatically increased in at least two of the Southern California localities. From 1977 to 1989, contributions over $100 to mayoral and city council candidates increased five hundred percent in Santa Barbara, and 1016 percent in Santa Monica—far higher than California as a whole (which increased 151 percent).[10] By the 1990s, real estate interests continued to play the primary role in local politics but, perhaps in contrast to most other communities, could no longer take their electoral power for granted.

THE STAKES FOR THE NEW URBAN ECONOMY

As for the new urban economy sectors, the previous chapters have already shown how the influence of the political environment on business varies by industry. On the one hand, the land-use needs of most software and entertainment firms do not cause many government-imposed "headaches." Of course, businesses vocalize concerns about excessively high taxes and fees in the three localities compared to neighboring jurisdictions. One widely read 1997 regional study confirmed Santa Monica's "high-cost" status among Southern California business settings; for instance, a law firm occupying thirty thousand square feet pays an average $95,680 in annual business and utility taxes.[11] What this high-cost status overlooks, however, is the fact that many firms accept the costs of doing business in Santa Monica in return for the agglomerative benefits and quality of life they obtain in the high-tech and entertainment districts of Los Angeles's Westside. Furthermore, the same study gave the city of Santa Barbara a "low-cost" grade and deemed the unincorporated areas of Santa Barbara County (including Goleta, home to a sizable high-tech corridor) "top spots" for doing business because county government does not levy business and utility user taxes.[12] At least Santa Barbara firms, then, have less reason to complain about the costs of doing business; with its lower property values, the same is even truer for San Luis Obispo.[13]

On the other hand, tourism firms regularly interact with the local government in their day-to-day business, even beyond the fees and permits shared by all businesses. The industry looks to the public sector for funds and subsidies; it sometimes also appeals to local government for relief from stiff competition, as Santa Monica's moratorium on new restaurant licenses illustrates. Hotels are especially concerned that cities use their bed taxes to promote tourism and not fund other city services. Large hotels that seek to expand more than local laws allow regularly lobby local government at planning commission hearings (or have local business groups appeal on their behalf). Tourism leaders frequently speak personally with city representatives or testify at city council hearings to advocate positions for improving downtown safety, containing the homeless, and opposing local cigarette-smoking bans. With many more forms of governmental intervention and taxation than software and entertainment firms face, "there's a tie that binds" tourism to government, as a San Luis Obispo economic development official explained.[14] Another political aspect of tourism stems from the fact that, perhaps more than for software and entertainment, community organizations and activists frequently single out the tourism industry when protesting the impacts of local growth.

MUNICIPAL CAMPAIGN CONTRIBUTIONS

These local traditions and industry trends yield competing expectations for the electoral interests of software, entertainment, and tourism firms. On the one hand, the ways that government impinges on the three sectors does not offer a compelling reason for at least software and entertainment firms to support the usual conservative candidates that the traditional urban business community supports. On the other hand, the long tradition of business antagonism toward progressive movements suggests that the traditional urban business community might influence firms to support the local "pro-business" candidates, if this is not already an ideological reflex of business leaders.[15] How do these competing expectations pan out? To answer this question, I have examined campaign contributions by software, entertainment, and tourism industries for mayoral and city council candidates in 1996 for Santa Monica and San Luis Obispo, and in 1997 for Santa Barbara.[16]

Figure 6.1 illustrates the substantive positions adopted by political candidates in these elections. Note that the "progressive," "centrist," and "conservative" categories reflect local perceptions of the political camps and not necessarily my own value judgments.

On the left, progressive candidates favor grassroots concerns, are typically products of community organizations, and regard business agendas for government with at least some degree of skepticism. Whereas "progressive" in Santa Barbara and San Luis Obispo is usually synonymous with slow

FIGURE 6.1

Recent political stances in Santa Monica, Santa Barbara, and San Luis Obispo

Locality	Progressive	Centrist	Conservative
Santa Monica	Support rent control.	Limit rent control (e.g., vacancy decontrol of rent-controlled apartments).	Oppose rent control.
	Favor more lenient laws restricting homeless.	Favor more lenient laws restricting homeless.	Favor tougher laws restricting homeless.
	Oppose pier entertainment permits based on resident complaints.	Grant pier entertainment permits over resident complaints.	Grant pier entertainment permits over resident complaints.
Santa Barbara	Support stricter limits on new housing development.	Favor weaker limits to boost affordable housing construction.	Oppose most limits on new housing development.
	Support municipal architectural requirements.	Support municipal architectural requirements.	Oppose municipal architectural requirements.
	Support city purchase of open space (Douglas Family Preserve).	Oppose city purchase of open space (Douglas Family Preserve).	Oppose city purchase of open space (Douglas Family Preserve).
San Luis Obispo	Restrict new water supply to one project only.	Restrict new water supply to one project only.	Support two new water-supply projects.
	Support no new major retail projects.	Support one new major retail project.	Support two new major retail projects.
	Support open space initiative (Measure O).	Support open space initiative (Measure O).	Oppose open space initiative (Measure O).

growth, Santa Monica's progressive candidates endorse a pro-renter agenda that has only a loose relation to growth issues. SMRR opposes certain development projects outright, but more often its city council majority simply imposes fiscal linkages to fund local services and amenities as a condition of approval. In the center, candidates may promote conventionally "liberal" urban issues (economic development for minority and working class communities, workplace unionization and labor politics, etc.) yet also support at least a moderately pro-growth agenda. Arguably, their position mirrors the ideological "Third Way" pursued by the Democratic Party since the Clinton administration. On the right, conservative candidates are pro-growth in the conventional sense and take their political cue largely from the traditional urban business community in the ways described earlier. Although many accept the preservation of certain environmental amenities (like beachfront parks), they do so only in step with the traditional urban business community.

Below, Table 6.1 shows how the software, entertainment, and tourism sectors give compared to local banks. The statistics I report are contributions per local firm (not just contributors, a much smaller group) and, in parentheses, the proportion of campaign contributions from each sector to candidates of each orientation; reading across rows, bold text indicates which sector gave the most to each political camp. Generally, the three sectors give insignificantly (i.e., less than local banks) overall, as well as to centrist and conservative candidates specifically. (San Luis Obispo departs from this pattern because no banks or bankers there gave money to any candidate.)

In almost all cases, software consistently ranks near the bottom for campaign contributions (per firm and proportionately) among the four sectors. The industry yields a very small group of contributors and appears to favor

TABLE 6.1

Campaign contributions per local firm (proportion of campaign contributions from local firms)

Locality	Orientation	Software	Entertainment	Tourism	Banks
Santa Monica	Progressive	$1.56 (0.4%)	**$9.26** **(5.9%)**	$8.11 **(9.3%)**	$0.00 (0.0%)
	Centrist	$11.57 (1.4%)	$6.34 (1.9%)	$15.96 **(8.5%)**	**$67.42** (2.5%)
	Conservative	$9.26 (1.0%)	$5.60 (1.5%)	$14.19 **(6.9%)**	**$36.36** (1.2%)
	All	$22.40 (1.0%)	$21.21 (2.5%)	$38.25 **(8.0%)**	**$103.79** (1.5%)
Santa Barbara	Progressive	$6.42 (1.6%)	**$11.70** (2.3%)	$2.38 **(3.5%)**	$4.90 (0.5%)
	Centrist	$3.19 (1.7%)	$0.00 (0.0%)	$4.27 **(11.2%)**	**$12.25** (2.3%)
	Conservative	$4.26 (1.0%)	$1.06 (0.2%)	$2.94 **(3.5%)**	**$16.20** (1.3%)
	All	$12.87 (1.3%)	$12.77 (0.9%)	$9.59 **(6.1%)**	**$17.65** (1.2%)
San Luis Obispo	Progressive	$0.00 (0%)	$0.00 (0%)	**$0.18** **(1.6%)**	$0.00 (0.0%)
	Centrist	$1.79 (2.1%)	**$4.55** (2.1%)	$1.06 **(12.6%)**	$0.00 (0.0%)
	Conservative	$0.00 (0.0%)	$0.00 (0.0%)	**$1.59** **(10.9%)**	$0.00 (0.0%)
	All	$1.79 (0.5%)	**$4.55** (1.0%)	$2.82 **(8.3%)**	$0.00 (0.0%)

SOURCE: campaign disclosure statements and Santa Monicans for Renters' Rights recipient committee campaign statement filed from Jan. 1 to Dec. 31 in the election year.

no particular political side consistently.[17] In stark contrast, entertainment gives substantially more to progressives than to other candidates, as well as more than software, tourism, and banks give to progressives.[18] This pattern holds even in Santa Barbara, although this may be a statistical artifact of its relatively minuscule industry; the same error likely explains entertainments' centrism in San Luis Obispo (from a single contribution by a local television station executive).[19] Proportionately, tourism contributes more in all campaign categories than the other two sectors, but its contributions per firm never rank first except in one case (to San Luis Obispo conservatives). This suggests that a small group of firms disproportionately comprises tourism contributors.[20]

Several software, entertainment, and especially tourism contributors give to more than one candidate, although local banks are more likely to yield multiple contributors proportionate to their sector, as Table 6.2 shows.

REPEAT PLAYERS IN LOCAL POLITICS

Another vehicle by which business elites extend their political influence is by serving on public commissions, task forces, and other public or quasi-public agencies. Often uninteresting or obscured to local voters, these hidden governments can make vital planning and allocation decisions and are therefore a common mechanism by which the traditional urban business community shapes the agenda in local politics.[21] Since placement on these entities usually comes by political appointment, it generally happens after a businessperson has gained access to politicians. In this way, service on such entities suggests that the businessperson is a "repeat player" in local government.

What kind of new urban economy elites pursue such political service? Since there is no central record for these activities (in contrast to campaign contributions), the evidence here is unsystematic yet suggestive. The city of San Luis Obispo appointed twelve local businesspeople to a 1997 "Targeted Industry Cluster Committee" to evaluate the fiscal benefits and local conditions for high-value sectors (of which high technology was deemed especially important). This committee included three executives from the largest

TABLE 6.2

Multiple contributors: proportion of local firms (number of multiple contributors)

Locality	Software	Entertainment	Tourism	Banks
Santa Monica	0.02 (2)	0.01 (4)	0.06 **(27)**	**0.09** (3)
Santa Barbara	0.02 (3)	0.01 (1)	0.00 **(4)**	**0.06** (3)
San Luis Obispo	0.00 **(3)**	**0.02** (1)	0.00 (2)	0.00 (0)

SOURCE: campaign disclosure statements and Santa Monicans for Renters' Rights recipient committee campaign statement filed from Jan. 1 to Dec. 31 in the election year.

local software firms and an Internet service provider; only the last was connected to campaign contributions. Also in San Luis Obispo, the founder of the oldest surviving software firm once sat on the school board and the city's "economic stabilization" task force. In Los Angeles, David Geffen and Lew Wasserman, respective studio moguls from DreamWorks SKG and MCA/ Universal (now Vivendi Universal), sat on a committee to bring the 2000 Democratic National Convention to the city.[22] In 1998, a Los Angeles County supervisor appointed a Sony Pictures executive to a Citizens Economy and Efficiency Commission.[23] The next year, a Paramount Pictures executive capped a six-year tenure as chair of the Community Redevelopment Agency, the city's urban renewal authority.[24] In Santa Monica, one of the most represented restaurateurs in campaign contributions and local business organizations also overheard public employees' grievances on the city's personnel committee.

Other combinations of electoral and civic participation open multiple paths to political influence. Accordingly, I cross-referenced multiple contributors with civic leadership in the traditional civic network to generate a supplementary list of repeat players. From software, I identified two repeat players from the industry's eight multiple contributors. In Santa Monica, a retired software tycoon gave money to a centrist and a conservative candidate. He is well known for his generosity to art galleries and local schools; a local land-use lawyer who has served on several candidates' election committees described his contributions as "eclectic and not partisan in nature." In Santa Barbara, a software executive gave money to two progressives and a centrist; he plays a leadership role on the local chamber, the local software booster association, and the local United Way.

From entertainment's six multiple contributors, the two repeat players had some relation to major development projects then pending before local government. The first was the president of Santa Monica Studios, whose new studio was the largest development project ever built in Santa Monica for a single entertainment tenant. In the same election cycle, he successfully ran as an SMRR-endorsed school board candidate and sat on the advisory board for the community college's "Academy of Entertainment and Technology." The second multiple contributor was a motion picture studio executive in charge of local community relations, whose company is the anchor tenant of one of Santa Monica's largest office complexes. He was also an officer of the National Conference of Community and Justice's Santa Monica chapter and was active in local school programs.

From tourism's thirty-three multiple contributors, I could identify six repeat players. From Santa Monica, three hotel managers were directors, respectively, of the local chamber, a neighborhood business association, and the Rotary Club. Two restaurateurs had been directors of at least three business associations (from the local chamber to the visitors and conference bureau); one told me he has served in about twenty-five civic organizations over the last two decades. Twelve of Santa Monica's twenty-seven multiple contributors, it should be noted, are tenants of or otherwise connected to the Santa Monica pier, which is governed by a quasi-city agency. From San Luis Obispo, one hotelier had been director at the local chamber, the local economic development organization, and the local university's sports foundation. Another hotelier gave significantly to the local community college.

In the three Southern California places, local business and government leaders report that these repeat player profiles are atypical; most new urban economy leaders, especially from software and entertainment, generally do not serve on local government agencies and task forces.[25] For one reason, business leaders in these sectors perennially claim to be "too busy" for such participation. This claim warrants some skepticism, since a lack of time seldom prevents the traditional urban business community from such participation, but it nevertheless shows how local politics are a discretionary activity in these sectors, especially for software and entertainment. Perhaps more importantly, the dynamic and unconventional ways that software and entertainment firms do business make their industries particularly opaque to most outside solicitors, including government. As a talent agent said of the entertainment industry,

> I don't think anybody who's not in this business gets how this business works, because it's not a business that you can describe to people. There are companies like 20th Century Fox or MCA or Disney that have hard assets; they have a lot of libraries, they have real estate, so on, and so forth. You can grasp the hard assets and how they are produced. What you can't grasp about the business is how it works, whatever standard operating procedure is. It's totally foreign to most people, because it's a very vague business in many ways.

Consequently, local politicians tend to solicit involvement from only the largest entertainment-media firms or most visible industry organizations. That could be all they need because "if you're doing politics, ninety-eight percent of the time [that] you need someone from the entertainment community, you're going to go to the movers and shakers," as a music industry organization executive observed. Nevertheless, the movers and shakers do not necessarily represent the typical entertainment company. These patterns of political participation suggest that local governments have no systemic access to most software and entertainment firms.

RATIONALES FOR POLITICAL PARTICIPATION

Tellingly, when I asked about their involvement in "local politics" in an open-ended manner, most software and entertainment executives did not usually bring up the issue of campaign contributions, unlike their counterparts from tourism and the traditional urban business community. Local politics appears to be rarely pondered by these information economy executives, whom I almost always had to prompt for specific details about campaign contributions. What reasons do corporate elites in the new urban economy sectors have to get involved in local politics?

POLITICS IS A DIRTY WORD

The late 1990s are generally thought to be a watershed moment in the politics of high-tech industries. After a legacy of widespread inaction, by 1999 "Silicon Valley's Peter Pans finally grew up," proclaimed one headline.[26] High-tech interest groups and firms heavily lobbied federal legislators regarding several landmark pieces of legislation, such as the Communications Decency Act, bills for R&D tax credits, federal moratoria on e-commerce sales taxes, and immigration reforms to ease the entry of foreign high-tech workers. Another goad to political activity came with the Justice Department's three-year antitrust lawsuit against the Microsoft Corporation, which "taught us," observed one dot-com CEO, "Better approach Washington preemptively rather than wait until there is a problem."[27] As a response, he and executives from Internet giants like Amazon.com, America Online, eBay, and Yahoo formed Netcoalition.com, the Internet's most prominent interest group, to lobby alongside older technology trade associations in Washington, DC.

The 2000 presidential race further fueled observers' interest in high-technology's political affiliations, in part because of widespread perceptions that technology industries do not conform to traditional business party lines. In "other kinds of old-time businesses, you tend to basically end up with a room full of Republicans," a software executive told me. "With a lot of high-tech businesses, that's not true. I find a wide range of ideas." Initially, the Democratic Party had the edge in industry favor, as exemplified by the "Gore-Techs," a group of high-tech executives whom presidential candidate Al Gore consulted regularly in the early years of his campaign.[28] Later, more conservative candidates were heartened by statements from industry leaders like John Chambers, CEO of Cisco Systems, who said at a 1999 fund-raiser for Republican candidate George W. Bush, "It's not Republicans versus Democrats. The Valley has respect for people who can make things happen."[29] Consequently, both major parties eyed high-tech leaders' money and endorsements as a major prize in 2000. As a consultant for Republican candidate John McCain observed, "It's only been relatively recently that Silicon Valley has realized that they don't have to choose between personal access and policy agreement. What you've got now is a situation where Gore isn't the only person spending a lot of time out here."[30]

As home to Silicon Valley, California also saw an unprecedented surge in high-tech political activity during this period. In 1996, the state's technology industries raised their political profile considerably to oppose a state initiative (Proposition 211) that would ease investor lawsuits against corporations for security violations. After defeating the initiative, high-tech business leaders formed the "Technology Network," a political action committee that funneled $915,000 to Democrats and $668,000 to Republicans in 1998 California and federal elections. High-tech interest groups lobbied unsuccessfully against 1999 California legislation mandating overtime pay for non-salaried workers who put in more than eight hours a day, which they feared would "fl[y] in the face of the entrepreneurial spirit of Silicon Valley," one CEO said.[31] A few executives entered the political arena apparently for reasons beside immediate business interest. In 1998, the top individual donor to California campaigns was Reed Hastings, a Silicon Valley software tycoon who spent $3.3 million to place a charter schools initiative on the ballot; he eventually withdrew the initiative after the state legislature adopted many of his reforms.[32] Still, many political observers believe that high-tech campaign contributions lag behind those given by other corporate communities. Explained the Technology Network's president, "To be giving a million dollars a year, you have to have some pretty significant government interests, and high tech, by and large, does not. The [Silicon Valley] giving is by individuals who are doing what they think is right for the country."[33]

Importantly, local politics appears to benefit little from the industry's newfound political energy. Most software executives told me they do not contribute money to local candidates, a claim borne out by campaign contribution records. Furthermore, they generally could not think of others in their local industries who *do* give money to local campaigns. In a characteristic statement, one executive asserted that "politics are [sic] probably a dirty word" in the software industry. Far more so than in entertainment and tourism, software executives express reluctance or even disdain for "doing politics," by which they also connote interacting with government, communicating with public and private decision-makers, or simply stating political opinions in a public forum. Occasionally, "politics" even includes participation in local trade associations and support for local nonprofits.

Apolitical and pragmatic attitudes specifically distinguish the ways that software leaders approach local politics. These attitudes usually correspond to different roles; CEOs and other firm executives tend to adopt the apolitical approach, while industry organizers adopt the pragmatic approach. Many *apolitical* software executives attribute their unease with politics to the turbulent nature of their company and industry. For some, this offers a clear rationale for avoiding politics: "If you're trying to run a business, you don't have time for that." Those who do take a stab at local politics often discover that their industry moves too fast for politics, which they find entails debate, consensus, and an inflexible adherence to procedure. Speaking about his advocacy on behalf of the local industry, a software executive complained,

> Part of the frustrating thing is the pace with which politics works. I couldn't do it; it's just way too slow. It takes forever to get stuff done . . . In this business, I can make things happen today. I can have an idea this morning, have it

implemented at noon, and have it make a difference in Paris when I wake up. Boom! Done, let's go, next! And I like that pace.

Another pervasive belief is that "politics" interferes with the industry's creative ethos.[34] In the "wired" culture, politics implies dependence on "tired" and old-fashioned ways of doing things that are at odds with the task of imagining possible futures and new innovations: "People in our industries tend to be extremely independent, almost libertarian in some ways; maybe there's where some of the apolitical nature comes from as well." Relatedly, many software executives uphold the perception of industry outsiders that, at an abstract level, their industry has no intrinsic "political" aspect:

> I think people in this business feel they are dealing with very broad questions . . . [This industry] realizes it's trying to appeal to all people, and therefore it's quite broad . . . [In] telecommunications and software, there's no underlying facet that I've been able to detect that would give you a clue as to anybody's politics. As a result, we don't see much politicization of those groups.

On a more mundane level, software leaders behave apolitically in order to maintain the broad local support that their industry has enjoyed so far. The industry is "something that all sides [in local politics] agree on universally. They may disagree on other industries, but for software, they all agree it's a win-win for everybody." Software firms generally face such minimal governmental intervention/regulation that executives can credibly claim, "For the most part, local politics don't influence the business." Additionally, in software-nascent localities where firms seek any boost they can get, "the industry is so fragile that it has to endear itself to both sides."

Because of these various apolitical rationales, most software executives refrain from making campaign contributions or engaging in other efforts to influence city hall. Many even withhold their political opinions from others in the industry; an Internet firm entrepreneur observed that, in all his dealings with other industry people, "I've never been in a situation where anyone starts ranting and raving about anybody particular in politics here. People are probably polite to each other because they don't know what each other's politics are." Some executives make special efforts to maintain their apolitical profile, as one explained when a local Rotary Club officer invited him to speak before the organization:

> I get these [speaking invitations] all the time, and I find out he's running for city council, and it's real important that he asked me to speak, which is seen as an endorsement of him. He asked me to come to this meeting, and that was okay, but I really started thinking about that. If I'm going to do that, do I get involved, and how much do I care about that stuff? I'm not sure that I do.

Even those who occasionally contribute funds do so in idiosyncratic and apparently non-partisan ways: "As a person, I'm not really political, [although] I guess once in awhile I get solicited for donations. Some times of the day I'm a Republican, other times I'm a Democrat."

Whereas individual companies may have little stake in local politics, occasionally the collective industry seeks laws, decisions, or resources from local government. Such political work typically falls to industry leaders, either officials from local software associations or (less commonly) voluntarily inclined executives, who tend to adopt a *pragmatic* approach to local politics. Via industry associations, they lobby local governments for favorable land-use zoning, improved telecommunications infrastructure, or government resources for marketing efforts. Informally, they use their expertise to influence local politicians on the issues where they can help. Few see themselves as habitually disposed to such activities; tellingly, they take pains (at least in interviews) to downplay the "political" nature of their advocacy efforts. One software leader who gave to progressive candidates stated,

> There's probably not a month that goes by that I don't talk to a city council member or a member of the [county] board of supervisors and give them an opinion about something. But if I'm on their case knocking on their door everyday—I'm not the one who sits there in the political forum and tries to make a political statement. I don't do that.

A very few industry leaders extend their pragmatic politics to contributing to local candidates whom they deem the most sympathetic to the industry's needs. Characteristically, they do so "from behind the scenes very, very quietly." For example, an executive who also presides over a local software booster association noted that when he gives money, "I have to do it so people don't confuse me as president of the [booster association] with my political positions." (Campaign contribution records reveal that he reported his occupation as "retired.") In keeping with their pragmatic approach, software leaders tend to give to candidates who they believe balance political extremes. The aforementioned executive, for instance, supports candidates who "are more in tune with the [booster association's] philosophy of combining economic vitality with quality of life. So I'm not going to go with a wild-eyed environmentalist who is not interested in one side, or someone who wants to open the barn doors to anybody." In San Luis Obispo, the sole software contributor (and a self-proclaimed libertarian) whose firm is heavily involved in the local software booster association gave to a centrist candidate.

THE SELF-PROCLAIMED LIBERALS

Whereas many outsiders puzzle over the affiliations of the software industry, there is little apparent mystery to entertainment's politics: liberal. Especially since Bill Clinton's 1992 presidential candidacy, much of the world knows of Hollywood's liberal leanings. To my surprise, no entertainment executive or elite worker I interviewed downplayed this reputation. An independent producer said she is "Democratic across the board," and other entertainment elites repeatedly pointed out that many high-level entertainment figures are "staunch supporters" of the Democratic Party. The political orientation of one of the most prominent entertainment talent agencies is "pretty far to the left," according to one agent, although officially the agency takes no political positions. Hollywood Republicans "exist," insiders concede, "but there aren't a lot of them." At a minimum, then, the industry does not shirk from political identities and party affiliations that corporate communities have traditionally deemed unreliable and even "anti-business."

Entertainment elites list a broad range of issues that comprise their liberal politics; tellingly, they associate these with their philanthropy as well as their politics. Civil libertarian causes rank highly among their political priorities—perhaps logically so, given that the industry faces regular criticisms for the sexual and violent content it produces. Just as prominent, if somewhat less coherent, is their support for social justice issues. Suggesting the breadth of these concerns, a director described his politics via the kinds of advocacy groups he supported: "groups that promote social equality, environmental sanity, having humans' basic needs taken care of, having a safety net for the most impoverished, and support systems, transition houses, women's shelters, all kinds of things like that." This does not mean the industry supports candidates and causes that might actually disturb the broader economic climate, as a record company executive explained:

> Like most people, entertainment people will be liberal on some things and conservative on others. For example, I don't see people calling for more progressive taxes. But yes, entertainment people are more liberal.

Still, entertainment's political priorities sometimes pose direct or indirect conflicts with other industries, a practice that is usually discouraged in business circles.[35] For example, director Rob Reiner led a successful 1998 California initiative to impose a fifty-cent cigarette tax that would fund early childhood development programs; he donated $1.55 million to this initiative campaign, making him the sixth largest individual donor to state campaigns that year.[36]

Entertainment politics tend to divide into liberal or pragmatic attitudes. As with software, these typically correspond to different roles; employees and independent contractors generally adopt the liberal approach, while executives of entertainment firms (particularly larger ones) take the pragmatic approach. *Liberal* entertainment talent, executives, and workers frequently support candidates, parties, and interest groups that do not focus on business climate issues, at least in the ways that "pro-business" Republicans do. In a few cases, entertainment figures even endorse more radical groups and candidates who oppose entertainment-related development projects, such as the DreamWorks studio proposal. This pattern supports insiders' belief that entertainment's liberal politics is largely motivated by the personal convictions of the industry's elite workers. One SMRR organizer attributed certain celebrities' financial support in the party's early years "largely to their personal predilection toward SMRR-type issues"; as evidence of his claim, these contributors did not even live in Santa Monica.

Perhaps a less visible factor behind entertainment's liberal reputation is that movers and shakers frequently support each other's personal politics in the course of doing business. For instance, a famous movie actor who is an executive director of a liberal advocacy group may solicit talent agencies, film studios, and other deep-pockets firms with which he has worked to buy tables (sometimes as much as $25,000 apiece) at a fund-raising benefit. Insiders contend that this sometimes expensive practice creates and protects business relationships with the high-status individuals who espouse those causes. An administrator from Barbra Streisand and Steven Spielberg's charitable foundations explained the process:

> It works like this: You find a celebrity who agrees to be honored and attract a crowd of professional peers. Twenty-five percent of the audience will be there because they believe in the organization, and the rest are there because they feel it's part of doing business . . . It's a quid pro quo. Everybody knows the honoree is a shill to bring in their friends. It's just a matter of, do they care enough about the cause to let themselves be used?[37]

In political or philanthropic fund-raisers and other events, entertainment workers find a more hospitable forum for business networking than media-frenzied film festivals or specific corporate events (like motion picture premieres) that take place on "somebody else's turf." Political activism and business networking mix casually in the company town, as evinced by a film director's unsolicited remark that "I'm going down tonight for a fund-raiser for a senator, and I'll bump into some studio people there." It does not matter that the entertainment firm has no direct interest in, or even sympathy for, its financial beneficiaries' activities. Simply to do business in a relationship-driven industry, entertainment elites often lend corporate resources to promote liberal issues that their colleagues personally advocate.

This practice is more common in philanthropy than political fund-raising—"the disease people started this," claimed the celebrity foundation administrator—since some firms prohibit corporate endorsements and contributions.[38] Still even philanthropy amplifies the industry's liberal profile. By giving money or in-kind services, the firm increases the resources with which a politically minded group pursues its activities. Fund-raising benefits also bring liberal political leaders in contact with a network of entertainment industry connections who can be solicited individually for campaign contributions. As the process is repeated, the attribution of firms' names and money to a variety of liberal causes reinforces the larger perception of a liberal entertainment industry. A corollary is that politicians and nonprofits that otherwise suit the convictions espoused by entertainment elites can find it extremely difficult to get their attention without prior access to industry networks. "In the entertainment world," a screenwriter who does philanthropic fund-raising explained, "making the ask"—in other words, soliciting support—requires "being invited in by friends. Friends have to call you up and say, 'You gotta come to this.' "

Entertainment directs its liberalism mostly at national and state levels. In local city council and mayoral campaigns, liberal entertainment figures appear to participate only to the degree that candidates, issues, and community movements pique their political interests. For example, a talent agent supports candidates at all levels except municipal "because I've never been that interested" in city politics. An independent producer with impressive experience in state and federal liberal campaigns does not follow local races because "primarily, I don't have enough time." Residential status may explain some of the industry's involvement in local campaigns. The entertainment workers I interviewed who *live* in Santa Monica were generally homeowners who do not belong to SMRR's renter constituency. However, if most SMRR supporters are renters, as SMRR organizers attest, then the party's entertainment contributors most likely consist of renters (perhaps lower-level employees not likely to be included among my interviewees) who benefit from SMRR's renter politics. (About three-fourths of progressive entertainment contributors in Santa Monica gave to the SMRR party directly.) For much the same reason, entertainment figures who live in Santa Barbara consistently endorse (if not financially support) progressive candidates because they can benefit from their slow-growth politics as local homeowners. Likewise, those with school-age children told me they followed school board races.

Executives of entertainment firms, particularly large ones, bring a business-minded *pragmatic* perspective in contrast or, more often, *addition* to the personal liberalism they might espouse. In federal elections, this pragmatism again leans them toward Democrats, since the Republican Party has long vilified the industry for its "unwholesome" and "anti-family" fare throughout the 1990s, although Democrats have joined them since the 1999 high school shootings in Littleton, Colorado. In public policy and closed-door benefits, Bill Clinton and other Democratic officials have repeatedly made overtures to entertainment executives that translate into significant financial support. As for Republicans' prospects, one studio executive predicted that "if Newt Gingrich came to town to raise money, he would have a hard time filling tables" with entertainment supporters. In the 1998 election, Republican candidates (e.g., for California governor) began advocating issues of entertainment interest. However, their party's legacy of antagonism appears to have given Democrats the first mover's advantage over entertainment firms' affiliations, at least in that election cycle. By September 2000, Democrats had collected $5.8 million for the November elections from entertainment, making the industry fourth on its list of industry supporters and exceeding by $2.1 million entertainment contributions to Republicans (for whom the industry ranked eleventh).[39]

By contrast, in the local arena, executives' political pragmatism often leads them to show bipartisan or even purely conservative support for city council and mayoral candidates. Entertainment firms with large real estate interests provide the archetypical case, as exemplified by a Santa Monica film studio executive who gave to candidates on all three political sides. He explained that the studio generally backs the same centrist and conservative city council candidates as its landlord-developer, even though the studio's employees tend to be "moderately left of center." As his rationale indicates, the film studio keeps its doors open to decision-makers and opinion-setters of competing political persuasions. (Perhaps coincidentally, this studio is a rare entertainment firm that belongs to the local chamber of commerce.) Los Angeles city elections also reveal large contributions across party lines by entertainment firms with vast office and studio properties. For example, film director and DreamWorks SKG chief Steven Spielberg gave substantially to all the major politicians who endorsed the Playa Vista development where the DreamWorks studio was slated. Spielberg was among the top contributors to the 1996 re-election campaign of former Republican mayor Richard Riordan (who ran against stalwart liberal and Playa Vista opponent Tom Hayden); he gave $50,000 to Republican governor Pete Wilson's 1994 re-election campaign; and with his DreamWorks partner David Geffen he reportedly helped raise *one-sixth* of the Clinton-Gore 1996 campaign chest via fund-raising parties and contributions.[40] Campaign contributions by MCA/Universal, Walt Disney Companies, Warner Brothers, and Paramount Pictures made entertainment the third highest sectoral contributor among the top twenty-five contributors to Los Angeles elective city office campaigns for the combined 1993 and 1997 elections. Between the two elections, eight lobbying firms represented the four entertainment-media firms at Los Angeles city hall.[41] Particularly revealing is entertainment support for former mayor Riordan, a moderate Republican who many feel "has made a real difference" on behalf of the industry.

Whereas land-use and real estate issues appear to motivate entertainment executives to get involved in local campaigns, other aspects of the political environment impinging on local production do not. Most notably, studios, networks, and independent production companies (particularly those working on lower-budget projects like TV movies, direct-to-video films, TV pilots, and independent films) often complain that the bureaucratic requirements and costs of filming in Los Angeles are prohibitive.[42] In response, local governments throughout the area have sought to bring "runaway production" back either to remaining soundstages or on location. Santa Monica's city government, for instance, actively promotes the use of its neighborhoods for film locations, to the chagrin of some residents; the city's film permit office can even be reached on one of the first menu choices on city hall's phone system. However, film producers and studio executives whom I interviewed expressed little interest in reforming the business climate in order to make local film shooting more cost-effective, despite this being a major policy goal of Riordan and other local politicians.

THE COMPULSION OF LAND USE

In contrast to software and entertainment, tourism leaders are far more likely to participate in local politics through campaign contributions. A few go even further. In San Luis Obispo, a hotelier is also a (centrist) city councilmember. In Santa Monica, a restaurateur ran for city council in the 1980s, while a second served on the campaign committee for a centrist councilmember who was re-elected in the election cycle covered in this chapter. This level of heightened activity, even if confined to a disproportionate few, supports the belief by traditional business leaders that, of the new urban economy sectors, tourism is the most involved in local electoral politics.

Tourism reveals four attitudes towards local politics and governmental regulation: apolitical, pragmatic, "pro-business," and slow growth. These correspond to variations in the vested interests that tourism companies have before local government. An *apolitical* attitude toward local politics seems most common among the tourism firms and entrepreneurs whose financial resources allow them to be indifferent to what goes on politically in any one place. The manager of a large corporate-owned hotel articulated this standpoint simply: "We certainly don't get involved in politics, so . . . we stay away from politics or donations to politicians, that type of thing." Campaign contribution records reveal that many of the largest hotels and highest-profile restaurants are conspicuously absent from the ranks of tourism contributors. The same appears to hold true for "vanity" establishments owned by entertainment celebrities. "Arnold Schwarzenegger may have a restaurant in town," an SMRR organizer observed, "but that doesn't mean he gets involved in Santa Monica politics." For some, the apolitical approach stems from the nature of multinational corporate business; for example, hotel managers are replaced as often as every three to five years, which gives them little time to grow sophisticated in the ways of local politics. Another factor is that apolitical tourism firms have already established themselves in the localities, and therefore have the luxury of staying apolitical. Had they more difficulty getting their site approved, they might espouse a different attitude towards local politics.

The latter plight describes tourism elites with the *pragmatic* approach. They might want to be apolitical, but they believe they cannot avoid getting involved in local politics, since their business tends to be explicitly politicized or subject to local governmental regulation. Consequently, they use campaign contributions to gain influence with local politicians of all orientations and, in the process, to stabilize the political environment for their business. Frequently more entrepreneurial than non-local hotel and restaurant chains, pragmatic firms invest great time and money in understanding the community "civically, charitably, and politically," observed a land-use attorney who represents several hotels. Tourism firms that make contributions to two or even all three sides epitomize the pragmatic approach. Consisting mostly of hotel developers, privately owned local hotels, and restaurants, their investments are held substantially or even exclusively in the locality. Another set of tourism companies inclined to political pragmatism is firms whose business depends on government subsidy, as exemplified by the tenants of the Santa Monica Pier and its new amusement park. These restaurant, bar, snack shop, and amusement park operators pay maintenance, security, and promotion fees to a nonprofit corporation whose directors are appointed by the city council; their contributions to candidates of all three orientations made up thirty-eight percent of all Santa Monica tourism contributions.

A third group of tourism firms takes a conventionally *"pro-business"* approach toward politics. Consisting predominantly of privately owned hotels, motels, and restaurants, these firms make conservative and often centrist contributions, since centrist candidates typically sit on a "pro-business" city hall coalition. Often, "pro-business" tourism firms do not limit their activities to campaign contributions; others include speaking publicly at city council meetings, serving on city task forces (like parking committees), and taking leadership roles in sympathetic candidates' campaign staff or local business organizations. At least in the three Southern California places, their stance appears to be a reaction to the slow-growth movements that shape local land-use and business policies. In their litany of complaints, "pro-business" tourism executives typically point their fingers not just at intrusive local government but also what they regarded as NIMBY (not in my backyard)–minded residents. Residential concerns about local growth, pro-business tourism elites insist, are behind protests against expanded parking or hotel projects, as well as small irritations like noise complaints or strict entertainment license standards. That this group reacts to slow-growth but not necessarily progressive government policies is suggested in Santa Monica, where the two agendas do not always coincide. For example, one restaurateur there backs SMRR's opponents because SMRR candidates (he believes) support "anti-business" policies; yet he claimed that "most restaurants like rent control" because they do more business when renters have more disposable income.

Finally, a small minority of tourism firms contribute to progressive candidates who promote *slow-growth* agendas. Their numbers are admittedly few (i.e., only ten tourism contributors to progressives, of which seven come from Santa Barbara), and none were among the recognized leaders I interviewed. Some are also benefactors of local environmental organizations that lead strong slow-growth efforts. Of course, many more tourism firms, including those in the three prior types described above, express concern to "maintain the specialness" of their locality, by which they mean maintaining ocean and coastal health, preserving scenic stretches of undeveloped land, and even slowing growth within the community. Yet this more widespread sentiment rarely compels them to make local campaign contributions. In a telling statement, one hotel owner who claims his firm and the larger tourism industry indirectly benefit from growth limits also believes he "can be more effective by staying unidentified as either pro-developer or no-growth."

THE NEW BUSINESS OF LOCAL POLITICS

For the most part, the software and entertainment industries do not collectively support the traditional urban business community's favored politicians, an important departure from business as usual. Just as importantly, most companies in these sectors have no need to build systemic relationships with local elected officials because they do not experience the primary factor that motivates business to get involved in local politics: governmental regulation. This pattern is underscored by the contrasting profiles of the sector and firms that give the most. Tourism firms donate more political money than the other sectors to a large extent because they are more regulated and overseen by local government. Likewise, certain corporate contributors tend to rely on government approval for land-use decisions or rent profits: software leaders seeking to expedite zoning changes benefiting the high-tech industry, film studios with extensive real estate holdings, hotels small enough to feel the financial squeeze of bed taxes, restaurants whose entertainment licenses and expanded parking require government approval, and tourism firms governed by quasi-city agencies.

To be sure, some people make campaign contributions out of personal conviction and not business needs.[43] The list of software, entertainment, and tourism contributors is sprinkled with a few individuals known for their political convictions, especially in entertainment. In many respects, the record of that industry's progressive contributions gives credence to its self-proclaimed and other-perceived liberalism. Although supporting talent's personal liberalism makes business sense in this relationship-driven industry, many of its favored candidates and causes do not promote a conventional "pro-business" agenda; a few of their candidates and causes even threaten the business climate for other companies.

Otherwise, campaign contributions tend to reflect a business rationality, which for many firms means avoiding local politics altogether. This, I believe, is a remarkable finding. Although the liberal, pro-environment regimes of Santa Monica, Santa Barbara, and San Luis Obispo have long been anathema to the traditional urban business community, they may serve the business and quality-of-life interests of most new urban economy firms, if the latter's insignificant support for conservative candidates is any indication. Tourism firms most resemble the traditional urban business community in their tendency to support "pro-business" candidates; even those that give to candidates on all sides do not support the ones who (they believe) support capricious noise complaints, revoke entertainment licenses, and deny expanded parking. Still, even tourism does not promote an unrestrained pro-growth agenda, for what are now I hope obvious reasons. Coupled with the widespread avoidance of local politics, these patterns demonstrate that the three sectors break in important ways from the traditional urban business community's mobilization around conservative candidates. Still, this sheds little light on the actual political good accomplished by the political camps strengthened by the new urban economy. I speak to the progressive possibilities embodied in the new political alignments in the next chapter, after I examine community philanthropy in the three sectors.

7

The New Local Philanthropy

The idea of the old establishment educating the new money is very much fading. The belief that new money ought to kowtow to and respect old money has been completely extinguished. People will be trying to break new ground . . . [High-tech millionaires will] be doing wonderful things, we just can't predict what.[1]

Corporate philanthropy may seem an odd choice for investigating the competitive imperatives of the new urban economy. Philanthropy's discourse of "doing good" suggests a discretionary activity that hardly represents corporate need, unlike choosing real estate, working with business associations, or even intervening in electoral campaigns. Some scholarly research supports the belief of many fund-raising professionals that corporate philanthropy mostly reflects business elites' personal interests and is therefore vulnerable to executive turnover and corporate turbulence.[2] For these and more bottom-line reasons, philanthropy and "corporate citizenship" are often the first casualties when competition forces companies to evolve or die.[3]

However, this way of looking at corporate philanthropy gives short shrift to the influence that charitable nonprofits wield, which stems less from the actual good works they achieve than from their abilities to shape discourses and mobilize collective action around the "civic good." In fact, corporate support for nonprofits embodies an important form of political behavior.[4] At the local level, the traditional urban business community has long used philanthropy to legitimate and even exercise community power. Regular support by corporate branches, regional banks, local newspapers, and utilities has made business strongholds out of nonprofits like the United

Way and local museums.[5] Corporate philanthropy embeds these and other nonprofits into the traditional civic network in at least three ways. First, non-profits offer settings for informal networking and deal-making opportunities that overlap other intercorporate interlocks, such as corporate directorates and policy-discussion groups.[6] Second, philanthropy allows business to influence the agenda of resource-dependent nonprofits.[7] To the extent that nonprofits compete for scarce business support, more controversial groups and causes that criticize business can go underfunded.[8] Third, nonprofits imbue business coalitions and agendas with the legitimacy that comes from their "harmonious" social service mission,[9] if they do not promote the business agenda outright.[10]

A NEW ERA OF CORPORATE PHILANTHROPY?

Does the new urban economy sustain these traditions of corporate philan-thropy? The existing evidence is unsystematic and mired in particular assump-tions about proper modes of corporate philanthropy. Much consternation about the philanthropic "failures" of new money comes from venerable nonprofits and their traditional business community benefactors. In a con-text where Fortune 500 corporations have fled central cities, nonprofits and urban business leaders alike fear that new urban economy corporations do not appear to be replacing the corporate citizens of old who sustained phil-anthropy and provided visible business leadership. For scholars, one diffi-culty in evaluating this claim rests upon whether the issue is philanthropic generosity *per se* or the apparent disinterest in older civic priorities. Al-though Hollywood, for instance, has a long tradition of philanthropy, it nevertheless received criticism recently for not supporting one of the down-town Los Angeles business community's pet projects, the construction of the Disney Concert Hall in downtown Los Angeles.

Still, Silicon Valley money has been conspicuous by its absence in the ranks of major philanthropists, at least before the late 1990s. One industry observer deems this characteristic of the region's "cyber-selfish" nature: "It's the Silicon Valley way to think foremost about the upside of all transac-tions," which makes high-tech firms notoriously stingy in philanthropic matters.[11] This accusation may unfairly single out the high-tech industry, since philanthropy officials like to remind one another that "corporate phil-anthropy is an oxymoron" in all sectors. Nevertheless, the characterization is upheld by a notable exception to the trend, Santa Monica software entre-preneur Peter Norton, who became a serious philanthropist after selling his eponymous firm. Commenting in 1993 on then-negligible high-tech phil-anthropy, he stated:

> . . . the new technology money is not interested much in these social involve-ments and thus will be relatively stingy with money, time and influence. First, the money is too new; traditionally, such social involvement comes late in the

lives of the makers or even in the next generation. Second, speaking stereo-typically, the personality of the tech-based newly wealthy is immature and self-involved.[12]

Other Silicon Valley tycoons seconded Norton's argument that "corporate maturity" must precede corporate philanthropy. In 1998 Bill Hewlett, the co-founder of the Hewlett-Packard Company, told a Silicon Valley civic leader, "Don't be so frustrated" by the apparent stinginess of technology firms. "These companies are so new. We weren't really known for our char-itable giving until we were twenty years old, but that was in 1964."[13] Inevitably, cultural factors are raised to explain the relative paucity of phil-anthropy within technology sectors, such as elite workers' utter absorption in work and personal lifestyle. Perhaps for this reason, more than one soft-ware executive I interviewed thought that mentoring young entrepreneurs was a significant act of charity.

Yet, outside of Silicon Valley, other philanthropy observers have pro-claimed an emerging new era of generosity.[14] In perhaps the most visible example, Bill Gates, the world's richest man, launched his philanthropic career in 1995 (some twenty years after Microsoft's founding) by endowing Harvard University and the University of Washington to the collective tune of $37 million.[15] By 1999, his foundation had spent an estimated $400 mil-lion a year for research to eradicate malaria, AIDS, and other diseases plagu-ing the developing world.[16] In 1997, broadcasting tycoon Ted Turner raised the ante by pledging $1 billion over ten years to United Nations agencies and encouraging others of his stature to give their share in turn. These highly visible gifts overshadow the myriad of smaller donations by firms, executives, and workers made rich by the "new economy." As the new-media director of the Philanthropy News Network observed, "In 1998 we were writing stories criticizing Gates and these other high rollers who weren't giving anything, and then in 1999 it all turned around."[17] His claim echoes other philanthropy insiders' expectation that generosity will increase as companies and the industry centers they establish grow older.

To what degree is philanthropy common among software, entertain-ment, and tourism firms in Santa Monica, Santa Barbara, and San Luis Obispo? New urban economy elites there reveal a mixed picture. Those from entertainment and tourism firms reported giving some kind of money, in-kind gift, or service, even when this was as modest as donating equipment to high school activities. However, between one-third and one-half of software executives I interviewed said their firm undertakes no sort of philanthropy at all. Although I did not randomly sample these executives, they dispropor-tionately represent local industry leaders, which suggests that corporate phil-anthropy is not normative among the most visible role models in the local software industry; moreover, philanthropy is probably even less common fur-ther down the three industries.[18] Executives from non-philanthropic firms usually explained, "We don't have the time or the money right now to participate very fully." Those from younger companies frequently cited insufficient profits for philanthropy ("venture capitalists will think their money is being thrown away"), although this factor does not necessarily deter all younger or unprofitable companies from giving; nor do older or more profitable companies consistently give. As for their failure to get personally involved through voluntary service, many executives cited their lack of free time. In a typical claim, a software CEO stated, "I travel for maybe forty percent of my time, so I can't get involved in projects where there are regular meetings. I end up dropping the ball because I've got to do my job."

TARGETS OF PHILANTHROPY

What kinds of community nonprofits benefit from the software, entertainment, and tourism firms that *are* philanthropic? This issue may be more important than overall rates of corporate philanthropy, since philanthropy is only now becoming more common among new firms, especially in software. In this context, philanthropic firms' decisions to give charitably should reflect the same local business structure shared by non-charitable firms. Along these lines, certain community nonprofits sustain "business as usual" better than others in local politics. If software, entertainment, and tourism firms support the older business community's favorite charities, this would suggest that they have structural incentives to access the traditional civic network. By contrast, if they support community nonprofits that the traditional urban business community does not usually support, this would imply that they had structural reasons to activate relationships outside the traditional civic network.

Below, I examine corporate support for three types of community nonprofits, one inside and two outside the traditional civic network. The first type, *traditional charities*, includes health, welfare, and social service nonprofits like the United Way, the Boys and Girls Club, Red Cross, and the Police Activities League. Corporate philanthropy and voluntary service to these groups generally confer upon business leaders status and acceptance in the local "old boys' network" and precede their ascendance into leadership circles of the traditional urban business community. These charities also tend to have a politically quiescent or centrist thrust that makes them suitable for emanating a "nonpolitical" legitimacy, in contrast to the "political" thrust of groups and causes that criticize business activities.[19]

Second, *environmental organizations* refer here to locally headquartered nonprofits (as opposed to local chapters of national groups) that address ecological impacts of human systems, habitat and animal conservation, and other environmental issues. These nonprofits lie well outside the traditional civic network. At least in Santa Monica, Santa Barbara, and San Luis Obispo, they frequently advocate policy and mobilize grassroots protest against unwanted development and growth, and they promote environmental regulations, land-use restrictions, and litigation that some view as hazardous to job growth and a "pro-business" climate.[20] For these legacies of adversity, the traditional urban business community and industry usually regard environmental organizations as "the enemy" in local politics.

Finally, *higher education* includes local universities and community colleges, institutions that assume greater significance in the new industrial space. Particularly in technology industries, companies often look to universities and colleges to conduct basic research and train future workers. At least in the three Southern California places, higher education institutions have had historically poor "town and gown" relations and weak ties to the traditional urban business community. Like environmental organizations, then, they institutionally reside outside the traditional civic network, although with less ideological antagonism to the "pro-business" agenda.

For these nonprofit fields, I examine three forms of corporate support. The first two are familiar forms of philanthropic involvement: corporate donations (of money or in-kind gift) and voluntary service (for example, on nonprofit boards of directors). The third, advocacy of community nonprofit goals, is a more episodic form of business support for groups that seek to change local policies and secure collective goods. My evidence comes from one year's development records for the most prominent nonprofit of each type in Santa Monica, Santa Barbara, and San Luis Obispo, for a total of nine nonprofits. I asked the fund-raising staff at these nonprofits to explain the trends in their development records and speculate about other local nonprofits likely to receive donations and service from software, entertainment, and tourism. For greater context, I also interviewed leaders (five environmental organizers and two social service nonprofit executives) of other important community nonprofits.

CHARITY AND THE OLD BOYS' NETWORK

In Santa Barbara and San Luis Obispo, the leading traditional charity is the United Way, the most endowed federated fund supporting community-based health/human service nonprofits in the U.S.[21] In Santa Monica, which has no local United Way branch, it is the Boys and Girls Club, the largest non–government funded local nonprofit in the city. The monetary statistics I report in Table 7.1 and subsequent tables in this chapter are donations per sector (i.e., from all local firms and not just the smaller group of contributors) and, in parentheses, absolute contributions. Once again, local banks provide a comparative baseline of significance; in each row, bold text indicates which sector gave the most. Since only the Santa Barbara County United Way made their development records available for public scrutiny, in the text below I cite verbal estimates from executives at the other two traditional charities.

Although Santa Barbara's software industry gives significant employee donations, a few firms and individuals skew its generosity for reasons I

TABLE 7.1

Donations per firm (total donations) to Santa Barbara County United Way

	Software	Entertainment	Tourism	Banks
Corporate	$142.80	$0.00	$0.00	**$320.73**
	($20,135)	($0)	($0)	**($16,357)**
Employee	**$823.43**	$0.00	$38.62	$320.73
	($116,104)	($0)	($25,606)	($16,357)

SOURCE: Santa Barbara County United Way, *1997–98 Thank You Report.*
NOTE: Individual gift amounts were calculated using mean values of reported gift ranges. Reported gifts only include the top twenty corporate gifts, the top thirty corporate employee gifts, and individual gifts over $1,000 (honored in the "leadership circle" ranks), which combined represent forty-eight percent of the 1997 campaign total.

explain later. Otherwise, the traditional urban business community sets a standard of generosity to traditional charities that the new urban economy sectors do not meet. Banks in Santa Monica contributed about ten percent of the traditional charity's 1997 income, equal to software and entertainment donations combined; likewise, banks gave more to San Luis Obispo's United Way than did any new urban economy sector. In Santa Monica, six software companies contributed roughly five percent (mostly in-kind gifts to set up a computer lab) of the Boys and Girls Club's total 1997 income. In San Luis Obispo, only the oldest software firm and the largest local Internet service provider represent the notably charitable software firms. Table 7.1 shows no entertainment philanthropy, although this is not surprising, given Santa Barbara's minuscule sector. Entertainment-heavy Santa Monica suggests a more typical picture; roughly five percent of the Boys and Girls Club's 1997 income came from four entertainment firms (a few other entertainment firms gave much smaller gifts). Tourism philanthropy appears to be negligible; one Santa Barbara hotel made the only cash donation, while no tourism firms in Santa Monica gave cash. However, this trend underestimates tourism's generosity in the form of donated door prizes or reduced rates for fund-raising benefits; for example, thirteen other Santa Barbara hotels and restaurants gave in-kind donations not incorporated into the table.

Voluntary service to traditional charities also shows that the three sectors lag behind banks and, by inference, the traditional urban business community. In Santa Barbara, nineteen bank executives sat on the United Way's board or served as lower-level campaign volunteers, in contrast to seven tourism executives, one software executive, and none from entertainment. In Santa Monica, the Boys and Girls Club board had two bankers, but no one from software, entertainment, or tourism. In San Luis Obispo, the only representative from any of the three sectors on the United Way board came (again) from the largest local Internet service provider.

Several features of local business structure inform these philanthropic patterns. First philanthropy to traditional community charities creates a visibility that can generate local business.[22] From software, San Luis Obispo's largest Internet service provider gives because its customers are local business, government, and nonprofit institutions, some of whose leaders also sit on the United Way board. Tourism's hidden philanthropy underscores its strong reliance on local markets because, as a Santa Barbara chamber executive told me, "The hospitality industry is interested in getting its name out locally." In addition to (and often the pretext for) their in-kind donations, some tourism firms host fund-raisers and other charitable events. In exchange, community nonprofits plan their special event logistics with local hotels and visitors and conference bureaus. By contrast, community philanthropy does not benefit most core firms, which comprise the stars of local software and entertainment industries; "there's no business reason, in the absolute classic business case," to undertake philanthropy, a CEO explained, "because we don't sell anything locally, and we're not like a retail company."

Another disincentive for philanthropy to traditional charities is suggested, if not adequately explained, by a charge that many human service executives level at software and entertainment firms: These companies feel no civic responsibility because employees and their families neither use nor need the charities' services. As the Santa Barbara United Way's executive director observed,

> When I first started meeting with CEOs of major corporations twenty-five years ago, much more often than not, I heard national, state, and local business leaders talk about the importance of services for their employees and families being available. In the past several years, except for a few standouts like Santa Barbara Bank & Trust, or Macy's, or United Parcel Service, more often than not, the discussion never discusses community or employee services but reaching targeted audiences of influence.[23]

This trend reached its height in Silicon Valley, where the United Way branch of Santa Clara County (the 30th largest in the nation) depleted its $11 million reserve fund in 1999. As its branch president opined:

> The Silicon Valley way of life is one of the best in the country, but I don't know that there is a grasp on the part of residents that there are people who need basic social services—shelters for battered wives, mental health services. I dealt with a number of companies whose officials said, "Our employees make this much money and they do not need these services, so why are you here?"[24]

It should be noted, however, that United Way donations were up in other high-tech centers like Seattle and North Carolina's Research Triangle at this time.[25]

CIRCUMVENTING THE TRADITIONAL CIVIC NETWORK

Regardless of the evidence for an employee-service mismatch—and certainly more than one executive I interviewed reiterated it without solicitation—the popularity of this hypothesis among traditional charity executives and older business community leaders does not quite square with the charity of software and entertainment firms in other cases. Specifically, many of these companies give to charities that deliver health, welfare, and social services but, unlike the United Way, operate *outside the traditional civic network*. In entertainment, many companies give to "industry standard" charities, such as the Entertainment Industry Foundation (Hollywood's equivalent of the United Way) and the T.J. Martell Foundation (a disease research nonprofit founded by music industry executives), that solicit paycheck deductions and corporate gifts—often to the exclusion of participation in United Way campaigns. Movie studios, record companies, talent agencies, and entertainment industry organizations also have their own philanthropic foundations. For example, via the National Academy of Recording Arts and Sciences, the music industry is the primary benefactor of nonprofits that promote music therapy and education.

To be sure, human service philanthropy is less frequent in software, at least among younger firms. Perhaps its closest industry standard counterpart is "venture philanthropy," a new mode of giving that evokes the entrepreneurialism and disdain for convention associated with Silicon Valley. In venture philanthropy, corporate donors "lend business expertise, identify and support 'social entrepreneurs' hungry to shake up the nonprofit world, and quantify their results."[26] Although many philanthropy observers are encouraged by the emerging trend of venture philanthropy, it quite likely portends further neglect of traditional charities by software leaders. "The problem with older charities is that after awhile it's like a company. You get wedded to one approach," one Silicon Valley CEO and venture philanthropist observed. "Giving to the World Wildlife Fund is a total waste of money. All of it goes to overhead. Just like United Way."[27]

An important factor, then, in philanthropy to charities in the traditional civic network, as opposed to human services more generally, is whether relationships exist between software firms and the traditional urban business community. If they do, local business leaders have a forum to urge software leaders to support their favorite charities and engage the traditional civic network as the older business community does. This seems to explain the atypical generosity of Santa Barbara's software sector to the United Way in Table 7.1. The four most generous software firms, whose combined gifts ($112,685) made up eighty percent of employee contributions and *all* corporate contributions from the industry, are older defense-related R&D branches that have resided in Santa Barbara since at least the mid-1980s. Atypical of the newer generation of software firms, they each employ well over one hundred employees. They also occupy large campuses in the high-tech corridors of suburban Goleta that, significantly, have been targeted by local environmentalists for growth controls. Because these firms can benefit from a local business agenda that vigilantly monitors growth controls, if not opposes them outright, they have more incentive than newer and smaller firms to be active in the traditional civic network. Perhaps unsurprisingly, executives from these four firms (as well as other older, defense-related firms that do not give) participate in the local chamber of commerce and high-tech trade associations more frequently and deeply than executives from newer and smaller software firms. Corporate philanthropy to the United Way may be the normative *quid pro quo* for the traditional urban business community's support in other settings, if this charity is not in fact a more instrumental site for collective action.

These firms are the apparent exception to the rule; otherwise, software philanthropy does not fall on the traditional urban business community's radar without preexisting relationships. A statement by a Santa Monica business leader who sits on the Boys and Girls Club's board is revealing:

> My sense is [software firms] are either doing a lot of wonderful things very quietly and I've missed it, or they're not doing a lot of wonderful things. I'm not aware of any of them taking an active role civically or charitably, although I may be out of the loop on that.

Another example reveals the limits of the older business community's reach. A Santa Monica software CEO began funding Los Angeles charities following his involvement in Rebuild LA, the nonprofit formed by metropolitan business and civic leaders after the 1992 Los Angeles riots.[28] Rebuild LA has brought together many of the most important corporate executives based in Los Angeles, which suggests that at least this software CEO participates in a traditional civic network. However, Rebuild LA's sphere of influence exceeds that of Santa Monica's traditional civic network, as the failure of any of Santa Monica nonprofit leaders to mention this foundation implies.

Entertainment's executives are similarly "hard to reach," as the president of a Santa Monica bank that manages several local nonprofits' assets acknowledged. "They haven't been here like we have. They don't belong to any service club." In large part, this stems from the insular, relationship-gatekeeping focus of entertainment executives. In the case of Santa Monica, traditional charity philanthropy from entertainment usually originates from mid-level employees whose children use the Boys and Girls Club. The club's executive director recalled how he found lower-level volunteers from the local branch of a cable channel:

> I didn't just walk into the door. I found out who knew the people there; I can get names and get me an introduction in the door . . . There's always

somebody who can track us down to get to their people. Sometimes you don't always get to the president.

While not negligible, entertainment's philanthropy to traditional charities does not necessarily bring high-level executives into the traditional civic network.

ENVIRONMENTALISM AS BUSINESS INTEREST

In terms of money and voluntary service, banks often give more to community environmental groups than do the new urban economy sectors—an ironic finding, perhaps, since the older business community usually perceives these nonprofits as their "enemies." Only entertainment diverges from this pattern, and it does so dramatically. Below, Table 7.2 reports contributions per local firm to (1) Santa Monica's Heal the Bay, a locally headquartered coastal advocacy-action group serving the Los Angeles region; (2) Santa Barbara's Community Environmental Council, a local sustainability-recycling foundation; and (3) the Environmental Center of San Luis Obispo County (ECOSLO), an environmental advocacy organization. Executives from the first two groups acknowledge that theirs are not the most "radical" of local environmental groups, which makes corporate philanthropy to them more acceptable to business leaders. Nevertheless, their organizations have origins in, and ties to, local grassroots coalitions that have long antagonized the traditional urban business community.

Software firms' environmental philanthropy is generally insignificant. One gave to Santa Monica's Heal the Bay, and three gave to Santa Barbara's Community Environmental Council, but their gifts equaled less than one percent of those nonprofits' annual incomes. For the years reported in Table 7.2, no software executives sat on the boards of the three environmental

TABLE 7.2

Donations per firm (total donations) to the largest community environmental organizations

Locality	Software	Entertainment	Tourism	Banks
Santa Monica	$27.77 ($3,000)	**$936.56** **($251,000)**	$26.04 ($11,250)	$272.73 ($9,000)
Santa Barbara	$14.11 ($1,990)	$0.00 ($0)	$0.00 ($0)	**$73.53** **($3,750)**
San Luis Obispo	$0.00 ($0)	$0.00 ($0)	$0.00 ($0)	$0.00 ($0)

SOURCE: *Heal the Bay* 11 (Spring 1998): 12–13; Community Environmental Council 1996 annual report; author's interview with ECOSLO executive director, May 27, 1998.
NOTE: Individual gift amounts were calculated using mean values of reported gift ranges. Heal the Bay gifts include cash value for in-kind donations.

organizations; however, two did serve as Community Environmental Council directors in 1995, and a third (from the firm QAD; see Chapter 4) served in 1998. Likewise, tourism gave insignificantly to environmental groups. Six tourism corporations and executives gave to Santa Monica's Heal the Bay; in Santa Barbara and San Luis Obispo, no tourism firm or executive contributed to Community Environmental Council or ECOSLO, respectively (although this did not include in-kind gifts). Tourism firms, however, may be important to other environmental organizations not included in the table. An executive from Santa Barbara's pro bono environmental law firm told me that its corporate donors include a handful of small firms in tourism and related sectors (outdoor activities retailers, fashion boutiques); unfortunately, he declined to estimate their donations.

Entertainment's philanthropy shows a remarkable contrast. In a year that Heal the Bay took in approximately $1.1 million in revenues, almost *one quarter* came from this industry. Firms comprised less than a third of the environmental organization's sixty-four entertainment donors; the rest were producers, actors, directors, composers, and other high-level entertainment individuals and couples. Seven high-level figures (e.g., a television network president, a television celebrity, two film producers) sat on its twenty-two-person board of directors in the same year; the fact that other board members came mostly from environmental and government backgrounds underscores this nonprofit's strong entertainment connection. Entertainment's philanthropy helps sustain, to varying degrees, two other Santa Monica environmental organizations (one founded by actors) not represented in the table. At all three Santa Monica nonprofits, celebrities and executives sit on boards of directors; studios and large entertainment companies buy tables at fund-raising benefits and awards ceremonies; and advertising agencies and production houses produce environmental TV spots at low or no cost.

As with fund-raisers for liberal candidates, environmental philanthropy provides useful opportunities for business networking and deal-making. Certain nonprofits outside of the environmental arena, like the Liberty Hill Foundation (founded by a film producer to fund grassroots community organizations) and the regional chapter of the National Conference for Community and Justice (a.k.a. the National Conference of Christians and Jews), also provide a setting for this business need and benefit from industry generosity. Yet, certainly business needs alone do not drive the industry's generosity to environmentalism or other causes; personal convictions also play an important role. In Santa Barbara, not an entertainment stronghold relative to Santa Monica, actor Michael Douglas paid the balance in a fund-raising campaign for the public purchase of a popular open space tract (subsequently dubbed the Douglas Family Preserve).

Notably, the industry's environmental beneficiaries are overwhelmingly moderate. During the Playa Vista controversy, the industry did not collectively support the more radical oppositional environmental groups, and Heal the Bay's executive director joined other officially recognized "stakeholder" groups in accepting the developer's environmental mitigations. Conceivably, this could indicate a cooptive rationale behind the industry's environmental philanthropy, although I could find no evidence of an explicit effort.[29] Entertainment donors to environmental groups comprise too broad a group to benefit directly from the project. More likely, of all the environmental organizations and campaigns supported by philanthropy, moderate ones hold the broadest ideological appeal; their social events can therefore draw from a wider base of industry liberals and provide a more profitable setting for the business of maintaining relationships.

QUALITY-OF-LIFE COALITIONS

In the new urban economy, environmental groups hold a relevance beyond their ideological opposition to the traditional urban business community. They articulate and organize the residential backlash against the uncontrolled growth and deteriorating quality of life that is found in many American communities, particularly in socioeconomically privileged ones.[30] In the three Southern California places, environmental groups have long been able to mobilize substantial numbers of voters and activists and frustrate, if not completely halt, the "pro-business" thrust of business as usual. Even the traditional urban business community has begun to adopt some notions of quality of life and the community "good" that liberals and environmentalists articulate. As an SMRR activist noted,

> Frankly, now the [Santa Monica] chamber has an environmental task force, and even a homeless task force. They're not just [espousing a] 'throw the bums out' kind of philosophy. So I think the business community has evolved.

When values like environmentalism shape the political discourse, business groups need not give money or service to environmental groups to enlist their political activism or civic legitimacy. Instead, they can acquire these episodically through advocacy coalitions with environmental organizations around specific issues. How likely are software and tourism, the sectors that support environmental groups the least, to join in such advocacy coalitions? Santa Monica, Santa Barbara, and San Luis Obispo are good places to pose this question, since environmental groups are recognized players in their local politics, to the chagrin of the traditional urban business community. The record of business-environmental coalitions in the late 1990s suggests that environmentalists' most persuasive appeal to these sectors lies in an important, if not central, factor for their local growth: the quality of life. However, the degree to which this latent interest becomes manifest varies between the two sectors.

Where its amenity infrastructure depends on environmental and aesthetic quality, tourism most readily joins environmentalists on issues of industry-wide interest. In Santa Monica, tourism firms and associations have supported lobbying by Heal the Bay and other environmental groups to require regional businesses to obtain "stormwater permits" to minimize urban runoff to the ocean. In Santa Barbara and San Luis Obispo, they endorse activists' efforts to restrict offshore and coastal oil and gas drilling. As the campaign manager for an anti-slant drilling initiative recalled, "all the local chambers of commerce opposed [our initiative]. The Santa Barbara Lodging Association was a crucial endorsement to balance the influence that the chambers had." Many San Luis Obispo hoteliers and other companies that depend on visitors (e.g., kayak shops, art galleries, gift shops) added their voices to local protests against the Hearst Ranch Resort and "big box" retail development, for fear that such development would mar the pastoral landscapes that (many felt) favorably distinguished the area from more urbanized areas. ECOSLO's director observed that tourism companies will "come out at meetings, and they'll speak out as a small business owner and say, 'Tourism is my life blood, and they come here because of the beautiful ocean and clean air, and we need to keep it that way.' " However, whereas industry-wide coalitions reliably endorse environmentalist efforts that benefit the entire local industry, they appear to break down around protests of individual development projects. "On land-use issues in general," ECOSLO's director explained, tourism endorsement "is pretty much a NIMBY thing. So, if they're talking about a development on the beach in South County, you may have some hotels that fight it for competition reasons, but not for the principles of land use or sustainable resource management kinds of things . . ."

The software sector cannot even boast this track record. Certain firms and business leaders occasionally back efforts to protect the local environmental quality, but with even less unanimity than their tourism counterparts. Indeed, how to reach the software industry at all is a question that vexes many environmental organizers. To a large degree, their question reflects the nature of firms' local business structure. Most firms have unsystematic land-use needs and no regulated activities—two factors that would most likely increase interaction, albeit perhaps of a negative kind, between the industry and environmental watchdogs. As with traditional charities, then, core software firms' short-term and globally focused orientation create a seemingly inscrutable public face, as Heal the Bay's executive director described:

> To be honest, we're completely ignorant of how to really make that connection with the high-tech industries. That's not to say we don't get a check here and there, but from the standpoint of real regular support and involvement, say, even at the board level, to find someone in his or her twenties [who] has

really made a mark at that point and could really help our organization
understand technology and see how it can work for what we're doing,
we haven't crossed that bridge; we haven't figured it out.

As Santa Barbara illustrates, many locals and environmental groups discern a paradox in the industry's ambiguous quality-of-life discourse. On the
one hand, individually and through software associations, companies often
proclaim that they value and enhance the local quality of life as a clean
industry that pays higher-than-average wages. The marketing materials for
Santa Barbara's high-tech booster association are fairly characteristic of
these sentiments: "The Economic Community Project is developing a path
where the quality of life and economic vitality of the region operate
together, rather than in opposition." On the other hand, to many environmentalists, software associations' support of projects like QAD's campus
looks suspiciously like the usual pro-growth efforts by the traditional urban
business community; as the latter's influence in software associations suggests, their suspicion is often correct. Although big projects and software
associations are not vital to most software firms, some locals nevertheless
fear that the industry's collective growth speaks more loudly than its com-
mitments to community well-being.

Amidst this legitimacy crisis, software leaders have looked for opportunities to demonstrate their industry's good will; in the late 1990s, they
seized upon the "Community Indicators" project. Initiated by environmentalists to help local decision-makers incorporate and monitor quality-
of-life concerns during regional and project planning, the project followed
a model used by other cities. First, input is solicited from citizens, businesses, and community leaders to identify "indicators" of the region's social
and environmental quality, ranging from grade school lunch program participation to indigenous bird species counts. Then, a steering committee of
public and private representatives operationalizes and oversees data gathering for these indicators (in addition to more common indicators of economic vitality).

By not regulating the business or growth of any firms, the Community
Indicators project offered a palatable form of business advocacy in a largely
symbolic effort that entailed little economic sacrifice. Yet, it also reveals software leaders' concerns for maintaining the sector's political legitimacy in a
community vigilant about quality of life. An environmental leader explained
how he exploited these concerns through his honorary seat on the Santa
Barbara Region Economic Community Project's "leadership group":

One of the things I've been doing is really haranguing them and saying, "You
know, you guys keep talking quality of life. What do you mean? Define your-
self." And they give me, "I don't know how." And here, here's the Indicators
program; this is what it's about. It's about defining the quality of life, sustain-

ability, community, whatever. It's a broader measurement of the standard of living; if the standard of living goes up, everything is good. And I had a number of conversations—well, one in particular—with [the Economic Community Project's founder] saying, "This is a step in this process, and you guys really need to be doing it as part of the [Economic Community Project], because you're saying that economic development supports quality of life, but you're not saying what that means. And so no one's going to trust you."

Thereafter, the local software association became instrumental in implementing the Community Indicators project: serving on the project's steering committee and trustees, helping to secure funding for the project, obtaining an economist to conduct the research, and soliciting business support for the project's mission.[31]

After the Community Indicators project, software and environmental leaders began collaborating on far less symbolic efforts. In the most far-reaching, environmental leaders agreed to support land-use densities for software and other targeted sectors that were higher than local growth-control ordinances previously allowed. In return, the Santa Barbara Region Economic Community Project endorsed the anti-sprawl intent of local growth controls and advocated strengthening urban limit lines and discouraging high-tech campus development along the coastline. This new land-use coalition eventually failed to alter local land-use policy for a few reasons, one being a simple lack of political momentum to make changes on linked policies unrelated to high-tech growth. This mundane political reality highlights a second, perhaps more germane factor; by their controversial collaboration, the software and environmental leaders threatened to disunite their respective constituencies, whose support would be needed to make the consensus law. Within the traditional urban business community, some developers backed the new land-use principles, while others resented how they would violate the ethos of investor prerogative and promote certain kinds of developments at the expense of other kinds. On the environmental side, the new land-use consensus alienated more diehard slow-growth activists. Subsequently, environmental leaders backed off from their advocacy coalition with the software industry. As one of them observed, "Seeking new allies [among software firms] is fine, but if it comes at the expense of old allies, that's a problem."

HIGHER EDUCATION: THE NEW CHAMBER OF COMMERCE

Although education has long been a beneficiary of corporate philanthropy,[32] the prominent roles that higher education institutions play in the new urban economy, exemplified by Stanford University's driving presence in Silicon Valley, are of special interest to university administrators with plans for institutional development. Administrators and faculty have been entrepreneurial in promoting their institutions through participation in local industry associations, R&D collaborations with local firms, training programs, and other ways to address industry needs. Consider, for example, this statement from the College of Engineering at the University of California at Santa Barbara (UCSB):

> The College is dedicated to building a solid high-technology community on the South Coast. The synergy between the community and the College is reflected in the critical role it has played in the development of [two local high-tech industry associations]; the existence of over twenty-five local companies founded by College alums or faculty; its proactive outreach into primary and secondary schools; and the tremendous talent pool and intellectual capital made available to the community.[33]

Local universities and colleges have also stepped up fund-raising efforts aimed at technology companies.[34] How have the new urban economy firms responded to their overtures? Table 7.3 reports contributions per firm to three higher educational programs with particular relevance to the the new urban economy in the three Southern California localities: (1) Santa Monica College's Academy of Entertainment & Technology, (2) the UCSB's College of Engineering, and (3) the (San Luis Obispo) Cuesta College fundraising campaign to establish a new campus, develop high-tech training and certification programs, and upgrade computers and laboratory equipment.

Clearly, the generosity of the software sector outpaces the other new urban economy sectors and local banks as well. Software's donations came from a relatively small number of firms (two for Santa Monica, twelve for Santa Barbara, and three for San Luis Obispo).[35] Not far behind software, entertainment shows a similar pattern; four entertainment firms gave over one sixth ($111,500) of donations to the Academy of Entertainment & Technology at Santa Monica College. At UCSB, one multinational electronics/media corporation represented the sole entertainment donor to

TABLE 7.3

Donations per firm (total donations) to selected higher education institutions

Locality	Software	Entertainment	Tourism	Banks
Santa Monica	**$1,657.41** **($179,000)**	$416.04 ($111,500)	$0.00 ($0)	$0.00 ($0)
Santa Barbara	**$4,485.82** **($632,500)**	$1,063.83 ($100,000)	$0.00 ($0)	$0.00 ($0)
San Luis Obispo	**$6,428.57** **($360,000)**	$0.00 ($0)	$543.85 ($300,750)	$3,888.88 ($105,000)

SOURCE: author's interview with Santa Monica College Dean of External Affairs, September 22, 1997; UCSB College of Engineering (1997); author's interview with UC Santa Barbara College of Engineering development director, May 21, 1998; Cuesta College Foundation's 1998 "Shareholders" report.
NOTE: Individual gift amounts calculated using mean values of reported gift ranges.

the College of Engineering. Finally, San Luis Obispo shows the only case of tourism contributions to the higher educational institutions that I found: two companies gave about one sixth ($300,750) of the San Luis Obispo community college's fund-raising campaign; almost all came from one of the area's more popular hotels. This idiosyncrasy suggests that predominantly information economy industries like software and entertainment give to higher education.

Tracking donations by geographical source reveals a philanthropic division of labor within the new industrial space. For community colleges, charitable support generally comes from local companies, perhaps because the amount of industry support needed is relatively little and therefore locally procurable. For high-profile research universities, by contrast, philanthropy can break down into different locations of origin. In industry centers, software donors are also mostly local, as exemplified by Silicon Valley firms' generosity to Stanford University and the University of California at Berkeley. In quality-of-life districts, however, *non-local* firms from Silicon Valley and other industry centers give more in contributions, and *local* firms give more in executive service. In fact, administrators of higher educational institutions value local companies for their executive service far more than for their money. At UCSB, for example, the dean of engineering's advisory board brings together thirteen executives, of which two came from local software firms and nine from local firms in other high-tech fields. As the dean explained, the local high-tech elites on his advisory board offer useful ideas about "how to work together, what kind of courses and training students need, how to partner in research and education, or just being a civic-minded citizen." UCSB's engineering college also lures other local CEOs for specific events, such as guest lectures on "entrepreneurial engineering," while about twenty local companies recruit actively at the College of Engineering.

Likewise, for Santa Monica College's Academy of Entertainment & Technology, entertainment's importance lies more in directorships, advice on curricular development, and other service gifts. Thirteen of the fifteen members of the Academy's advisory board to the college president were high-level executives from a cross section of important Hollywood firms. Additionally, by the end of its first year, forty-eight entertainment-related firms and organizations supported the Academy, either in a consulting role or as a "partnership company" offering student internships. For both software and entertainment, the returns that corporate donors receive are often indivisible but still quite tangible: a local labor market of skilled employees, external research shaped around their priorities, and contact with other local industry executives.

Importantly, software and entertainment executives' voluntary service involves face-to-face interactions and systemic relationships between higher education officials—precisely what the traditional civic network has largely failed to sustain elsewhere. Industry and scientific leaders meet at university advisory committees and activities to share their considerable knowledge about local and often national business circles they represent, the direction of the information economy, and its relevance for the places their industries inhabit. For these and other reasons, a variety of locals—chambers of commerce, local politicians, nonprofit fund-raisers, and newspaper reporters (as well as social scientists like myself)—compete for the limited time and resources that these business leaders allocate to non-business and non-educational issues. ("This group is pretty hard to cold call," a local software association executive conceded.) Thus, higher education institutions serve as information economy "chambers of commerce" far more effectively, albeit perhaps unintentionally, than real chambers. More to the point, business-university gatherings siphon off industry elites from traditional civic settings like the chamber of commerce or traditional charities. The latter can hardly compete with universities to organize core firms, promote their local sectors, get personal access to the most important industry leaders, and anticipate the local economy's shifting directions.

BRIDGING THE CAMPUS/PRIVATE INDUSTRY GAP

Even for those that do not donate money or voluntary service, many new urban economy firms see value in advocating university development, as the California Polytechnic University at San Luis Obispo (Cal Poly) illustrates. Many San Luis Obispo high-tech executives are involved in the university's research and collaboration opportunities, while virtually all the rest advocate "bridging the campus/private industry gap" (the theme of a recent San Luis Obispo industry conference) to improve their access to research opportunities and entry-level labor as well as lay the foundation for local industry growth. In tourism, industry leaders readily acknowledge how the university brings visitors to the area: students' parents, visiting scholars and administrators, attendees at university functions, and so on. Yet until recently, the campus did not combine civic and economic roles; town and gown relations were somewhat chilly, especially with the traditional urban business community. As a Cal Poly administrator described,

> We existed in our own little island here and didn't pay any attention to what was going on. We didn't have to, because all of our money came from outside, all our support came from outside, and we sent our projects back outside. So we didn't do a very good job of letting the locals know what we were producing, and we're trying to turn that around now.

In another source of conflict, Cal Poly's for-profit business ventures, ranging from college merchandise to agricultural marketing to business services, sparked protests from some in San Luis Obispo's traditional business community about unfair competition.[36]

Recently, Cal Poly has stepped up its civic presence with two major contributions to the technology and amenity infrastructures; in the process, the university has become possibly the most important local developer of large projects to date. In 1996, Cal Poly and the city jointly funded construction of a $30-million, twelve-hundred-seat campus performing arts center that tourism officials hope will upgrade the caliber of culture and entertainment for locals and visitors alike. Although the center's long-term fiscal benefits still have to be ascertained, tourism leaders and other local boosters have nevertheless deemed it a success and anticipate construction of a Cal Poly sports complex.[37]

Cal Poly also spearheaded a proposal for a high-tech research park. Local high-tech firms and others had long circulated the idea of a joint public-private research park but lacked the political currency to move it past the "white paper" stage and attract a developer. Slow-growth city councils carried out three prior studies that disapproved of the research park because of its potential growth impacts. Consequently, local high-tech firms and the local software booster association looked to a Cal Poly–sponsored study for the political "juice" to galvanize support from local government:

> We believe that the proposed project has the potential to assist in the formation of new businesses, create a positive impact on the local economy, while having little or no adverse impact on the quality-of-life issues that are important to our local area. Technology transfer from Cal Poly to the business community gives our local businesses a competitive advantage while increasing revenue flow into the community. Knowledge-based high-tech businesses are well known for high paying jobs and low environmental impact, both of which are key issues to our group.[38]

Cal Poly obtained the services of the Bechtel Infrastructure Corporation, an internationally prominent engineering and construction firm, to conduct a feasibility study and lend credibility to the proposal (Bechtel was also the former employer of the Cal Poly administrator appointed to oversee the study). The fact that a new research park development would belong to the university first and foremost (i.e., most likely built on Cal Poly property) did not stop various local entities, from the booster association to a county-wide economic development organization, from adding their resources to the task. Even the chamber did not let members' frustrations with Cal Poly overshadow its stakes in the R&D park; it co-authored a city study investigating the quality of the local technological infrastructure for the R&D park and local high-tech industry.

Released in 1998, Bechtel's study disappointed the park's advocates and pleased many growth opponents when it determined, "A research park based on a large real estate development is not an appropriate model for San Luis Obispo."[39] In part, this was due to insufficient demand for such facilities;

despite the wishes of local boosters and some software leaders, San Luis Obispo's growth as a quality-of-life district for technology companies has proceeded at too slow a pace to necessitate such an extensive project. As of this writing, the university-sponsored research park task force continues to investigate ways to establish incubator facilities using existing infrastructure, in what some call a "virtual park." In whatever form it may eventually take, the research park proposal illustrates how Cal Poly adds tremendous muscle to the policy agenda of San Luis Obispo's software firms, whose political resources in this modest industry outpost pale by comparison. Perhaps just as importantly, the software-university coalition has not engendered controversy and threatened disunity among political constituencies, as software-environmental coalitions have elsewhere.

TRAJECTORIES OF BUSINESS/NONPROFIT ALIGNMENTS

The evidence presented in this chapter does not decisively refute widely held fears that the new urban economy portends an overall decline in local philanthropy and "corporate citizenship." A good number of firms, especially in software, have yet to undertake any philanthropy whatsoever; only time will tell if their future philanthropy will eventually converge or, as the cases of software and entertainment suggest, further diverge from the traditional urban business community's philanthropic patterns. However, many other firms are currently "doing good" in the community—just not always with the traditional urban business community's favorite nonprofits. Fears are warranted, then, only if civic responsibility means participation in the usual set of charities and activities that comprise the nonprofit front of the traditional civic network. Indeed, the patterns for software, entertainment, and tourism firms that are philanthropically active suggest that the new money may never completely adopt older philanthropic modes.

The advocacy coalitions described here, although not widespread, illustrate the most far-reaching alignments between software, entertainment, and tourism sectors and nonprofits outside the traditional civic network. Their relevance lies less in the three sectors' apparent liberal or green tendencies, which may simply reflect industry leaders' pragmatism in places where quality of life shapes the political discourse. Rather, the fact that the three sectors reach out to those outside of (e.g., higher education) and even antagonistic to (e.g., environmental groups) the older business community *in order to do business* highlights the industry's independence from the traditional civic network and its business norms. Throughout the new industrial space, the characteristic of local business structure that consistently aligns companies with the older business community is dependence on local markets and local elite networks. Yet even tourism, the sector most embedded in the traditional civic network, fails to remain in a strident and coherent coalition with any one side, including the older business community.

Alongside the three sectors' general failure to support conservative local politicians, the new corporate philanthropy signals an important break from the traditional urban business community's civic modes. Thus, it is tempting to conclude that these new business alignments empower community actors and issues that overturn the traditional urban business community's hegemony in local politics. Is the picture so clear-cut? Prudence is in order here, since forecasting the political consequences of the new business-nonprofit alignments requires further attention than I have given here to how both the traditional urban business community and liberal urban regimes accommodate these alignments. At this point, a case can be made for both a pessimistic and a somewhat more optimistic scenario.

In the pessimistic scenario, the new business alignments perpetuate traditional business hegemony. For one reason, the new local philanthropy exacerbates political divisions on the left (between progressive and center, among environmentalists and other liberal policy-advocacy nonprofits) by increasing moderates' influence and pushing more hard-line groups to the political margins. Environmentalists and politicians supported by the new firms face pressures to endorse contributors' development projects, as illustrated by the controversial Playa Vista project. Finally, it is worth recalling a Santa Barbara environmental organizer's ambivalence about the QAD campus proposal: "no one wants to be seen as saying no to everything." At a minimum, the new business-nonprofit alignment reinforces an indirect convergence of the new players who are then asked to help shape, but not reject, the new urban economy's local growth.

If environmentalists and progressive candidates represent important signatories to a new growth consensus, then the less obviously ideological universities may be the strongest executors of local growth. The broad support that local software and entertainment firms give to research park proposals and entertainment academies shows how the higher education mission now extends well beyond the campus. Universities and colleges throughout the new industrial space have secured unprecedented local consensus to construct sports stadia, performing arts centers, and other large-scale cultural amenities, with the understanding that such projects should benefit local industries.[40] As San Luis Obispo illustrates, these new nonprofit-private coalitions can even break historic growth limits more effectively than can the traditional business community.

Yet at least for software and entertainment, however, a more optimistic scenario can be imagined in which the new business alignments diminish the centrality of the traditional civic network because the new corporate elites conduct their face-to-face work on college advisory boards and at environmental benefits and fund-raisers for liberal candidates.[41] These settings provide a crucial outlet for systemic relationships with software and entertainment leaders who wield considerable influence in local and often national business circles. Environmentalists and progressive politicians might flinch at the instrumentalization of their respective spheres. Yet, perhaps they should take solace in some evidence suggesting that even episodic business-progressive coalitions can undermine the all-for-one solidarity that characterizes the usual growth coalition.[42] Considering the special visibility that the new high-tech and entertainment industries command in local newspapers, the defection of even a few firms or industries from the traditional business consensus can send tremors through the business community.[43]

Both of these scenarios presume a degree of stability in the new urban economy sectors, if not the durability of local firms in these sectors. Given the volatile nature of these industries and the broader capitalist economy, should such stability be assumed? Having completed my review of the local business structure in software, entertainment, and tourism, I offer a final assessment of the sectors' connections to place and the political implications thereof.

8

Rethinking Rootlessness

A round the time I finished gathering data for this book, three events dramatically upset the environments for software, entertainment, and tourism companies. First, in the spring of 2000, the technology-heavy NASDAQ lost twenty percent of its trading volume and set in motion the "dot-com crash" that deflated the stock market's exuberance for companies operating on or developing technologies for the Internet. Subsequently, many technology firms cancelled IPOs, replaced executives from the prior boom era, laid off employees, or went out of business altogether. This presaged the second event, a broader recessionary downturn in the global economy by 2001 that has persisted as this book goes to press. Entertainment and tourism joined software in facing industry consolidation, as the discretionary consumer spending upon which the three sectors depend dropped dramatically. Although box-office receipts earned Hollywood a record eight billion dollars in 2001, TV, cable, and commercial production remained mired in an alarming slump, with industry employment its lowest in four years.[1] Finally, on September 11, 2001, terrorists destroyed the World Trade Center in New York City among other attacks on U.S. soil. By literally wiping out a substantial amount of capital assets from the global economy, the catastrophe exacerbated existing recessionary trends; additionally, traveler confidence eroded substantially, and the airline sector pled for a public-sector bailout.

As I write eight months after this last event, it is still too early to assess the definitive and cumulative impacts upon economies new and old, and so at this juncture I hesitate to speculate whether a new military-industrial complex, an end to urban tourism, or any other outcome will ravage or renew the three sectors examined in this book. Most certainly, the post-2000 consolidation in the software and PC industry has already curbed the labor market demand that allowed elite workers to command income and workplace premiums, including freedom in the location of their work; this trend may very well slow the growth of quality-of-life districts. Yet recessionary trends have only increased the need for cost-cutting technologies and innovations throughout most sectors of the global economy, and it is not clear that these can be produced through corporate strategies other than flexible organization. High-technology sectors reveal and, even more, embody a perennial contradiction of capitalism; namely, transforming the means of production to cut costs and extract greater surplus labor value inevitably requires the work of innovative labor, which in turn maintains a role for elite workers in the corporation. Although elite workers may avoid speculative enterprises and return to large companies after the dot-com crash, their socialization within creative milieux and networking across firms will most likely remain critical elements of their innovative capacity. For this reason, I suspect that the organizational medium of the new industrial space will not likely disappear any time soon.

Furthermore, events since 2000 can be understood as merely exacerbating the sectoral turbulence that always surrounds new urban economy sectors. How has this turbulence affected the three industries in Santa Monica, Santa Barbara, and San Luis Obispo? Of the three sectors, the software industry has probably experienced the greatest upheaval. Only forty-five percent of software companies are still doing business in the same form as when I interviewed their executives; another thirty percent were acquired by other companies, ten percent moved to another location, and fifteen percent are out of business. Additionally, only half the executives are still with the same company; the rest moved on, including eight percent who started new companies and another eight percent who became venture capitalists. Entertainment has shown a little more stability, at least outside of "new media" niches like Internet broadcasting and content distribution that were swept up in the dot-com crash. Among the companies I studied, only nine percent no longer exist, and this is largely attributable to the music industry consolidation following the acquisition of MCA and its subsidiary record labels by Seagram and later Vivendi. Industry consolidations may still be on the horizon, especially as the film industry anxiously follows the music industry's struggles with intellectual property "piracy" via Internet-based digital distribution.[2] Since September 11, 2001, tourism has suffered a major setback, not only in New York City but also in other urban destinations that depend substantially on non-regional visitors who arrive by air. Yet, at least at this early stage, tourism companies have proven the most stable of the three sectors; turnover has been limited to ownership changes at two hotels, although my sample's skew toward industry leaders most likely underestimates the fallout among smaller and more entrepreneurial companies.

LESSONS FROM THE NEW URBAN ECONOMY

Overall, these trends undermine the arguments raised by a few community leaders I interviewed that the new elites will assume the civic and political profiles of traditional "corporate citizens" once they "have been here long enough." Personal commitment by executives may no longer be a stable foundation for corporate citizenship because this group may simply not work or have companies in the community for much longer. Here it should also be recalled how executives kept their firms financially lean by not renewing memberships in industry associations and local chambers they deemed "unnecessary." Without stable and routine settings for interaction with their community counterparts, new urban economy firms and executives will participate in urban affairs, I believe, largely based on the imperatives imposed by their local business structures.

BUSINESS CLIMATE UNCERTAINTY MOTIVATES POLITICAL PARTICIPATION

The new urban economy has not altered capital's control of inward investment or, subsequently, the context for corporate power in cities that urban scholars have elaborated through decades of research. Local governments' capacities to set land-use policy, impose fees and taxes, and shape the local business climate in other ways continue to introduce uncertainty into corporate bottom lines. For traditional manufacturers and big-box retailers, profit margins are sensitive to material cost factors like rent and wages that differ across localities. These and other variables of local business costs increase corporate interest in lobbying local government, either directly or via the traditional urban business community, for favorable policies and public subsidies that minimize the effect of material cost factors. Therefore, the need that traditionally motivates business to intervene in local politics—namely, to shape local land-use decisions and policy in ways that promote a "pro-business" climate—endures in the new urban economy. What has changed is the prevalence of this need among software, entertainment, and tourism companies.

A critical factor here is each sector's knowledge intensiveness, which sets software and entertainment apart from tourism. Most of the software and entertainment firms in the three Southern California localities depend little on traditional cost factors and particularly scarce sites for their profits, due to the intellectual nature of their work, their small size, and their intensive use of workspace. In particular niches, software and entertainment firms can also do business in "virtual," technologically mediated ways that reduce the advantages of locating in industry centers. Thus, most software and entertainment firms have little incentive to enlist traditional urban business communities in undoing restrictive governmental policies that constrain corporate land uses. This is not to say that these companies are ideologically opposed to permissive land-use policies or public subsidies, but only that for most of them, their profits do not usually hinge on these. Furthermore, certain business perspectives can push software and entertainment firms further from the traditional business land-use agenda. Many new business leaders speak a language about quality of life that, while too ambiguous to place them squarely in the liberal-environmentalist camp, is also too unconventional to be mastered by a local business community accustomed to viewing community in terms of exchange values and growth potentials. The transnational outlook of many software and entertainment executives sits uneasily next to the parochial viewpoint of the traditional urban business community. With such structural and ideological indifference to traditional criteria for a "pro-business" climate, most local software and entertainment firms do not intervene in the local political and civic scene.

However, a subset of actors retains a conventional pro-growth interest in local land use and therefore participates in local politics in more conventional ways. Larger firms that seek to build spacious office complexes, studio facilities, and research campuses are one example; another is industry leaders who address the "collective need" for more space that in fact most individual firms do not experience. While often prominent, these actors tend to be few, and do not represent the typical software and entertainment firm. Moreover, even with a conventional interest in land-use policy, these atypical actors may forego traditional business community alliances.

This finding that local business climate uncertainty does not substantially affect the software and entertainment sectors, and therefore does not motivate their political participation, suggests an important break with long-standing business practices. It therefore raises the issue of its generalizability. Although Santa Monica, Santa Barbara, and San Luis Obispo exemplify important new thrusts in urban and economic restructuring, they nevertheless differ from many other sites of industry. Specifically, they contain mostly R&D branches, "boutique" firms, and corporate headquarters that do not cover the entire range of industrial activities in high-tech sectors; among those underrepresented are hardware manufacturers and the especially massive branches and headquarters seen in Silicon Valley. These latter firm types are more sensitive to material cost factors because they require particular locations, extensive land parcels, and/or lower-skilled workers. Also, hardware manufacturers frequently produce noxious by-products that trigger environmental regulations that further squeeze profits. This more capital-intensive aspect remains a part of the high-tech economy and clings to more conventional settings of industry, such as flexible districts (for specialized production) and satellite platforms in developing nations (for more standardized production). Likewise, the increasing role that tourism properties and themed entertainment districts play in the portfolios of the largest entertainment firms suggests that these companies may be edging further toward a local politics motivated by land-use concerns, simultaneous with the knowledge-intensive mode I have focused on to this point.[3] By emphasizing the more knowledge-intensive firms, this book could underestimate the extent to which traditional land use remains a factor in more capital-intensive sites for the software and entertainment sectors.

Tourism illustrates how manual labor-intensive and cost factor–dependent work persists in the new urban economy. Most hotels and restaurants face considerable land-use uncertainty and government regulation; consequently, they are more disposed than software and entertainment to participate in local politics in order to shape policy to their benefit. Special tourism districts are sometimes located on public land or governed by quasi-city agencies; these explicit dimensions of politicization especially compel tourism firms to intervene in local politics. Only this industry's collective interests in preserving a locality's quality of life put it at odds with the traditional urban business community's pro-growth agenda and even their own individual stake in growth. Otherwise, tourism underscores how the new urban economy does not break completely with the traditional business stake in local business climates.

How generalizable is the moderate path in local growth pursued by the tourism industry in Santa Monica, Santa Barbara, and San Luis Obispo? The answer, I believe, lies in the particular kind of place representations that tourism firms sell. These Southern California destinations offer natural amenities and village ambiance that sustain visitors' perceptions that they can "get away from it all," by which many visitors mean their usual urban and suburban settings. It certainly helps that many visitors consume these local features with ideas of coastal California's "uncommon" beauty and glamour in their heads. Although one can debate whether such amenities and images are *simulations* of nature and community, it is nevertheless clear that tourism in these places commodifies a quality of life that depends heavily on the natural environment and the fragile pleasures of a rarified urban village. This kind of tourism, which relies on *preserving* amenities, contrasts sharply with the industry's trajectory elsewhere toward themed parks and destinations, package vacations, urban entertainment zones, and other capital-intensive forms of tourism that entail *constructing* new amenities, environments, and experiences. These forms of tourism probably promote more virulent "pro-business" politics since they usually entail speculative and capital-intensive development, for which localities may offer regressive subsidies or cede over public authority altogether.[4] Themed tourism brings extensive development that bodes ill for existing qualities of life; indeed, sometimes the latter are replaced wholesale by the construction of new destinations, like amusement parks, heritage districts, and urban entertainment districts.[5] The same is likely true for the companies that serve business travelers with generic hotel and restaurant accommodations. To the extent, then, that the construction and representation of more "artificial" places typify the industry elsewhere, the moderate path taken by the firms that I studied could underestimate tourism's pro-growth thrust.

DISORGANIZING THE TRADITIONAL CIVIC NETWORK

Through mutual interests and effective cooperation, an urban business community coheres as a *social group,* "a collection of people who regularly interact with one another on the basis of shared expectations concerning behavior, and who share a sense of common identity."[6] This textbook definition, however, describes a reality from which the business communities in Santa Monica, Santa Barbara, and San Luis Obispo seem to be moving away. To varying degrees, the new urban economy sectors have abandoned the collective organizations, activities, and interests that usually tie local firms together, simply because the new sectors have no need for them.

For knowledge-intensive sectors, the reasons to stay out of the traditional civic network follow straight out of their business needs. Software and entertainment firms rarely need the local services offered by chambers of commerce. They tend not to retain developers or make campaign contributions that might improve the chances of a successful development project. They largely avoid local banks when they seek financing. They channel their philanthropic energies outside venerable traditional charities. The effect of their disconnect from the traditional civic network appears in more idiosyncratic circumstances as well. For instance, when firms or the collective industry are entangled in local land-use controversies, they appear willing to negotiate with environmental groups on the terms for their projects' success. This may represent pragmatic engagements with local players and discourses specific to the liberal places I studied, but it nevertheless shows that these firms enjoy a political free will that is reinforced by their remove from the traditional civic network.

To the extent that local economies develop in the direction of knowledge-intensive sectors, these trends diminish the centrality of the traditional civic network in the local political and civic scene. Ironically, no conflict or hardball maneuvering between the new sectors and old business community is required to weaken the latter's power. As global companies, software and entertainment firms generally pay little attention to local politics, local business communities, or even the local costs of doing business; they simply want a competitive and sometimes "nice" place to work and live in, at least for a few years before they move on. Yet by refraining from the customary organizations and practices of the traditional civic network, software and entertainment firms upset the "ecology of games" that traditionally binds local businesses to one another.[7] In short, the growth of software and entertainment sectors means that local businesses no longer interact with each other in regular ways, anticipate each others' interests adequately, or identify with each other as a larger social group—as an *urban business community.*

Tourism, by contrast, is more integrated into the traditional civic network. Many tourism firms use the services of local chambers and visitor conference bureaus. Hotels, restaurants, and other tourism firms have incentives to contribute money to local candidates. Many tourism firms give to local charities as part of their business. The industry's concerns to maintain the "specialness" of the locality make tourism a moderating influence *within* the traditional urban business community, although this influence comes *despite* its greater integration into the traditional civic network. Tourism, then, illustrates how the new urban economy may not completely erode the collective organizations and activities that make up the traditional civic network.

However, the traditional civic network may soon be overshadowed by a new one. Universities and colleges increasingly draw the resources, voluntarism, and collaboration of software and entertainment firms. They sponsor the development of industrial parks, performing arts centers, and other facilities in local industry and amenity infrastructures as well. In these ways, they can serve as rival chambers of commerce for the new urban economy. Environmental groups defend the natural and urban amenities that tourism commodifies, and their endorsement can legitimate the local growth of new urban economy sectors. As I noted in the last chapter, the emergence of business-nonprofit alignments outside the traditional civic network says little about the social good they actually accomplish; raising vast sums of money for environmental groups, for instance, did not preclude liberal entertainment figures from supporting controversial developments. Nevertheless, at least in the places I studied, local environmental nonprofits and higher educational institutions appear to be negotiating a different ecology of games with sectors in the new urban economy—one in which the traditional urban business community assumes a diminished role.

CHANGING THE THRUST OF URBAN POLITICS

Does the new urban economy allow for a more democratic *process* in urban politics? The evidence from Southern California suggests that without a regular stake in shaping land use and maximizing business subsidies, software and entertainment firms lack the conventional motivation of businesses to intervene in urban governance. Without a routine presence in the traditional civic network, these same firms abdicate their capacity for systemic power in the locality, even though they retain the political leverage that comes with their control of capital investment. Tourism firms retain these traditional concerns, but they moderate their influence with an important slow-growth interest. These patterns suggest much that is unprecedented in the local politics I observed. For some time, "pro-business" advocates and their activist opponents have expected the new firms to make a dramatic political stand that has arguably yet to materialize. When these industries mobilize, they seldom arouse the collective support of all their members; they appear willing to negotiate on community quality; and they bestow political outsiders like grassroots nonprofits and higher educational institutions an unusual degree of political legitimacy. Outcomes like these, I believe, represent important strides in local democracy away from the conventional business hegemony that rarely concedes a role to residents and interest groups outside the usual growth coalition.

Perhaps even more unprecedented is that new urban economy firms share with residents an interest in community "use value" that outweighs their interest in exchange values. For knowledge-intensive sectors, place-based quality of life is no longer just a local cost of doing business; its value to elite workers makes it an important (if collectively unresolved) problem for many companies in flexible districts and a competitive opportunity for quality-of-life districts. For tourism firms, local amenities represent assets to sell to visitors—a goose that lays a golden egg. As firms in the new urban economy articulate their assorted interests in local amenities, they valorize residents' long-standing concerns for the use values of place. Not surprisingly, grassroots organizations like environmental groups assume a new importance in local politics; perhaps they now represent the interests of new urban economy firms as well as, if not better than, the traditional urban business community. This new affinity between business and community at least creates the possibility that a more grassroots consensus can be reached on how local growth and development should proceed.

Since by many standards, these political processes appear far more democratic than in most localities, the question should be asked: Can software, entertainment, and tourism firms sustain a progressive urban regime? Regime theory suggests that the central dynamic in any urban regime is the distribution of public goods, over which business and community typically fight in a zero-sum battle.[8] Usually, business demands that government regressively direct tax revenues and other public goods to subsidize private accumulation; any concessions that residents gain to preserve community use value can then only come at the expense of business. If sufficiently antagonized by redistribution for residential benefit, business usually seeks to roll back these gains or flees for more "pro-business" settings.

Does this zero-sum battle over the politics of redistribution characterize Santa Monica, Santa Barbara, and San Luis Obispo? In these places, the new sectors are largely undeterred by whatever "anti-business" climate they inherit, because local policies like restrictive land-use zoning and environmental regulations do not affect them for the most part. Moreover, they show little interest in rolling back these policies or promoting business subsidies in order to attract new businesses. In short, they appear to be relatively immune to regressive policies at the level of locality; state and federal subsidies are far more enticing, it seems. Even more, in many ways they *benefit* from policies that sustain social goods because they enable competitive advantage: employee productivity, workforce stability, visitor appeal, and so on. This breaks from the zero-sum dynamics of urban regimes; business and residents now mutually advocate community use value.

Again, how generalizable is this dynamic? In the Southern California places, environmental regulations and other policies protect natural and cultural amenities of the kinds enjoyed by middle and upper classes. There is a self-serving interest in the new sectors' tolerance of the political climate, since firms concede to local costs that, in fact, maintain a quality of life consumed by their elite workers or desirable tourist markets. Would the new sectors remain inactive in localities that tax businesses to support services that, by contrast, benefit minority and working-class communities? If Santa Monica's rent control policies (which activists insist serve such constituencies) are any indication, then new urban economy firms' tolerance of the SMRR regime could suggest an affirmative answer. It is also worth recalling how large firms like entertainment studios agreed to support "justice-for-growth" efforts, apparently as an acceptable cost of doing business. However, where policies benefiting minority and working-class communities *dominate* regime agendas, I suspect a more pessimistic scenario. If the context for new urban economy growth is a quality of life that appeals to elite workers, then the kinds of firms I studied would probably not locate in predominantly minority and working-class communities in the first place. Moreover, the systematic exceptions to the corporate interest in quality of life may erode the progressive outcomes. When corporate pursuit of profit entails physical growth, few firms show any qualms regarding the effects of their own local growth. At least for software and entertainment, one distinction is that they engage the politics of local growth, both pro and con, with much less collective solidarity than either the traditional urban business community or liberal-environmental coalitions—the result, I believe, of their polarized industry structure. Otherwise, insofar as local growth externalizes social costs onto the larger community, then the *benefits* of the new urban economy appear less than totally democratic.

In his study of San Francisco's progressive coalition of the 1980s, Richard DeLeon conceptualized the urban anti-regime as a "transitional political order set up defensively to block the Lazarus-like reemergence of the old pro-growth regime."[9] Shorn of its defensive quality, this sounds much like what results from the ascendance of software, entertainment, and tourism sectors in urban economies. DeLeon also argued that an anti-regime cannot sustain itself without a stable business alliance. Through their quality-of-life interests, the new sectors may be allies to growth opponents; by their disorganization of the traditional civic network, they may disturb the capacities of the old pro-growth regime. However, the level of their political involvement is a critical issue, particularly for software and entertainment. Their aloofness from the local political and civic scene means that whatever positive impact they make comes largely from local agents: industry-specific organizations, universities, and environmental groups. Under what conditions will the new business leaders directly and systematically intervene in the political and civic scene to promote community use value? A more definitive answer awaits further study.

DEEPENING THE STRATIFICATION OF PLACES

Whatever the future holds for urban regimes, one consequence is quite clear: The new urban economy deepens the stratification of places. Here, I refer to how Santa Monica, Santa Barbara, and San Luis Obispo belong to a global hierarchy of production and consumption sites. As any chamber director or mayor knows, core firms contribute greatly to the socioeconomic fate of their locations by generating high wages and tax revenues that multiply through the local economy. In software and entertainment, the core firms I studied occupy a high value-added niche shared by many firms in Silicon Valley and Hollywood; indeed, the quality-of-life district effectively carves slices of economic activity away from these centers. So, too, the tourism firms I studied serve a tourism market that an increasing number of localities seek to tap. Although Santa Monica, Santa Barbara, and San Luis Obispo attract different volumes and types of visitors, they do so with attractions like beaches, village ambiance, pleasant weather, wilderness, and enticing place representations that few localities can create from scratch. To the degree that their kind of nature-based leisure remains popular, these localities have a "place luck" envied by other cities.

Their place luck derives from an unconventional factor: not a "pro-business" climate, but the *absence* of this traditional advantage. What some business advocates deride as "anti-business" climates has been revalorized by broader economic shifts: the decline of conventional industry, the growth of knowledge-intensive sectors and leisure industries, and the new role that lifestyle plays in production (via elite workers) and consumption (via leisure, retirement, and domestic services). These places have prospered not due to attributes that are common to other places—for instance, public subsidies to attract new firms, which none of the three areas offer—but for the attributes that *distinguish* them from other places. Although these elements of place luck suggest a critique of "race to the bottom" strategies that many localities undertake to compete for capital investment, the prosperity of quality-of-life districts nevertheless raises the stakes of that competition.

Place luck also has a local history. My study examined a type of political setting that is familiar to many non-corporate middle-class communities, where public services, the environment, slow growth, and urban amenities set the terms of community use value. These terms and their specific community gains were established only through struggles by neighborhood organizations, environmentalists, liberals, and progressives. Now, with the articulation of these places into the new industrial space, their place luck may be sustained by a new dynamic. Insofar as it disorganizes the traditional urban business community (as software and entertainment do), moderates the pro-growth agenda (as tourism does), and gives "outside" civic sectors a new role (as all three sectors do), the new urban economy potentially weakens the ability of growth coalitions to roll over use-value amenities. Insofar as the competitiveness of the quality-of-life district overshadows the agenda of traditional business leaders, the new urban economy potentially undermines the legitimacy of value-free development. I say "potentially" because only future human agency by grassroots community groups will guide the structural thrust of the new urban economy toward specific outcomes.

To be sure, the traditional strategies that places employ to attract capital investment have not completely lost their value. Flexible districts will continue to offer irreplaceable advantages for business that adopt flexible strategies, and "pro-business" climates will continue to attract businesses and sectors that regard high rents, high wages, environmental regulations, and growth restrictions as critical costs of business. In fact, the fate of the quality-of-life district is indelibly tied to the flexible district; they comprise two spaces that structure the regulation of labor control. Moreover, the new industrial space and traditional corporate geography are inextricably linked to one another, dual landscapes in the uneven development created by capital accumulation. As such, they are landscapes with unequal advantage. So long as core firms in knowledge-intensive sectors and tourists represent the new goods for which places compete, localities like Santa Monica, Santa Barbara, and San Luis Obispo are likely to maintain advantage in the stratification of places.

CORPORATE POWER FOR THE TWENTY-FIRST CENTURY

Although the differences that new urban economy sectors make in local politics occasionally materialize in the form of mistrust and even antagonism between software, entertainment, and tourism companies and the traditional urban business community, it is misleading to depict their interactions as one of necessary conflict. The three sectors wield the same non-local exercise of urban power that has long trained urban business communities in the United States to advocate a pro-growth agenda. Only when that agenda threatens corporate local dependence—on elite workers, localized business relationships managed by deal-makers, and visitors' distinctions of quality-of-life superiority—does local conflict between global and local fractions of capital ensue. This potential for conflict is the final difference that the new urban economy makes for urban politics. It is time to contextualize the many differences uncovered by this study within a broader theory of corporate power.

SLIDING SCALES OF DIFFERENCE

Particularly in software and entertainment, companies often claim that "for the most part, local politics doesn't influence the business." Their claim is true insofar as the local level is only one arena where business profit is achieved. As this book has shown, when the importance of material cost factors decreases, the local level becomes far less relevant than it has been, say, for traditional industry. However, once the analysis of corporate power moves above the local scale, familiar patterns reappear. Indeed, the three sectors direct far more collective resources and effort at broader geographical scales that shape the political environment for business profit. To name some of the more obvious examples, software industry organizations lobby state governments to prevent shareholder lawsuits and overtime wage laws that can cut into profits; at the federal and state level, the industry seeks special protection from anti-monopoly regulation and e-commerce taxation. Software and entertainment companies appeal to the federal government to enforce intellectual property rights and obtain other protections in international trade negotiations. Software and tourism trade groups join other industries in lobbying for expanding (or at least loosening controls on) immigration of foreign workers. Their causes may have economic and social merits, yet what is telling is *how* industries make their case: through campaign contributions, personal relationships between industry and government elites, and the ubiquitous public-private ties that inevitably accompany governmental regulation and taxation. Needless to say, grassroots groups cannot claim such systemic access to government's ear, and so beyond the local level, the three sectors are far more likely to engage in politics as usual.

However, although the fear of capital's rootlessness reinforces government's receptivity, capital in the new urban economy is in some ways less mobile compared to the industry of old. Corporate capital in tourism is the least mobile of the three sectors, since it depends on visitor amenities that are fixed in place, quite costly to re-create wholesale, and valorized by non-local place representations that are not usually their own creation. Except for major theme park developers, tourism companies can seldom pick up and move without setting in motion their own demise. The threat of rootless capital is more real for software and entertainment, where companies have stepped up the outsourcing of standardized and material activities out of their original locations. However, these same competitive forces have also given rise to elite talent and imbued certain places with new strategic value as a medium of industrial organization. Thus, flexible districts and quality-of-life districts exert a compelling attraction on other activities in these sectors—an attraction from which capital itself has profited. As competitive sites for knowledge-intensive production, they manifest a source of local dependence, of rootedness in place, that capital cannot entirely escape. Granted, it may be worthwhile to lament the exodus of more material forms of production like manufacturing or film production, since these tend to employ a broader base of workers and portend less socioeconomic stratification than knowledge-intensive activities. The opposite has unfortunately come to pass in the new industrial space.

More generally, exercising corporate power *from* particular industry locations should not be confused with exercising corporate power *on* those same locations. Silicon Valley and Hollywood give "local" form to global industries. Hence the simultaneity of regionally skewed memberships and far-flung influence in software and entertainment's major trade associations. Local political environments affect Silicon Valley and Hollywood only to the extent that production is sensitive to spatial variation in business costs. When this work is material and standardized in nature, the local effect is indeed substantial. Historically, many of the workforces who performed material and standardized activities have leveraged the industries' local dependence to mobilize labor; in some cases, governmental regulation has also increased local business costs. In response, software and entertainment companies have increasingly shifted material and standardized production elsewhere; the exodus finished in Silicon Valley by the 1990s and is presently underway in Hollywood.

As these flexible districts lose their material industry, local politics, at least as capital traditionally conceives the issue, becomes less relevant to companies there. The political environments in industry settings *elsewhere* (like Bangalore, India for software coding or Vancouver, Canada, for film production) are now more likely to affect Silicon Valley and Hollywood companies than what goes on in their backyards. As this transnational geography suggests, the most relevant scale of political concern for software and entertainment capital is global, not local. The quality-of-life district should also be understood as a global setting for knowledge-intensive activities, even if the agglomerative pull of industry networks confines its dispersal to a day's journey out of existing industry centers. Quality-of-life districts' fortunes hinge on globally oriented companies based in Silicon Valley and Hollywood and other industry centers, not the "pro-business" nature of their own local political environment.

HOW CAPITAL LIVES

The disparity between local and non-local exercises of corporate power is a striking feature in cities and regions that thrive in the new industrial space. With less need to engage locally in hardball tactics, companies of the kind described in this book have perhaps lulled some observers and activists into a false optimism about their political "enlightenment" in contrast to corporations of old. The fact that politics as usual continues beyond the local scale suggests that this optimism is misplaced, at least literally. Nevertheless, it captures an element of truth about corporate power in the twenty-first century: Capital increasingly has to take a human dimension into account in its bottom-line quest for profits. In software and entertainment, this dimension manifests in elite workers whose expertise and relationships drive productivity in these flexible industries. In tourism, it comes in the form of visitors whose leisure and lifestyle concerns fuel the demand for the sector's services.

I believe it is unlikely that capital can eradicate these human dimensions from its structure any time soon for a number of reasons. It takes elite workers' expertise to routinize, de-skill, and outsource production. To the extent that capital's quest to extract greater surplus value from labor requires further innovations in corporate strategies and production technologies, a demand for expert labor that is competitively deployed in flexible districts seems assured. This is the fundamental contradiction of the high-tech age. Furthermore, in a world where collective resistance to the dehumanizing terms of work and life has been episodic at best, consumer industries like entertainment and tourism offer the escapes and recreations that help legitimate (or at least distract attention from) this alienation.

Finally, and perhaps least expectedly, capitalists increasingly view their own careers and lives through humanistic criteria like the "challenge" of work and the "rewards" of quality of life. At least in software, entertainment, and other flexible sectors like finance, their self-conception is no simple delusion. In fact, capital's human agents are themselves deployed via specialized labor markets, ad hoc recombinations, and the cycles of prosperity and recession. As talent headhunters will attest, executives have little attachment to their own companies—perhaps as little as capital is thought to have to places. The fact that capital's interests are served, at least in the short term, by its managers' self-exploitation does not dismiss the point that capitalists themselves seek to "get a life," and thereby embody the structural contradiction of elite workers.

In this context of corporate impermanence and elite workers, place matters for the coordination of capital accumulation and the regulation of its contradictions in bold new ways. Affirming the claims of economic geographers, this book has shown how one kind of industry location, the flexible district, has become a privileged site for knowledge-intensive production and innovation. A new kind of industry location, the quality-of-life district, reveals the power of elite workers to leave industry centers that develop unchecked toward a tragedy of the commons. The tourist destination is a different kind of industry location, where visitors' tastes valorize place-based amenities against a backdrop of industrialization and urban sprawl. These three industry locations illustrate how capital's mobility generates new forms of local dependence that root it back in particular places.

An altogether separate issue, however, is the awareness of their collective plight—in short, the class consciousness—that corporate elites in the three sectors show in these locations. Like the traditional urban business community (albeit with less enthusiasm for value-free development), tourism firms acknowledge their local dependence when they collectively mobilize to promote their locality and attract visitors. Software and entertainment firms in the flexible district have consciously sought to escape the most burdensome costs of their local dependence by moving material production elsewhere. They may fail to address the environmental and cost-of-living strains that push away many elite workers, but the continual arrival of new replacements lessens that problem's urgency for most companies.

However, in quality-of-life districts, flexible firms mostly arrive as elite workers seeking lifestyle opportunities. Corporate elites there show no local class consciousness, reactionary or progressive, that motivates them to cast their lot with either the traditional urban business community or its opponents. Most ominously, when their attachment to the quality-of-life district is threatened—because the industry boom has turned bust, or because the "lifeboat" has tipped over with too many companies seeking the same amenities—they have little incentive not to move on, perhaps to a more pristine or exclusive locale. Like hotel guests who demand a different room when the view from the window is marred or the towels are not sufficiently fluffy, cosmopolitan elite workers threaten rootlessness in their very quest for place-specific amenities. This is the new uncertainty that emerges out of capital's local dependence. It does not bode well for the economic sustainability of quality-of-life districts, especially if they are abandoned as no longer "a place to get away from it all," yet not quite a bona fide industry center. Nor should it encourage optimism among residents and grassroots organizations willing to make concessions to potential allies in new urban economy sectors in the fight to preserve community use value.

The quality-of-life district offers a glimpse into other industries and economies where elite workers are found. If labor market privilege gives elite workers freedom from any concerns but their own lifestyle satisfaction, then this class can choose not to get involved in the struggles over labor and community. The fear of a "free agent" society is not new, and it echoes current polemics against gentrification, "bourgeois bohemians," and the selfish communitarianism of the "new geography."[10] Although a narcissistic generation, the aestheticization of social difference, or other cultural factors may be to blame, the crucial enabling mechanism is an industrial organization that lets the labor market "flexibly"—that is, without collective planning and moral regulation—drive corporate productivity and industrial location. Furthermore, if capital is not a group but a social relation to the means of production, so, too, is elite labor. In flexible industries, the people who make things happen with knowledge and money often embody both class relations, a very real and common paradox. It is worth pausing to consider what this means for urban power. For better or worse, "old" capital clearly understood its local dependence on the communities and places it created, even if this supported the politics of reactionary paternalism or corporate exodus. It is not clear that the new capitalists have even this awareness of their local dependence, at least for those who do not need to be at the center of the action.

At the risk of discounting how conventional modes of corporate power will continue to haunt much of the world into the foreseeable future, this new face of corporate power poses a challenge to anyone concerned about corporate accountability and social justice. Old understandings of capitalists as rootless colonists of place may no longer be totally viable, but they have their political value by stating very plainly what capital's interests are in the places it touches down; whether this is seen as legitimate bottom-line concerns or inhumane exploitation can be left for debate. In the current moment, by contrast, capital shows a human face that seduces not only localities seeking the fortunes of the new urban economy, but even *capitalists themselves* into believing that the framework of urban power—the private ownership of capital, competition among localities for inward investment, and the local hegemony of the traditional urban business community to attract this investment—has somehow qualitatively changed.

With its destabilizing effects upon the traditional urban business community, whose customary role has been to articulate and enact rules of urban power that are not entirely of their making, the hope that the new urban economy promises a better future is perhaps understandable. Nevertheless that future remains to be proven by capital itself. In flexible districts, companies must acknowledge and address the environmental and social strains that their unchecked collective prosperity has set in motion. In quality-of-life districts, elite workers must go beyond a superficial appreciation of amenities and show commitment to locally forged ideals of community. In places where tourism revolves around natural and cultural amenities, tourism firms must demonstrate their concern for the destination's fragility in word and deed. Tourism firms that commodify simulated and themed environments obviously have little incentive to protect community use value; perhaps tourists—that is, every one of us—should stem the demand for such environments and take better care of the places from which they seek to get away. Until then, all bets are off. Even as scholars refine their understandings of corporate power to take account of capital's unforeseen evolution, cities and their grassroots advocates might do best to hold on to traditional standards of "corporate power," with all their ruthless, rootless, and inhumane connotations, and challenge capital to prove them false.

Methodology Appendix

T his study examines the local business structure of software, entertainment, and tourism companies in three Southern California locations in order to investigate the difference that the new urban economy makes for local politics. My methodology was comparative in three ways. First, I compared the software, entertainment, and tourism industries with each other in order to identify specific features of local business structure that motivate business and political activities in each sector. Second, to find out whether any of these features makes a significant difference from the usual ways industry and local business approach urban politics, I compared the three sectors to traditional urban business community patterns documented by prior urban research. Where sector-specific comparisons were meaningful, I used local banks as a proxy for the traditional urban business community, since this sector provides the most reasonable baseline of business participation in local politics. Why local banks? With their centrality in financial and civic networks, they are a bastion of the traditional urban business community.[1] However, local banks do not intervene in city politics as much as rentier groups like developers or construction firms, which tend to be the primary business actors in local politics.[2] Third, rather than analyze the data solely along sectoral categories, I retained locality as a comparative dimension. This means I looked for common patterns in Santa Monica, Santa Barbara, and San Luis Obispo to make claims about the sectors, but I also considered locality when a particular sector behaved differently in one place. For instance, I was able to distinguish differences in software companies' civic participation between Santa Monica, a flexible district with quality-of-life appeal, and Santa Barbara and San Luis Obispo, the bona fide quality-of-life districts.

It can be argued that a sample size of three research sites is too small to make scientific generalizations about new urban economy firm behavior in

all cities. This is true, and I have willingly sacrificed statistical generalizability for the in-depth analysis that qualitative interviews and fieldwork
allow. In regards to my sampling rationale, I analyzed Santa Monica, Santa
Barbara, and San Luis Obispo as three diverse nodes in the new industrial
space. Following scholarship on economic globalization, I analyzed these
Southern California places not as random elements of a larger universe of
cities in the U.S. or even the world, but rather as elements of the smaller set
of actual and potential locations in the new industrial space.[3] I then referred
to prior research on industrial geography and urban politics to get a sense
of my research sites' "generalizability" within this singular context.

DATA GATHERED

I combined qualitative and quantitative methods and accumulated data
from several sources to discern the patterns in local business structure for
the software, entertainment, and tourism sectors. I gathered data from 1996
to 2000, a five-year period that I treated as a single point in time representative of the new urban economy.

INTERVIEWS

I conducted, tape recorded, and personally transcribed interviews with
ninety-five individuals who did business, held political office, or staffed
community nonprofits in (or occasionally around) Santa Monica, Santa
Barbara, and San Luis Obispo. I sampled informants so as to reach the most
important executives in new urban economy sectors, leaders of the traditional urban business community, and key organizers in local nonprofits
and politics. Interviews were almost always held at informants' workplaces
during the weekday, although a few informants chose instead to meet me at
coffee shops, restaurants, or their homes. Interviews typically lasted from
thirty to ninety minutes; those with software and entertainment informants
usually ran toward the shorter end. Although this length of time was shorter
than I hoped for, many informants told me they could not give me more
time because thirty minutes with a high-level executive was quite valuable
in their circles, and because they were simply too busy to talk for longer. I
compensated for this short interview length by sampling a greater number
of informants than I originally intended, particularly in software and (with
less success) entertainment.

I did not count each individual whom I interviewed as a single informant. In three interviews, I interviewed pairs of informants from the same
organization; I count each pair as a single informant. Eleven informants
came from sectors like high-technology manufacturing or art that I later
excluded from the industries I would study; I consider these preliminary
interviews outside of my bona fide informant pools. I called or e-mailed
eight informants to ask specific questions, while a ninth informant (an
entertainment executive) e-mailed his response to my interview schedule in

a very cursory format. I count these partial interviews as one-fourth of an informant. This resulted in 77.25 bona fide informants, whom I divided into two pools; see Table A.1, below.

In the first informant pool, forty-three of my informants (or fifty-six percent of all bona fide informants) came from the new urban economy sectors. I sampled them using snowball sampling methods designed to emphasize the reputed leaders of the industries. More than half of my new urban economy informants came from the software industry, which reflects how my rejection rates varied by sector. I was rejected by or could not contact eight software referrals, seven entertainment referrals, and four tourism referrals. Thirteen of these nineteen rejections came from Santa Monica, the research site with the largest entertainment industry. To compensate for shortcomings in finding entertainment informants, I interviewed seven high-level entertainment executives whom academic colleagues personally knew and referred to me. Three of these informants worked outside the city limits of Santa Monica (in West Hollywood, Beverly Hills, and Hollywood proper, although one lived in Santa Monica); thus, I asked them about political and civic participation in their respective communities and later assessed how their civic interests and behavior might parallel or diverge from their Santa Monica counterparts. I applied the same rationale to one software executive from my original snowball sample who worked at a firm near Santa Monica, in Marina Del Rey. To compensate for the weakness in tourism informants, particularly in Santa Barbara and San Luis Obispo, I relied on indirect evidence about this industry that I had gathered in previous research I conducted on these localities.[4] Since tourism is the most familiar and "home-grown" of the new urban economy sectors, it was also easier to get indirect accounts of this industry from community informants (my second informant pool; see below) than for software and entertainment.

With my new urban economy informants, I used an interview schedule that I frequently modified to make it appropriate for and comprehensible to the informant; see Figure A.1. I regularly prompted informants to

Table A.1

The informant pools

| Locality | New Urban Economy | | | Community | | |
	Software	Entertainment	Tourism	Business	Civic	Total
Santa Monica	5.5	7.25	5	5	8.5	31.25
Santa Barbara	8.25	2	1	4	5.5	20.75
San Luis Obispo	11	1	2	4	7.25	25.25
Total	24.75	10.25	8	13	21.25	77.25

Figure A.1

Interview schedule for new urban economy informants

Locational motivations

1. How did you get to this city and locate your business here? How long has your business been here? Do you also live here? Do most of your employees live in or around this city?

2. Some people suggest that businesses in your industry are attracted to places with a high quality of life, for example, in regards to recruiting competitively for the best employees. Would you say your industry has a particular affinity for places with a desirable quality of life? Is quality of life something that other companies in your industry have raised as an issue?

Local business associations

3. How did you get involved in [local business association]? What is the extent or magnitude of your participation in this association?

4. Is your involvement in [local business association] a company decision or a personal project?

5. What other business or trade associations do you participate in: chamber of commerce, American Electronics Association? Are these particularly concerned with the local growth of your industry? Which associations do you devote more time to?

6. If you don't get involved in local business associations, how do you get access to business information about hiring employees, potential investors, lobbying policy-makers, and so on?

7. How concerned are you about attracting to this area other companies that are like yours or that could support your company? Is this a requirement for your company's prosperity?

8. Do other local companies in your industry take the stance toward these issues that you do? Do they get involved like you do? What do you perceive the level of leadership to be from other local industries like software/entertainment/tourism?

Political involvement

9. How would you describe the level of interaction you have with local representatives and government?

10. Do you get involved in local politics by endorsing or giving money to local candidates, campaigns, or political parties? Which ones? Ever get involved in an electoral race?

11. Do you consider your support for [politicians/campaigns/parties] a company decision or a personal project?

12. Are there constraints on participating in community organizations or local politics due to being privately owned/publicly traded/a corporate headquarters or branch?

13. Have you ever received any criticism within your industry or the community for your civic or political involvement?

14. Have you been unduly burdened by local environmental regulation or land-use planning? Other local issues that have impacted you? What about state or federal regulations?

15. Are there certain issues that no local organization or politician is raising that you think need to be addressed?

Participation in community nonprofits

16. Are you, either through work or [local business association], involved in organizations outside of the industry that seek to enhance the local quality of life, such as local nonprofits, education, environmental organizations, etc.?

17. What is the range of causes you are willing to support? What causes would you not get involved in? Does your participation have anything to do with your business?

Figure A.1 *Continued*
Interview schedule for new urban economy informants

18. What's your perception of the caliber of community nonprofits in this community: professional/ grassroots, moderate/radical? Has this influenced your decision to get involved?

19. Time for participation in honorary roles: If you don't have it, then who does? (Certain age? Occupation? Industry?)

20. Are there other companies or business leaders in town that get involved to the extent you do in supporting community nonprofits or getting politically involved? Which organizations/politicians do they support?

Case study development proposals

21. Did you take a personal position on the proposed QAD research campus [for Santa Barbara informants]? The proposed Dreamworks studio in Playa Vista [for Santa Monica informants]? The proposed Hearst Resort Ranch [for San Luis Obispo informants]? What about others in your industry?

Conclusions

22. Can you refer me to other businesspeople who get involved like you do?

23. Can I contact you if I have some follow-up questions? [Get business card.]

describe not only their own attitudes and behavior concerning the issues of study, but also those of their colleagues and counterparts—an effective way to expand my analytical scan on their industries. In interviews, I tried to be very transparent about my intellectual agenda. For instance, I asked informants directly about the unconventional role of quality of life in the industry's growth or particularly contentious local development proposals. Although some researchers believe that direct questions on controversial issues lead informants to give distorted or socially expected responses, I believe that my direct approach better engaged my informants, especially those who continually checked their watches to see how much time remained in the interview.

In the second pool of informants, 34.25 informants (or forty-four percent of all bona fide informants) represented "the community" in some way. Thirteen were traditional urban business leaders (listed as "business" in Table A.1), while 21.25 came from local politics or community nonprofits (listed as "civic"); they generally consisted of executives from local banks, development firms, business associations, political office-holders or staff, and executive directors or development officers from the most important community charities. I used purposive sampling techniques to find these informants, selecting them for their first-hand perspectives on how the new urban economy sectors participated in local development projects, business associations, electoral campaigns, and philanthropy. Because I had researched local politics and philanthropy in Santa Barbara and San Luis Obispo in prior studies, I interviewed additional business and civic leaders from Santa

Monica to get comparable depth of knowledge about how that place operates on these dimensions.

For my community informants, I gave a different emphasis to the interview schedule shown in Figure A.1. I asked them less about themselves and more about the new urban economy firms and leaders, for example, to name particular companies involved in local organizations, to identify particular forms of civic involvement, and to attempt to explain the various reasons why companies in the three sectors did or did not get involved in the locality. Second, I asked community informants to elaborate on how their organizations and, more generally, the traditional urban business community or the liberal-environmental coalitions to which they belonged have accommodated the new urban economy firms and leaders.

FIELD NOTES

During all of my interviews, I took field notes about my informants' settings and activities, as well as other things occurring within my view. In a few cases, informants took me on tours of their workplaces. My field notes provided valuable information on the workplace in software, entertainment, and tourism: employee activities, companies' site needs, comparability to conventional workplaces, accessibility to the public (through storefront signs and doors, framed newspaper articles about the company hung in the lobby, etc.), and so on.

I attended at least one meeting for almost all the local business associations that I studied. During these meetings I engaged in small talk with other participants and, when asked, explained that "I'm a sociologist studying the local software/entertainment/tourism industry." Otherwise I kept silent and took notes on a small notepad, from which I made more elaborate field notes within a day. These events provided useful data on the ways the three sectors were organized, the kinds of individuals and companies that did or did not participate in business groups, the topics of local concern to industry, and the industry "culture" that did or did not materialize in these meetings. A few events featured business speakers who described their companies and their companies' local origins; these made useful surrogates for interviews, although I did not count them as informants.

I gained access to business association meetings in various ways. Some groups explicitly opened events to the public, so I simply attended the scheduled meeting, dinner, cocktail hour, or lecture (in one case, an informant paid my entrance fee to a dinner event). Other groups held regular meetings of task forces or subcommittees, access to which required a prior invitation from an association leader. I could not attend some meetings because they were private, unannounced, or prohibitively expensive; most entertainment industry associations fell in this category. In these cases, I would try to ask informants about what went on in these kinds of meetings or turn to news reports and scholarly research about these associations for supplementary evidence. Overall, even many ostensibly public meetings were closed settings. In a few meetings, my presence as an outsider was certainly conspicuous to the participants, although generally not enough to distract them from their intended activities.[5] In at least one case, participants felt comfortable enough with my presence to ask me what I thought "as a sociologist" about a particular topic; I would answer honestly, but not so as to reveal any intellectual concerns and speculations that might derail the meeting.

SECONDARY DATA ANALYSIS

Quantitative data came from existing datasets, such as the U.S. Census Statistical Abstract. To count the number of local firms in the new urban economy sectors (reported in Chapter 1, Tables 1.2–1.4), I used the Select Phone 99 phone book CD-ROM set, which contains 1998 phone book listings for every business in the United States and can sort them by city and standard industrial code (SIC).[6] Although this dataset was not specifically designed to count the total number of firms in a local industry, it provides the most reliable enumerations of firms in particular industries at a city level for a non-census year, and I converted it to this purpose fairly easily.[7]

In Chapters 5–7, I incorporated these local firm counts into the tables where I compare software, entertainment, and tourism sectors with each other and with local banks on participation in local chambers of commerce (Tables 5.1–5.2), campaign contributions (Tables 6.1–6.2), and philanthropy (Tables 7.1–7.3). In addition to reporting absolute values, I also incorporated sector size by calculating and comparing mean statistics *per firm,* which indicate how typical or widespread a form of participation is among all local firms in that sector. For each statistic, denominator values came from the industry totals reported in Tables 1.2–1.4; below, Table A.2 reports the number of local banks that I used to calculate a comparative baseline of significance. Numerator values came from quantitative data that I gathered from chamber membership directories, campaign disclosure statements, and nonprofit development records that listed individuals and firms involved in (respectively) local business associations, electoral campaigns, and community nonprofits.

Table A.2

Number of local banks

SIC	Description	Santa Monica	Santa Barbara	San Luis Obispo
602	Commercial banks	33	51	27

SOURCE: Select Phone, 1999 version, InfoUSA Inc., Omaha, Neb.
NOTE: Different branches of the same firm are counted as separate firms.

I gathered other documents from the field. After each interview, I asked informants for any brochures, annual reports, or other publicly available materials on their firm or organization. I looked at corporate websites on the Internet about company history, directorate, membership in industry associations, and activities in the local community; these proved especially useful in preparing for interviews. Business associations and community nonprofits provided organization charts, mission statements, member directories, newsletters, calendars, Internet mailing lists for group discussion (I subscribed to as many of these as possible), promotional materials, and so on. Finally, during the five years I conducted research, I clipped local newspaper stories (in print or from newspaper websites) on local economies, sectors, particular companies, and case studies that I analyzed for this research. I compiled as many of these documents as possible onto a computerized database along with my interview transcripts, field notes, and any secondary data that I could enter in digital form. I especially took care to include the names of individuals and companies found in the boards of directors, task-force committees, member directories, meeting participants, and corporate sponsors for as many local business organizations and community non-profits as I could find in my research sites.

As I gathered data about political fund-raising and community philanthropy, I discovered that campaign contribution and nonprofit development records often gave little or no sign of a person's industry affiliation. This is why my computerized database of interview transcripts, field notes, field documents, and news clippings proved especially valuable. By cross-referencing the names of the individuals and organizations listed in the campaign and philanthropy documents with my database, I could identify which ones belonged to the sectors I studied, as well as list the other groups and activities in which they participated (which I report in Chapter 6, "Repeat players in local politics"). Additional cross-referencing sources I used included Internet search engines that were specific to certain industries (e.g., Hollywood Online's "MoviePeople Database"). For my philanthropy analysis, I also asked a staff member from each nonprofit to identify the directors and benefactors from software, entertainment, and tourism companies.

ADDITIONAL METHODS AND DATA FOR CAMPAIGN CONTRIBUTION ANALYSIS

In Chapter 6, my data on campaign contributions to mayoral and city council candidates came from election-year campaign disclosure statements from 1996 for Santa Monica and San Luis Obispo and from 1997 for Santa Barbara.[8] These statements identify the names, occupations or employers, and contribution amounts of all individuals and organizations who gave $100 or more.[9] I recorded this information for all contributors and then pooled it into progressive, centrist, or conservative candidate datasets for each research site based on the political orientation of each candidate, which is reported on page 193 in Table A.3.

Table A.3

Candidates for office

Candidate	Political orientation	Office sought	Incumbent or Challenger	Election results
Santa Monica (1996)				
Alvarez, Donna Dailey	conservative	city council	challenger	lost
Bloom, Richard	progressive	city council	challenger	lost
Feinstein, Michael	progressive	city council	challenger	won
Genser, Ken	progressive	city council	incumbent	won
Greenberg, Asha	conservative	city council	incumbent	won
Olsen, Kelly	progressive	city council	incumbent	lost
Rosenstein, Paul	centrist	city council	incumbent	won
Schwengel, Frank	conservative	city council	challenger	lost
Santa Barbara (1997)				
Beaver, Helene	conservative	mayor	challenger	lost
Garcia, Gil	centrist	city council	incumbent	won
Guzzardi, Joe	centrist	city council	challenger	lost
Lodge, Sheila	progressive	city council	challenger	lost
Miller, Harriet	progressive	mayor	challenger	won
Roberts, Tom	progressive	city council	incumbent	won
Secord, Dan	conservative	city council	challenger	won
San Luis Obispo (1996)				
Parker, Lance	conservative	city council	challenger	lost
Romero, Dave	conservative	city council	incumbent	won
Settle, Allen	centrist	mayor	incumbent	won
Smith, Kathy	centrist	city council	incumbent	won
Veesart, Pat	progressive	city council	challenger	lost

These individuals comprise the group of candidates whose campaign contributions I analyzed in Chapter 6. Several candidates for office either accepted no campaign contributions or did not file campaign disclosure statements at the city clerk's office and were therefore not included in my campaign contribution analysis: in Santa Monica, Shari Davis, Jeffery Hughes, Susan Mearns, Jonathan Metzger, Larry Swieboda (all city council candidates); in Santa Barbara, Christopher Allen (city council candidate),

Aaron Gray (city council candidate), Bill Hackett (mayoral candidate), Bob Hansen (city council candidate), Ajay Patel (city council candidate); in San Luis Obispo, Lark Jursek (mayoral candidate). For Santa Monica's progressive candidate dataset, I also incorporated contributions to Santa Monicans for Renters' Rights (SMRR), the city's progressive party, reported in its recipient committee campaign statement. Each election cycle, SMRR collects contributions to fund *party* campaigns for its slate of municipal candidates for all elected city offices.[10] Contributors to SMRR did not appear in the individual campaign disclosure statements of any SMRR-endorsed candidates, who independently raise their own campaign finances. Still, contributions to SMRR played an important role in municipal elections by providing a second funding source for Santa Monica progressives. From this pool of money, I added the twenty-nine percent that the party allocated to its mayoral and city council endorsees into Santa Monica's progressive candidate dataset.

From the three candidate databases for each research site, I grouped together contributions from software, entertainment, tourism, and banks based on contributors' self-reported occupations. However, in campaign disclosure statements, employer names did not always clearly denote the sector that contributors came from; some contributors also obscured their affiliation by listing ambiguous titles ("self-employed," "investor," "retired," etc.) or contributing via relatives in apparently unrelated sectors. Such misreporting underestimates a sector's actual campaign contributions.[11] For this reason, I triangulated my data in two ways. First, I reviewed various business directories, using the names of contributors and their employers to look for information on sectoral affiliation. Second, I cross-referenced the names of contributors and their employers in my computerized database for additional information on their sectoral/organizational affiliation.

Notes

CHAPTER ONE

1. Rebecca Solnit and Susan Schwartzenberg, *Hollow City* (London: Verso, 2000); and Christopher Mele, *Selling the Lower East Side* (Minneapolis: University of Minnesota Press, 2000).

2. For arguments about the rise of "post-materialist" values, see Ronald Inglehart, "Public Support for Environmental Protection: Objective Problems and Subjective Values in 43 Societies," *PS: Political Science and Politics* 28 (1995): 57–72, and *Culture Shift in Advanced Industrial Society* (Princeton, N.J.: Princeton University Press, 1990); Paul R. Abramson and Ronald Inglehart, *Value Change in Global Perspective* (Ann Arbor: University of Michigan Press, 1995); and William R. Catton and Riley E. Dunlap, "A New Ecological Paradigm for Post-Exuberant Sociology," *American Behavioral Scientist* 24 (1980): 15–47; see also Lester W. Milbrath, "The World is Relearning Its Story about How the World Works," in *Environmental Politics in the International Arena: Movements, Parties, Organizations, and Policy,* ed. Sheldon Kamieniecki (New York: State University of New York Press, 1993), 21–39. For evidence that "new money" shows greater liberalism than its older counterparts, see Val Burris, "The Myth of Old Money Liberalism: The Politics of the *Forbes* 400 Richest Americans," *Social Problems* 47 (2000): 360–378.

3. Karl Marx, *Capital: A Critique of Political Economy,* vol. 1, trans. B. Fowkes (New York: Vintage Books, 1976).

4. Kevin R. Cox and Andrew Mair, "Locality and Community in the Politics of Local Economic Development," *Annals of the Association of American Geographers* 78 (1988): 307–325.

5. The distinction between local dependence and local independence should not be confused with differences in firm ownership or scale. For example, a chain bookseller may have the financial leverage that comes from hundreds of stores, yet each store is locally dependent, prospering or perishing based on the local economy that anchors the store's market. By contrast, a financial adviser may be privately owned and work out of a single office, but by selling her services to customers all over the world, she effectively constitutes a big business immune from the vicissitudes of the local economy outside her office.

6. Matthew A. Crenson, *The Un-Politics of Air Pollution: A Study of Non-Decisionmaking in the Cities* (Baltimore: Johns Hopkins Press, 1971).

7. John R. Logan and Harvey L. Molotch, *Urban Fortunes: The Political Economy of Place* (Berkeley: University of California Press, 1987).

8. Stella M. Capek and John I. Gilderbloom, *Community Versus Commodity: Tenants and the American City* (Albany, N.Y.: State University of New York Press, 1992).

9. J. Allen Whitt, *Urban Elites and Mass Transportation: The Dialectics of Power* (Princeton, N.J.: Princeton University Press, 1982).

10. Joe R. Feagin, *Free Enterprise City: Houston in Political Economic Perspective* (New Brunswick, N.J.: Rutgers University Press, 1988).

11. Mark Gottdiener, *The Social Production of Urban Space* (Austin: University of Texas Press, 1985); John Mollenkopf, *The Contested City* (Princeton, N.J.: Princeton University Press, 1983); and Harvey Molotch, "The City as a Growth Machine," *American Journal of Sociology* 82 (1976): 309–330.

12. Clarence N. Stone, "Systemic Power in Community Decision Making: A Restatement of Stratification Theory," *American Political Science Review* 74 (1980): 978–990.

13. Kee Warner and Harvey Molotch, "Power To Build: How Development Persists Despite Local Controls," *Urban Affairs Review* 30 (1995): 394–395.

14. David Harvey, *The Urbanization of Capital* (Baltimore: Johns Hopkins University Press, 1985), 16.

15. Roger Friedland and Donald Palmer, "Park Place and Main Street: Business and the Urban Power Structure," *Annual Review of Sociology* 10 (1984): 393–416.

16. Joseph Galaskiewicz, *Exchange Networks and Community Politics* (Beverly Hills, Calif.: Sage, 1979); and R. O. Schutze, "The Bifurcation of Power in a Satellite City," in *Community Political Systems,* ed. M. Janowitz (Glencoe, Ill.: Free Press, 1961), 19–80.

17. Michael Storper and Richard Walker, *The Capitalist Imperative: Territory, Technology, and Industrial Growth* (Oxford: Blackwell, 1989).

18. Joe R. Feagin and Robert Parker, *Building American Cities: The Urban Real Estate Game,* 2d ed. (Englewood Cliffs, N.J.: Prentice Hall, 1990); Mollenkopf, op. cit.; and Whitt, op. cit.

19. Harvey Molotch, "The City as a Growth Machine," 317.

20. Crenson, op. cit.

21. Friedland and Palmer, op. cit.

22. Roger Friedland, *Power and Crisis in the City: Corporations, Unions, and Urban Policy* (New York: Schocken Books, 1983).

23. Harvey Molotch, "Capital and Neighborhood in the United States: Some Conceptual Links," *Urban Affairs Quarterly* 14 (1979): 289–312.

24. Logan and Molotch, op. cit.

25. Gottdiener, op. cit.; John Logan, "Growth, Politics, and the Stratification of Places," *American Journal of Sociology* 84 (1978): 404–416.

26. David Harvey, *The Condition of Postmodernity: An Enquiry into the Origins of Cultural Change* (Cambridge, Mass.: Blackwell, 1989).

27. See, e.g., Kevin R. Cox, "Ideology and the Growth Coalition," in *The Urban Growth Machine: Critical Perspectives Two Decades Later,* ed. Andrew E. G. Jonas and David Wilson (Albany, N.Y.: State University of New York Press, 1999), 23.

28. Joe Painter, "Regulation, Regime, and Practice in Urban Politics," in *Reconstructing Urban Regime Theory,* ed. M. Lauria (Thousand Oaks, Calif.: Sage Publications, 1997), 127.

29. M. Goodwin and J. Painter, "Concrete Research, Urban Regimes, and Regulation Theory," in *Reconstructing Urban Regime Theory,* 13–29.

30. Steven L. Elkin, *City and Regime in the American Republic* (Chicago: University of Chicago Press, 1987).

31. Clarence N. Stone, "Urban Regimes and the Capacity to Govern: A Political Economy Approach," *Journal of Urban Affairs* 15 (1993): 1–28, and *Regime Politics: Governing Atlanta, 1946–1988* (Lawrence, Kans.: University of Kansas Press, 1989); and Barbara Ferman, *Challenging the Growth Machine* (Lawrence, Kans., University Press of Kansas, 1996).

32. Clarence N. Stone, op. cit.; and Elkin, op. cit.

33. Harvey Molotch, "Growth Machine Links: Up, Down, and Across," in *The Urban Growth Machine: Critical Perspectives Two Decades Later,* ed. A. E. G. Jonas and D. Wilson (Albany, N.Y.: State University of New York Press, 1999), 247–265; and Stone, "Urban Regimes and the Capacity to Govern." For a typology of agendas that urban regimes pursue, see John R. Logan, Rachel Bridges Whaley, and Kyle Crowder, "The Character and Consequences of Growth Regimes: An Assessment of Twenty Years of Research," in *The Urban Growth Machine: Critical Perspectives Two Decades Later.*

34. As I have defined it, the traditional civic network could also include other frequent sites for interaction among urban businesses and other community institutions and members not covered in this book, like local firm directorates, public school boards, and fraternal orders.

35. Andrew Sayer and Richard Walker, *The New Social Economy: Reworking the Division of Labor* (Cambridge, Mass.: Blackwell, 1992), 134; and Paul Baran and Paul Sweezy, *Monopoly Capital* (New York: Monthly Review Press, 1996).

36. Leonard Nevarez, "Efficacy or Legitimacy of Community Power? A Reassessment of Corporate Elites in Urban Studies," in *Understanding the City: Contemporary and Future Perspectives,* ed. J. Eade and C. Mele (Oxford: Blackwell, 2002), 379–396.

37. See, e.g., G. W. Domhoff, *Who Rules America? Power and Politics in the Year 2000,* 3d ed. (Mountain View, Calif.: Mayfield Publishing Company, 1998).

38. AnnaLee Saxenian, *Regional Advantage: Culture and Competition in Silicon Valley and Route 128* (Cambridge, Mass.: Harvard University Press, 1994); and Allen J. Scott, *Technopolis: High-Technology Industry and Regional Development in Southern California* (Berkeley: University of California Press, 1993).
39. Saskia Sassen, *The Global City: New York, London, Tokyo* (Princeton, N.J.: Princeton University Press, 1991).
40. Dennis R. Judd, "Constructing the Tourist Bubble," in *The Tourism City*, ed. Dennis R. Judd and Susan S. Fainstein (New Haven, Conn.: Yale University Press, 1999), 35–53; and Sharon Zukin, *The Cultures of Cities* (Cambridge, Mass.: Blackwell, 1995).
41. Richard Florida and Gary Gates, "Technology and Tolerance: The Importance of Diversity to High-Technology Growth," Brookings Institution Center on Urban and Metropolitan Policy Survey Series paper, Brookings Institution Center on Urban and Metropolitan Policy Survey Series, Washington, D.C., 2001; and Richard Florida, "Competing in the Age of Talent," report prepared for the R. K. Mellon Foundation, Heinz Endowments, and Sustainable Pittsburgh [database online] (Pittsburgh, 2000); available from http://www.heinz.cmu.edu/~florida/talent.pdf; INTERNET.
42. Feagin, op. cit.
43. Feagin and Parker, op. cit.
44. Kee Warner and Harvey Molotch, *Building Rules: How Local Controls Shape Community Environments and Economies* (Boulder, Colo.: Westview Press, 1999), and "Power To Build: How Development Persists Despite Local Controls," *Urban Affairs Review* 30 (1995): 378–406; and Feagin and Parker, op. cit.
45. Cliff Kono et al., "Lost In Space: The Geography of Corporate Interlocking Directorates," *American Journal of Sociology* 103 (1998): 863–911.
46. Beth Mintz and Michael Schwartz, *The Power Structure of American Business* (Chicago: University of Chicago Press, 1985); Todd Swanstrom, *The Crisis of Growth Politics: Cleveland, Kucinich, and the Challenge of Urban Populism* (Philadelphia: Temple University Press, 1985); and R. Perrucci and M. Pilisuk, "Leaders and Ruling Elites: the Interorganizational Basis of Community Power," *American Sociological Review* 35 (1970): 1040–1057; cf. Michael Useem, *The Inner Circle: Large Corporations and the Rise of Business Political Activity in the U.S. and U.K.* (New York and Oxford: Oxford University Press, 1984).
47. Cf. Val Burris, "The Two Faces of Capital: Corporations and Individual Capitalists as Political Actors," *American Sociological Review* 66 (2001): 361–381.
48. Mark Gottdiener, *Planned Sprawl: Private and Public Interests in Suburbia* (Beverly Hills, Calif.: Sage Publications, 1977).
49. Cf. Mark S. Mizruchi, *The Structure of Corporate Political Action: Interfirm Relations and their Consequences* (Cambridge, Mass.: Harvard University Press, 1992); and Dan Clawson, Alan Neustadtl, and James Bearden, "The Logic of Business Unity: Corporate Contributions to the 1980 Congressional Elections," *American Sociological Review* 51 (1986): 797–811.
50. Joseph Galaskiewicz, *Social Organization of an Urban Grants Economy: A Study of Business Philanthropy and Nonprofit Organizations* (Orlando, Fla.: Academic Press, 1985).
51. William S. Hendon and Douglas V. Shaw, "The Arts and Urban Development," in *The Future of Winter Cities*, ed. G. Gappert (Newbury Park, Calif.: Sage, 1987), 209–217; and Sylvia Tesh, "In Support of 'Single-Issue' Politics," *Political Science Quarterly* 99 (1984): 27–44.
52. Alberta M. Sbragia, "Pittsburgh's 'Third Way': The Nonprofit Sector as a Key to Urban Regeneration," in *Leadership and Urban Regeneration*, ed. D. Judd and M. Parkinson (Newbury Park, Calif.: Sage, 1990), 51–68; and J. Allen Whitt, "Mozart in the Metropolis: The Arts Coalition and the Urban Growth Machine," *Urban Affairs Quarterly* 23 (1987): 15–36.
53. Daniel Bell, *The Coming of Post-Industrial Society* (New York: Basic Books, 1973); and Alain Touraine, *The Post-Industrial Society* (New York: Random House, 1971).
54. Ronald Inglehart, "Public Support for Environmental Protection: Objective Problems and Subjective Values in 43 Societies," *PS: Political Science and Politics* 28 (1995): 57–72; and Abramson and Inglehart, op. cit.
55. Harvey, op. cit.
56. Ash Amin, *Post-Fordism: A Reader* (Cambridge, Mass.: Blackwell, 1994); and Alain Lipietz, *Mirages and Miracles: The Crises of Global Fordism* (London: Verso, 1987).
57. Scott Lash and John Urry, *The End of Organized Capitalism* (Cambridge: Polity, 1987).
58. Thierry Noyelle, *Services and the New Economy: Toward a New Labor Market Segmentation* (New York: National Center on Education and Employment, 1988); Karl Albrecht and Ron Zemke, *Service America! Doing Business in the New Economy* (Homewood, Ill.: Dow Jones-Urwin, 1985); and Thomas M. Stanback, Jr. et al., *Services: The New Economy* (Towota, N.J.: Allanheld, Osmun, 1981).
59. Manuel Castells, *The Rise of the Network Society* (Cambridge, Mass.: Blackwell, 1996).

60. Manuel Castells, "Materials for an Exploratory Theory of the Network Society," *British Journal of Sociology* 51 (2000): 10–12.
61. See, e.g., Martin Neil Baily and Robert Z. Lawrence, "Do We Have a New Economy?" working paper no. 8243, National Bureau of Economic Research, Cambridge, Mass., 2001; William D. Nordhaus, "Productivity Growth and the New Economy," working paper no. 8096, National Bureau of Economic Research, Cambridge, Mass., 2001; and Michael A. Kouparitsas, "Is There Evidence of the New Economy in the Data?" working paper No. 99–21, Federal Reserve Bank of Chicago, Chicago, Ill., 1999.
62. Graham Tanaka, *Digital Deflation: Solving the Mystery of the New Economy, Ushering in a New Era of Prosperity* (London: McGraw-Hill, 2001).
63. R. D. Norton, *Creating the New Economy: The Entrepreneur and the U.S. Resurgence* (Cheltenham, U.K.: Edward Elgar, 2001); and Sandra E. Black and Lisa M. Lynch, "What's Driving the New Economy: The Benefits of Workplace Innovation," working paper no. 7479, National Bureau of Economic Research, Cambridge, Mass., 2000.
64. Kenichi Ochmae, *The Invisible Continent: Four Strategic Imperatives of the New Economy* (New York: Harper Business, 2000).
65. Peter Fingar and Ronald Aronica, *The Death of "E" and the Birth of the Real New Economy: Business Models, Technologies and Strategies for the 21st Century* (Tampa, Fla.: Meghan-Kiffer Press, 2001).
66. David Asch and Brian Wolfe, *New Economy—New Competition: The Rise of the Consumer?* (New York: St. Martins, 2001); and David Lewis, *The Soul of the New Consumer Authenticity: Why We Buy and What We Buy in the New Economy,* (London: Nicholas Brealey, 2000).
67. James D. Underwood, *Thriving in E-Chaos: How 10 Traditional Companies are Using Leadership, Technology, and Agility to Succeed in the New Economy* (Roseville, Calif.: Prima Venture, 2001).
68. Thomas Winninger, *Full Price: Competing on Value in the New Economy* (Chicago: Dearborn, 2001); and Philip Evans and Thomas S. Wurster, *Blown to Bits: How the New Economics of Information Transforms Strategy* (Boston: Harvard Business School Press, 2000).
69. Tony Smith, *Technology and Capital in the Age of Lean Production: A Marxian Critique of the "New Economy"* (Albany, N.Y.: State University of New York Press, 2000).
70. Cf. Sayer and Walker, op. cit.
71. Logan, op. cit.
72. To keep the proliferation of new and often redundant concepts to a minimum, I borrow the "new industrial space" from Manuel Castells, who conceptualizes it more narrowly to describe the geographical dynamics of technology sectors; Manuel Castells, *The Rise of the Network Society* (Cambridge, Mass.: Blackwell, 1996), 386–393. In this book, I invest the term with a broader concern in industrial geography (which Castells shares) for how industries and their endogenous growth dynamics create industrial sites and their locational qualities; see, e.g., Sayer and Walker, op. cit. chap. 3; and Storper and Walker, op. cit.
73. Manuel Castells, "Materials for an Exploratory Theory of the Network Society," *British Journal of Sociology* 51 (2000): 12.
74. Harvey Molotch, "The Political Economy of Growth Machines," *Journal of Urban Affairs* 15 (1993): 29–53.
75. Norman Krumholz and Pierre Clavel, "Snapshot, 1978," in *Reinventing Cities: Equity Planners Tell Their Stories,* ed. N. Krumholz and P. Clavel (Philadelphia: Temple University Press, 1994), 190.
76. Derek Shearer, "Interview with Derek Shearer," in *Reinventing Cities: Equity Planners Tell Their Stories,* ed. N. Krumholz and P. Clavel (Philadelphia: Temple University Press, 1994), 192–206; and Pierre Clavel, *The Progressive City: Planning and Participation, 1969–1984* (New Brunswick, N.J.: Rutgers, 1986).
77. Kee Warner, Harvey Molotch, and Amy Lategola, *Growth Control: Inner Workings and External Effects* (Berkeley: California Policy Seminar, University of California, 1992).
78. Kenneth Starr, *Material Dreams: Southern California Through the 1920s* (New York: Oxford University Press, 1990).
79. Otis L. Graham Jr. et al., *Stearns Wharf: Surviving Change on the California Coast,* Public Historical Studies Monograph No. 11. (Santa Barbara, Calif.: Graduate Program in Public Historical Studies, University of California, Santa Barbara, 1994), 57.
80. Harvey Molotch and William Freudenburg, *Santa Barbara County: Two Paths,* OCS Study MMS 96-0036 under contract no. 14-35-001-30663 (Camarillo, Calif.: U.S. Department of Interior, Minerals Management Service, Pacific Region, 1996).
81. Barbara Epstein, *Political Protest and Cultural Revolution: Nonviolent Direct Action in the 1970s and 1980s* (Berkeley: University of California Press, 1991).

82. Rose McKeen, *Parade Along the Creek: Memories of Growing Up with San Luis Obispo* (San Luis Obispo, Calif.: Rose McKeen, 1988).

83. Reported in Karen Kaplan, "The Sky's the Limit," *Los Angeles Times,* June 16, 1988.

84. Matthew A. Zook, "The Web of Consumption: The Economic Geography of Commercial Internet Content Production in the United States," *Environment and Planning A* 32 (2000): 416.

85. Quoted in Ben Fritz, "Study of L.A. VC Investment Illustrates Dominance of Westside, Names Top Area Investors," in *Digital Coast Daily* [electronic bulletin] (cited January 25, 2001); available from http://www.digitalcoastdaily.com; INTERNET.

86. See Edward J. Malecki, *Technology and Economic Development: The Dynamics of Local, Regional, and National Change,* 2d ed. (New York: Longman Scientific & Technical and John Wiley & Sons, 1997), 17.

87. Reported in Kaplan, op. cit.

88. Many so-called entertainment firms in Santa Barbara and San Luis Obispo are actually broadcasting stations and motion picture production services. One might reasonably argue that these standard industrial codes inaccurately correspond to my definition of entertainment firms; however, they accurately classify important entertainment firms in Santa Monica (such as cable networks and post-production facilities), which is why I kept them here.

89. Dean Runyan Associates, *California Travel Impacts by County, 1992–1995* (Portland, Ore.: Dean Runyan Associates, 1997), 12.

90. David L. Gladstone and Susan S. Fainstein, "Tourism in U.S. Global Cities: A Comparison of New York and Los Angeles," *Journal of Urban Affairs* 23 (2001): 30.

91. Christopher M. Law, *Urban Tourism: Attracting Visitors to Large Cities* (London: Mansell, 1993), 109.

92. See Richard Pillsbury, *From Boarding House to Bistro* (Boston: Unwin Hyman, 1990), 183.

93. Stephen L. J. Smith, "Defining Tourism: A Supply-Side View," *Annals of Tourism Research* 13 (1988): 179–190.

94. See Susan S. Fainstein and Dennis R. Judd, "Global Forces, Local Strategies, and Urban Tourism," in *The Tourism City,* ed. Dennis R. Judd and Susan S. Fainstein (New Haven, Conn.: Yale University Press, 1999), 4.

CHAPTER TWO

1. Greg Miller, "Pretenders to Silicon Valley's Throne," *Los Angeles Times,* March 8, 1998.

2. Alfred Weber, *Alfred Weber's Theory of the Location of Industries* (Chicago: University of Chicago Press, 1929).

3. Allen J. Scott, *Technopolis: High-Technology Industry and Regional Development in Southern California* (Berkeley: University of California Press, 1993), and *New Industrial Spaces: Flexible Production, Organisation and Regional Development in North America and Western Europe* (London: Pion, 1988); and Michael Storper and Richard Walker, *The Capitalist Imperative: Territory, Technology, and Industrial Growth* (Oxford: Blackwell, 1989).

4. Ash Amin, *Post-Fordism: A Reader* (Cambridge, Mass.: Blackwell, 1994); and David Harvey, *The Condition of Postmodernity: An Enquiry into the Origins of Cultural Change* (Cambridge, Mass.: Blackwell, 1989).

5. Andrew Sayer and Richard Walker, *The New Social Economy: Reworking the Division of Labor* (Cambridge, Mass.: Blackwell, 1992); see also M. Goodwin, S. Duncan and S. Halford, "Regulation Theory, the Local State, and the Transition of Urban Politics," *Environment and Planning D: Society and Space* 11 (1993): 67–88.

6. Peter Dicken et al., "Chains and Networks, Territories and Scales: Towards a Relational Framework for Analysing the Global Economy," *Global Networks* 1 (2001): 89–112.

7. Andrew E. G. Jonas, "Local Labour Control Regimes: Uneven Development and the Social Regulation of Production," *Regional Studies* 30 (1996): 323–338; and Storper and Walker, op. cit.

8. David Harvey, *The Limits to Capital* (Chicago: University of Chicago Press, 1982).

9. Ann Markusen, "Sticky Places in Slippery Space: A Typology of Industrial District," *Economic Geography* 72 (1996): 294–314.

10. Allen J. Scott, *Technopolis: High-Technology Industry and Regional Development in Southern California* (Berkeley: University of California Press, 1993).

11. Storper and Walker, op. cit.

12. Ibid.

13. Neil Gabler, *An Empire of their Own: How the Jews Invented Hollywood* (New York: Crown, 1988); and Danae Clark, *Negotiating Hollywood: The Cultural Politics of Actors' Labor* (Minneapolis: University of Minnesota Press: 1995).

14. David Harvey, *The Condition of Postmodernity: An Enquiry into the Origins of Cultural Change* (Cambridge, Mass.: Blackwell, 1989).

15. Markusen, op. cit.

16. Amy Glasmeier, "Factors Governing the Development of High Tech Industry Agglomerations: A Tale of Three Cities," *Regional Studies* 22 (1988): 287–301; and Roger Friedland and Donald Palmer, "Park Place and Main Street: Business and the Urban Power Structure," *Annual Review of Sociology* 10 (1984): 393–416.

17. John Mollenkopf, *The Contested City* (Princeton, N.J.: Princeton University Press, 1983).

18. Manuel Castells, "Materials for an Exploratory Theory of the Network Society," *British Journal of Sociology* 51 (2000): 12. Robert Reich offers a similar explanation with his idea of "symbolic analysts"; Robert B. Reich, *The Work of Nations* (New York: Vintage, 1992), 177.

19. Jeremy Howells, "The Location and Organisation of Research and Development: New Horizons," *Research Policy* 19 (1990): 133–146.

20. Edward J. Malecki, "Corporate Organization of R and D and the Location of Technological Activities," *Regional Studies* 14 (1980): 219–234.

21. Ibid.

22. Mark Van de Kamp, "Local Defense Industry Pioneer Dies," *Santa Barbara News-Press*, June 29, 1996.

23. Susan S. Fainstein and David Gladstone, "Evaluating Urban Tourism," in *The Tourism City,* ed. D. R. Judd and S. S. Fainstein (New Haven, Conn.: Yale University Press, 1999), 21–34; and John Urry, *The Tourist Gaze: Leisure and Travel in Contemporary Societies* (London: Sage, 1990).

24. Dennis R. Judd, "Constructing the Tourist Bubble," in *The Tourism City,* ed. D. R. Judd and S. S. Fainstein (New Haven, Conn.: Yale University Press, 1999), 35–53. I borrow the term "amenity infrastructure" from William S. Hendon and Douglas V. Shaw, "The Arts and Urban Development," in *The Future of Winter Cities,* ed. G. Gappert (Newbury Park, Calif.: Sage, 1987), 215.

25. Susan S. Fainstein and Dennis R. Judd, "Global Forces, Local Strategies, and Urban Tourism," in *The Tourism City,* ed. D. R. Judd and S. S. Fainstein (New Haven, Conn.: Yale University Press, 1999), 11.

26. John Urry, *Consuming Places* (London: Routledge, 1995).

27. But see John Hannigan, *Fantasy City: Pleasure and Profit in the Postmodern Metropolis* (New York: Routledge, 1998); and Maureen G. Reed, "Power Relations and Community-Based Tourism Planning," *Annals of Tourism Research* 24 (1997): 566–591.

28. Christopher M. Law, *Urban Tourism: Attracting Visitors to Large Cities* (London: Mansell, 1993), 113.

29. Harvey, op. cit.

30. Susan Christopherson, "Flexibility and Adaptation in Industrial Relations: The Exceptional Case of the U.S. Media Entertainment Industries," in *Under the Stars: Essays on Labor Relations in Arts and Entertainment,* ed. L. S. Gray and R. L. Seeber (Ithaca, N.Y.: ILR Press/Cornell, 1996), 86–112.

31. Amin, op. cit.

32. AnnaLee Saxenian, *Regional Advantage: Culture and Competition in Silicon Valley and Route 128* (Cambridge, Mass.: Harvard University Press, 1994); and Scott, op. cit.

33. A. Marshall, *Elements of Economics of Industry* (New York: Macmillan Marshall, 1900).

34. Markusen, op. cit.; and Michael J. Piore and Charles F. Sabel, *The Second Industrial Divide: Possibilities for Prosperity* (New York: Basic Books, 1984).

35. Michael Storper, "The Resurgence of Regional Economies, Ten Years Later: The Region as a Nexus of Untraded Interdependencies," in *The Economic Geography Reader: Producing and Consuming Global Capitalism,* ed. J. Bryson et al. (New York: John Wiley & Sons, 1999), 209–215.

36. Storper and Walker, op. cit., and Paul David, "CLIO and the Economics of QWERTY," *American Economic Review* 75 (1986): 332–337.

37. See Peter Dicken, *Global Shift: The Internationalization of Economic Activity,* 2d ed. (New York: Guilford Press, 1992).

38. E.g., Dennis Hayes, *Behind the Silicon Curtain: The Seduction of Work in a Lonely Era* (Boston: South End Press, 1989).

39. Douglas Henton, "Lessons from Silicon Valley," in *Global City-Regions: Trends, Theory, Policy,* ed. Allen J. Scott (Oxford: Oxford University Press, 2001), 394; and Martin Kenney and Urs von Burg, "Institutions and Economies: Creating Silicon Valley," in *Understanding Silicon Valley: The Anatomy of an Entrepreneurial Region,* ed. M. Kenney (Stanford, Calif.: Stanford University Press, 2000), 218–240.

40. Hillary Atkin, "IBM Brings its E-Business to Santa Monica Next," in *Digital Coast Weekly* [e-mail listserv] (2000 [cited March 30, 2000]).

41. See also Allen J. Scott, *The Cultural Economy of Cities* (London: Sage, 2000), 2–23; and Manuel Castells, *The Rise of the Network Society* (Cambridge, Mass.: Blackwell, 1996), 159.

42. Storper and Walker, op. cit., p. 48.

43. Homa Bahrami and Stuart Evans, "Flexible Recycling and High-Technology Entrepreneurship," in *Understanding Silicon Valley: The Anatomy of an Entrepreneurial Region,* ed. M. Kenney (Stanford, Calif.: Stanford University Press, 2000), 165–189.

44. This corporate strategy of impermanence also manifests itself in the circuits of capital, in which firms may receive massive infusions of capital from private investors and, later, the stock market, only to merge with a larger company upon the success of their product or go bankrupt upon its failure. The notion that firms can be "built to flip" (Jim Collins, "Built to Flip," *Fast Company,* March, no. 32 [2000]: 131) may have lost favor since the dot-com crash, but its rationale nevertheless poses analytical problems for organizational ecology and other schools of thought that presume that organizational survival is the primary goal for firms. Bahrami and Evans, op. cit.; cf. James N. Baron, Michael T. Hannan, and M. Diane Burton, "Labor Pains: Change in Organizational Models and Employee Turnover in Young, High-Tech Firms," *American Journal of Sociology* 106 (2001): 960–1012.

45. Mark C. Suchman, "Developers and Counselors: Law Firms as Intermediaries in the Development of Silicon Valley," in *Understanding Silicon Valley: The Anatomy of an Entrepreneurial Region,* ed. M. Kenney (Stanford, Calif.: Stanford University Press, 2000), 71–97; and Martin Kenney and Richard Florida, "Venture Capital in Silicon Valley: Fueling New Firm Formation," in *Understanding Silicon Valley: The Anatomy of an Entrepreneurial Region,* ed. M. Kenney (Stanford, Calif.: Stanford University Press, 2000), 98–123.

46. Christopherson, op. cit.

47. See, e.g., Neil M. Coe, "On Location: American Capital and the Local Labour Market in the Vancouver Film Industry," *International Journal of Urban and Regional Research* 24 (2000): 79–94.

48. Reported in James Bates, "Productions Flee to Canada," *Los Angeles Times,* June 25, 1999. For a rebuttal to the Screen Actors Guild and the Directors Guild of America report, see Allan King, "Canada Replies to Alarmed U.S. Filmmakers Who Want It All," *Los Angeles Times,* July 30, 1999.

49. Allen J. Scott, "The U.S. Recorded Music Industry: On the Relations Between Organization, Location, and Creativity in the Cultural Economy," *Environment and Planning A* 31 (1999): 1965–1984.

50. Richard Sennett, *The Corrosion of Character: The Personal Consequences of Work in the New Capitalism* (New York: W.W. Norton, 1998); and Barry Bluestone and Bennett Harrison, *The Deindustrialization of America: Plant Closings, Community Abandonment, and the Dismantling of Basic Industry* (New York: Basic Books, 1982).

51. Cf. Richard Florida and Martin Kenney, *The Breakthrough Illusion: Corporate America's Failure to Move from Innovation to Mass Production* (New York: Basic Books, 1990).

52. Salim Lakha, "The New International Division of Labour and the Indian Computer Software Industry," in *The Economic Geography Reader: Producing and Consuming Global Capitalism,* ed. J. Bryson et al. (New York: John Wiley & Sons, 1999), 148–155.

53. E. J. Davelaar and P. Nijkamp, "The Role of the Metropolitan Milieu as an Incubation Centre for Technological Innovations: A Dutch Case Study," *Urban Studies* 26 (1989): 517–525.

54. Paulina Borsook, *Cyberselfish: A Critical Romp Through the Terribly Libertarian Culture of High-Tech* (New York: Public Affairs, 2000); Richard Barbrook and Andy Cameron, "The Californian Ideology," *Science as Culture* 6 (1996): 44–72; and Stephen S. Cohen and Gary Fields, "Social Capital and Capital Gains: An Examination of Social Capital in Silicon Valley," in *Understanding Silicon Valley: The Anatomy of an Entrepreneurial Region,* ed. M. Kenney (Stanford, Calif.: Stanford University Press, 2000), 190–217.

55. See David Hesmondhalgh, "Flexibility, Post-Fordism and the Music Industries," *Media, Culture & Society* 18 (1996): 469–488; and A. Aksoy and K. Robins, "Hollywood for the 21st Century: Global Competition for Critical Mass in Image Markets," *Cambridge Journal of Economics* 16 (1992): 1–22.

56. Richard E. Caves, *Creative Industries: Contracts between Art and Commerce* (Cambridge, Mass.: Harvard University Press, 2000); and William T. Bielby and Denise D. Bielby, "Organizational Mediation of Project-Based Labor Markets: Talent Agencies and the Careers of Screenwriters," *American Sociological Review* 64 (1999): 64–85.

57. Scott Lash and John Urry, *Economies of Signs and Spaces* (London: Sage, 1994).

58. Susan Christopherson and Michael Storper, "The Effects of Flexible Specialization on Industrial Politics and the Labor Market: The Motion Picture Industry," *Industrial and Labor Relations Review* 42 (1989): 340.

59. Janet Wasko, *Hollywood in the Information Age: Beyond the Silver Screen* (Austin: University of Texas Press, 1995).

60. Christopherson and Storper, op. cit.

61. See Richard Florida, *The Rise of the Creative Class* (New York, Basic Books, 2002), 224.

62. One trade journal article advises, "Programming, senior management, and occasionally marketing are generally the only positions worth using a recruiter for." Stacy Cowley, "Employee Finders and Keepers," *Silicon Alley Reporter* 4(2) (2000): 88.

63. The currency of American technology sectors' demand for skilled foreign labor is the H-1B, a three-to-six-year visa issued to foreign job candidates who demonstrate a specialized knowledge. For a discussion of how the immigration of skilled workers has dramatically transformed Silicon Valley, see AnnaLee Saxenian, *Silicon Valley's New Immigrant Entrepreneurs* (San Francisco: Public Policy Institute of California, 1999).
64. Lisa Ammerman, "Choosey Pays," *Silicon Alley Reporter* 5(5) (2001): 54.
65. Data gathered by Joint Venture Silicon Valley indicated that wages for software employees in Silicon Valley averaged $95,800 in 1998, thereby outpacing all other Silicon Valley sectors (e.g., semiconductors, bioscience, professional services). In 1999, after accounting for inflation Silicon Valley's average wage grew 5.1 percent to $53,700, compared to a national increase of 3.4 percent to $33,700. See http://www.jointventure.org/resources/2000Index/trends.html.
66. Markusen, op. cit.
67. Manuel Castells, *The Informational City: Information Technology, Economic Restructuring and the Urban-Regional Process* (Oxford: Blackwell, 1989), 82.
68. E.g., Baron, Hannan, and Burton, op. cit.
69. David Alm, "Code and Corona: Corporate Life in Silicon Alley," *Silicon Alley Reporter* 4(3) (2000): 36.
70. Manuel Castells and Peter Hall, *Technopoles of the World* (Oxford: Blackwell, 1994); and AnnaLee Saxenian, *Regional Advantage: Culture and Competition in Silicon Valley and Route 128* (Cambridge, Mass.: Harvard University Press, 1994).
71. Borsook, op. cit., p. 178.
72. "Company town" is also the business section heading for the *Los Angeles Times*'s entertainment industry news.
73. Perhaps the most famous film industry gathering, the annual Academy Awards, is usually held at one of two downtown Los Angeles venues, the Dorothy Chandler Pavilion or the Shrine Theater—a rare occasion when the industry collectively congregates in a local setting outside the usual territorial limits of the company town. As of this writing, there are plans to move the ceremonies to a similarly peripheral facility in the new "Hollywood and Highland" development, an urban entertainment district in Hollywood proper spearheaded by the developers responsible for the Times Square renovation in New York City.
74. Scott, op. cit., 1972; see also Paul M. Hirsch, "Processing Fads and Fashions: An Organization-Set Analysis of Cultural Industry Systems," *American Journal of Sociology* 77 (1972): 650.
75. Saxenian, op. cit.
76. Michael Storper and Susan Christopherson, *The Changing Location and Organization of the Motion Picture Industry: Interregional Shifts in the United States* (Los Angeles: School of Architecture and Urban Planning, University of California, Los Angeles, 1985).
77. Quoted in Lynell George, "Hollywood Balancing Act," *Los Angeles Times,* May 20, 2001.
78. Linda Beth Mothner, "Modest Beginnings" *Los Angeles Times,* August 30, 1998.
79. Richard Florida, *The Rise of the Creative Class* (New York: Basic Books, 2002), 135.
80. David Brooks, *Bobos in Paradise: The New Upper Class and How They Got There* (New York: Simon and Schuster, 2000), 134.
81. See Florida, op. cit., 10; Piore and Sabel, op. cit., and Larry Hirshhorn, *Beyond Mechanization* (Cambridge, Mass.: MIT Press, 1984).
82. Charles S. Varano, *Forced Choices: Class, Community, and Worker Ownership* (Albany, N.Y.: State University of New York Press, 1999).
83. David L. Gladstone and Susan S. Fainstein, "Tourism in U.S. Global Cities: A Comparison of New York and Los Angeles," *Journal of Urban Affairs* 23 (2001): 34.
84. In this regard, tourism trade associations reinforce lobbying by the Alliance of Small Businesses, the National Manufacturers Association, the Chambers of Commerce, and agricultural associations to reduce national enforcement of illegal immigration. See Claudio Sanchez, "September 11th's Effect on Immigration Politics," *All Things Considered,* National Public Radio, October 22, 2001.

CHAPTER THREE

1. Miguel Helft, "Sun, Sand & Silicon," *Los Angeles Times,* January 20, 1997.
2. Richard V. Knight, "City Development and Urbanization: Building the Knowledge Based City," in *Cities in a Global Society,* ed. R. V. Knight and G. Gappert (Newbury Park, Calif.: Sage, 1989), 237.
3. Paul D. Gottlieb, "Amenities as an Economic Development Tool: Is There Enough Evidence?" *Economic Development Quarterly* 8 (1994): 276.
4. Richard Florida and Gary Gates, "Technology and Tolerance: The Importance of Diversity to High-Technology Growth," Brookings Institution Center on Urban and Metropolitan Policy Survey Series paper, Brookings Institution Center on Urban and Metropolitan Policy Survey Series, Washington,

D.C., 2001; and Richard Florida, "Competing in the Age of Talent," report prepared for the R. K. Mellon Foundation, Heinz Endowments, and Sustainable Pittsburgh [database online] (Pittsburgh, 2000); available from http://www.heinz.cmu.edu/~florida/talent.pdf; INTERNET.

5. Joel Kotkin, *The New Geography* (New York: Random House, 2000); and Richard Florida, *The Rise of the Creative Class* (New York, Basic Books, 2002).

6. Michael Storper and Richard Walker, *The Capitalist Imperative: Territory, Technology, and Industrial Growth* (Oxford: Blackwell, 1989), 172.

7. Edward J. Malecki, *Technology and Economic Development: The Dynamics of Local, Regional, and National Change*, 2d ed. (New York: Longman Scientific & Technical and John Wiley & Sons, 1997), 126; and Manuel Castells, *The Informational City: Information Technology, Economic Restructuring and the Urban-Regional Process* (Oxford: Blackwell, 1989), 52.

8. On random locational effects, see C. Thompson, "High-Technology Theories and Public Policy," *Environment and Planning C: Government and Policy* 7 (1989): 135.

9. I refer to the ideas of "public choice" theorists, e.g., Paul E. Peterson, *City Limits* (Chicago: University of Chicago Press, 1981); and Charles M. Tiebout, "A Pure Theory of Local Expenditures," *Journal of Political Economy* 64 (1956), 416–424.

10. Roberto Camagni, "The Economic Role and Spatial Contradictions of Global City-Regions: The Functional, Cognitive, and Evolutionary Context," in *Global City-Regions: Trends, Theory, Policy*, ed. A. J. Scott (Oxford: Oxford University Press, 2001), 96–118.

11. AnnaLee Saxenian, "The Urban Contradictions of Silicon Valley: Regional Growth and the Restructuring of the Semiconductor Industry," in *Sunbelt Snowbelt: Urban Development and Regional Restructuring*, ed. L. Sawers and W. K. Tabb (New York and Oxford: Oxford University Press, 1984), 163–197; Philip J. Troustine and Terry Christensen, *Movers and Shakers: The Study of Community Power* (New York: St. Martin's Press, 1982); and Karl Belser, "The Making of Slurban America," *Cry California* 5 (1970): 1–18.

12. Median home price data come from the California Association of Realtors. In 1990, San Francisco and San Jose, the urban poles of Silicon Valley, ranked second and third, respectively, in highest median housing values in the United States.

13. Quoted in Charles Piller, "High-Tech Model of Inconsistency," *Los Angeles Times,* January 9, 1999.

14. On "technostress" see Manuel Castells and Peter Hall, *Technopoles of the World* (Oxford: Blackwell, 1994), 23.

15. Ulrich Beck, *Risk Society: Towards a New Modernity* (London: Sage, 1992).

16. Castells and Hall, op. cit., p. 26.

17. Richard Sennett, *The Corrosion of Character: The Personal Consequences of Work in the New Capitalism* (New York: W. W. Norton, 1998); and William T. Bielby and Denise D. Bielby, "The Hollywood 'Graylist'? Audience Demographics and Age Stratification among Television Writers," *Current Research on Occupations and Professions* 8 (1993): 141–172.

18. Paulina Borsook, *Cyberselfish: A Critical Romp Through the Terribly Libertarian Culture of High-Tech* (New York: Public Affairs, 2000). A 1984 survey of Silicon Valley workers found that job satisfaction increased with number of hours worked. Cited in Castells and Hall, op. cit., p. 22.

19. Quoted in Marianne Cooper, "Being the 'Go-To Guy': Fatherhood, Masculinity, and the Organization of Work in Silicon Valley," *Qualitative Sociology* 23 (2000): 383–384.

20. Brooke Wirtschafter, "Get a Life!" *Digital Coast Reporter* 4(2) (2001): 8.

21. Reuters, "Tech Workers Turning Tail?" *Wired News* [electronic bulletin], February 10, 2000, http://www.wired.com/news/business/0,1367,34274,00.html.

22. Florida, op. cit., 16.

23. On spatial structures of regulation, see Marshall M. A. Feldman, "Spacial Structures of Regulation and Urban Regimes," in *Reconstructing Urban Regime Theory: Regulating Urban Politics in a Global Economy*, ed. M. Lauria (Thousand Oaks, Calif.: Sage, 1997), 31.

24. On "affluent downshifters," see Juliet B. Schor, *The Overspent American* (New York: Harper Collins, 1999).

25. Quoted in Silas Lyons, "Film Sound System Company is Planting Some Local Roots," *San Luis Obispo Telegram-Tribune*, July 23, 1997, n.p.

26. Quoted in Lynell George, "Hollywood Balancing Act," *Los Angeles Times,* May 20, 2001.

27. Michael Storper and Susan Christopherson, *The Changing Location and Organization of the Motion Picture Industry: Interregional Shifts in the United States* (Los Angeles: School of Architecture and Urban Planning, University of California, Los Angeles, 1985).

28. For example, working on three- to six-month projects like motion pictures allows special effects houses to be located within a day's drive to a studio or other site of production coordination; geographically, this means as far away from Hollywood as Santa Barbara or ostensibly San Luis Obispo. Two- to four-week projects like commercials, however, require more rapid face-to-face interaction;

when firms and workers work on several projects simultaneously (up to five projects is not unusual), their interaction will be shorter and more frequent than in longer projects. Shorter projects disadvantage firms and workers located outside the metropolis and therefore reinforce the territorial concentration of production activities and networks in Hollywood.

29. Harvey Molotch, John Woolley, and Teri Jori, "Growing Firms in Declining Fields: Unanticipated Impacts of Oil Development," *Society and Natural Resources* 11 (1998): 145; and P. Reynolds, "New Firms: Enhancing their Growth," *Economic Development Commentary* 13 (1989): 8.

30. Quoted in Silas Lyons, "SLO Company's Epic Computer Game Poised for Worldwide Debut," *San Luis Obispo Telegram-Tribune*, September 16, 1997.

31. See Gottlieb, op. cit., p. 280.

32. Manuel Castells, *The Informational City: Information Technology, Economic Restructuring and the Urban-Regional Process* (Oxford: Blackwell, 1989).

33. Sarah E. Moran, "Best New Places To Do Business for Tech. Companies," *The Industry Standard*, February 19, 2001, 80–84.

34. Rebecca Solnit and Susan Schwartzenberg, *Hollow City* (London: Verso, 2000); Christopher Mele, *Selling the Lower East Side* (Minneapolis: University of Minnesota Press, 2000); and Richard Lloyd, "The Digital Bohemia" (paper presented at the annual meeting of the American Sociological Association, Anaheim, Calif., August 21, 2001).

35. P. Haug, "Regional Formation of High-Technology Service Industries: The Software Industry in Washington State," *Environment and Planning A* 23 (1991): 880.

36. In its 1998 list of America's 300 most livable cities, *Money* ranked San Luis Obispo as the second-best place to live among smaller towns in the West; Fort Collins, Colorado, came in first.

37. Although, by many standards, San Luis Obispo's median housing costs are still prohibitive, for Silicon Valley migrants it often represents a benefit. One software executive told me, "Selling my home, which was nothing spectacular, in Sunnyvale to move down here, I sold it for nearly $600,000 and came down here and found that I couldn't spend that much on a house; there's no way."

38. Mark Gottdiener, *The Theming of America: Dreams, Visions, and Commercial Spaces* (Boulder, CO: Westview, 1997); and John Urry, *The Tourist Gaze: Leisure and Travel in Contemporary Societies* (London: Sage, 1990).

39. Stella M. Capek and John I. Gilderbloom, *Community Versus Commodity: Tenants and the American City* (Albany, N.Y.: State University of New York Press, 1992), 58.

40. Mele, op. cit.

41. Walker A. Tompkins, *Santa Barbara Past and Present* (Santa Barbara, Calif.: Tecolote Books, 1975).

42. Robert A. Beauregard, *Voices of Decline: The Post-War Fate of US Cities* (Cambridge, Mass.: Blackwell, 1993).

43. Mike Davis, *Ecology of Fear: Los Angeles and the Imagination of Disaster* (New York: Metropolitan Books, 1998), and *City of Quartz: Excavating the Future in Los Angeles* (London: Verso, 1990).

44. Urry, op. cit., p. 2.

45. E.g., C. M. Hall and S. J. Page, *The Geography of Tourism and Recreation: Environment, Place and Space* (London: Routledge, 1999); and Christopher M. Law, *Urban Tourism: Attracting Visitors to Large Cities* (London: Mansell, 1993).

46. Scott Lash and John Urry, *Economies of Signs and Spaces* (London: Sage, 1994).

47. Urry, op. cit., p. 57.

48. This is not to say that tourists and quality-of-life migrants consume the *same* set of place amenities. Indeed, their respective sets can comprise conflicting landscapes, as revealed when residents avoid congested "tourist bubbles" and complain about visitors "running over" their town. Sometimes the two landscapes, however, are sequentially related. Future quality-of-life migrants may first discover their soon-to-be hometown as a visitor and later inhabit the less-well-known residential areas, or they may first visit as guests of residents who show them firsthand "how we live here." On "tourist bubbles," see Dennis R. Judd, "Constructing the Tourist Bubble," in *The Tourism City*, ed. D. R. Judd and S. S. Fainstein (New Haven, Conn.: Yale University Press, 1999), 35–53.

49. Pierre Bourdieu, *Distinction* (London: Routledge, 1984).

50. Shared also, e.g., by Mike Savage et al., *Property, Bureaucracy and Culture: Middle-Class Formation in Contemporary Britain* (London: Routledge, 1992); and Urry, op. cit.

51. On reliability wages, see Annemieke Roobeek, "The Crisis of Fordism and the Rise of a New Technological Paradigm," *Futures* 19 (1987): 129–154.

52. Quoted in Karen Kaplan, "Tech Coast: Entrepreneurs and Officials Seek to Ride an Innovation Wave to Rival That of Silicon Valley," *Los Angeles Times*, March 9, 1998.

53. Urry, op. cit.

54. Richard Lloyd and Terry Nichols Clark, "The City as an Entertainment Machine," *Critical Perspectives on Urban Redevelopment* 6 (2001): 357; and Lash and Urry, op. cit., p. 271.

55. Richard Lloyd, "The Digital Bohemia" (paper presented at the annual meeting of the American Sociological Association, Anaheim, Calif., August 21, 2001), 26; see also Mele, op. cit.

CHAPTER FOUR

1. See Clarence N. Stone, *Regime Politics: Governing Atlanta, 1946–1988* (Lawrence, Kans.: University of Kansas Press, 1989), and "Systemic Power in Community Decision Making: A Restatement of Stratification Theory," *American Political Science Review* 74 (1980): 978–990.
2. Cf. Donald A. Palmer and Roger Friedland, "Corporation, Class, and City System," in *Intercorporate Relations: The Structural Analysis of Business,* ed. M. S. Mizruchi and M. Schwartz (Cambridge, U.K.: Cambridge University Press, 1987), 166–167.
3. E.g., George F. Colony, "My View: Hollow.Com," Forrester corporate website [database online] (2000 [cited May 26, 2000]); available from http://www.forrester.com/ER/Marketing/0,1503,183, FF.html; INTERNET.
4. In Santa Barbara, a developer of R&D campuses and other high-technology office sites explained his "rule of thumb" to calculate spatial dimensions for software firms: roughly two hundred square feet per employee. Thus, a one-thousand-square-foot space can comfortably house two to three employees. In denser urban settings like New York City, by contrast, "modest estimates" go down to one hundred to 125 square feet per employee. Andy Pelander, "Real Estate Blues," *Silicon Alley Reporter* 4(2) (2000): 104.
5. Rebecca Solnit and Susan Schwartzenberg, *Hollow City* (London: Verso, 2000), 120.
6. See Paul D. Gottlieb, "Residential Amenities, Firm Location and Economic Development," *Urban Studies* 32 (1995): 1413–1436.
7. Anna Dorfman, "Real Estate: Finding Office Space in a Tight Market," *Digital Coast Reporter* 3(4) (2000): 60.
8. Richard Lloyd, "The Digital Bohemia" (paper presented at the annual meeting of the American Sociological Association, Anaheim, Calif., August 21, 2001); Solnit and Schwartzenberg, op. cit.; and Christopher Mele, *Selling the Lower East Side* (Minneapolis: University of Minnesota Press, 2000).
9. Reported in Karen Kaplan, "The Sky's the Limit," *Los Angeles Times,* June 16, 1998.
10. Quoted in Melinda Fulmer, "Clean Sweep: Landlords Woo Tech and Show Biz Firms, Turn Others Away," *Los Angeles Times,* February 24, 1998.
11. Quoted in Duke Helfand, "Artists Fight to Save their Endangered Retreat," *Los Angeles Times,* January 19, 1997.
12. James Bates, "Reality Is, DreamWorks Never Needed a Studio," *Los Angeles Times,* July 30, 1999.
13. In the contentious negotiations over the expansion proposal, MCA/Universal volunteered to recognize the city's living wage ordinance (which usually applies only to city contractors) for its Universal Studios employees. Its agreement was seen by many as a major and unexpected concession to Los Angeles's labor movement, which has emphasized living wages in recent voter registration and unionization efforts.
14. Cf. Christopher M. Law, *Urban Tourism: Attracting Visitors to Large Cities* (London: Mansell, 1993), 115–116.
15. Richard Foglesong, "Walt Disney World and Orlando: Deregulation as a Strategy for Tourism," in *The Tourism City,* ed. D. R. Judd and S. S. Fainstein (New Haven, Conn.: Yale University Press, 1999), 89–106.
16. Dorfman, op. cit., p. 60, and "The Westside Market: One Dot-com's Hell May Be Another One's Heaven," *Digital Coast Daily* (electronic bulletin), May 3, 2001.
17. Andrew Wood, "Organizing for Local Economic Development: The Growth Coalition as a Cross-National Comparative Framework," in *The Urban Growth Machine: Critical Perspectives Two Decades Later* (Albany, N.Y.: State University of New York Press, 1999), 163–176, and "Analysing the Politics of Local Economic Development: Making Sense of Cross-National Convergence," *Urban Studies* 33 (1996): 1281–1295.
18. Martin Kenney and Urs von Burg, "Institutions and Economies: Creating Silicon Valley," in *Understanding Silicon Valley: The Anatomy of an Entrepreneurial Region,* ed. M. Kenney (Stanford, Calif.: Stanford University Press, 2000), 227.
19. Quoted in C. J. Hughes, "Heading for the Exit Doors," *Silicon Alley Reporter* 5(5) (2001): 36.
20. This occurred after I gathered data on corporate philanthropy to environmental organizations and so is not reported in Chapter 7, Table 7.2.
21. Peter Katz, co-author of *The New Urbanism* (Peter Katz and Vincent Scully, *The New Urbanism: Toward an Architecture of Community* [New York: McGraw Hill, 1994]), is a notable supporter of the Playa Vista project, having advocated the project in his book as well as an April 8, 1996 letter to the editor of Santa Monica's local newspaper (*The Outlook*).

22. Under the settlement terms of the lawsuit settlement, Maguire Thomas Partners scaled down the proposed development and pledged $12.5 million toward wetlands restoration agreed to by the Friends of the Ballona Wetlands coalition. In a claim that other environmentalists have contested, Friends co-founder Ruth Lansford argued that Maguire Thomas Partners had thus "cede[d] the most crucial wetlands area back to Friends of the Ballona Wetlands." Pat Kramer, "The Dream is Alive: Why Environmentalist Ruth Lansford Likes the SKG Development, " n.d. [database online] (cited May 11, 1999); available from http://www.boxoff.com/sneak1aapr.html; INTERNET.

23. DreamWorks SKG, the Building Trades Union, the Irvine Foundation, and the city of Los Angeles also discussed participating (contingent upon the studio's move) in a "Playa Vista Job-Link" program to give economically disadvantaged residents training for jobs in entertainment, multimedia, and construction industries. Jill Leovy, "Colleges Pin Hopes on DreamWorks for Entertainment Training Centers," *Los Angeles Times,* February 24, 1999.

24. James Bates and Claudia Eller, "Work Speeds Up as Hollywood Braces for Strikes," *Los Angeles Times,* July 23, 2000.

25. Harvey Molotch, "Growth Machine Links: Up, Down, and Across," in *The Urban Growth Machine: Critical Perspectives Two Decades Later,* ed. A. E. G. Jonas and D. Wilson (Albany, N.Y.: State University of New York Press, 1999), 248–249; and Mark Gottdiener, *The Social Production of Urban Space* (Austin: University of Texas Press, 1985), 224.

CHAPTER FIVE

1. Andrew Wood, "Organizing for Local Economic Development: The Growth Coalition as a Cross-National Comparative Framework," in *The Urban Growth Machine: Critical Perspectives Two Decades Later,* (Albany, N.Y.: State University of New York Press, 1999), 163–176; Kevin R. Cox and Andrew Mair, "Locality and Community in the Politics of Local Economic Development," *Annals of the Association of American Geographers* 78 (1988): 307–325; and Michael Useem, *The Inner Circle: Large Corporations and the Rise of Business Political Activity in the U.S. and U.K.* (New York: Oxford University Press, 1984).

2. Cliff Kono et al., "Lost In Space: The Geography of Corporate Interlocking Directorates," *American Journal of Sociology* 103 (1998): 863–911; and Beth Mintz and Michael Schwartz, *The Power Structure of American Business* (Chicago: University of Chicago Press, 1985).

3. Philip J. Troustine and Terry Christensen, *Movers and Shakers: The Study of Community Power* (New York: St. Martin's Press, 1982).

4. See Clarence N. Stone, "Urban Regimes and the Capacity to Govern: A Political Economy Approach," *Journal of Urban Affairs* 15 (1993) 11–12.

5. Wood, op. cit., and "Analysing the Politics of Local Economic Development: Making Sense of Cross-National Convergence," *Urban Studies* 33 (1996): 1281–1295.

6. Quoted in "Chamber, ECOSLO blast fed oil study," *San Luis Obispo Business* (published by the San Luis Obispo Chamber of Commerce), June, 1998, 1.

7. On Silicon Valley, see Troustine and Christensen, op. cit. The chamber of commerce in Hollywood proper has had a degree of success in drawing the entertainment industry's attention, thanks primarily to its role in selecting and organizing fanfare for inductees to the famous "Walk of Fame," where entertainment celebrities and insiders are honored with star plaques paved into the sidewalks. See Jan Lin, "Dream Factory Redux: Mass Culture, Symbolic Sites, and Redevelopment in Hollywood" in *Understanding the City: Contemporary and Future Perspectives,* ed. J. Eade and C. Mele (Oxford: Blackwell, 2002), 397–418. Outside of this function, however, the chamber appears to lose significant industry participation.

8. Victoria Duff, "Networking Outside the Net World," *Digital Coast Reporter* 3(4) (2000): 36.

9. A precedent for this lack of rapport is the ethnic resentment and different geographical centers that characterized Los Angeles's historical elites; WASP business leaders presided over downtown, while predominantly Jewish film moguls helped develop the Westside. Neil Gabler, *An Empire of their Own: How the Jews Invented Hollywood* (New York: Crown, 1988).

10. Cf. James S. Post et al., "Managing Public Affairs: The Public Affairs Function," *California Management Review* 26 (1983) 135–150; and Michael J. Merenda, "The Process of Corporate Social Involvement: Five Case Studies," in *Research in Corporate Social Performance and Policy,* vol. 3, ed. L. E. Preston (Greenwich, Conn.: JAI Press, 1981), 17–41.

11. I do not count the "film commissions" or "film councils" sponsored by local business associations as entertainment subcommittees, since these offices primarily help film and television productions obtain local permits for location filming.

12. Briavel Holcomb, "Marketing Cities for Tourism," in *The Tourism City,* ed. D. R. Judd and S. S. Fainstein (New Haven, Conn.: Yale University Press, 1999), 54–70; and R. J. Bennett, "Business

Associations and Their Potential to Contribute to Economic Development: Reexploring an Interface Between the State and Market," *Environment and Planning A* 30 (1999): 1367–1387.

13. W. F. Wetzel, "Informal Risk Capital: Knowns and Unknowns," in *The Art and Science of Entrepreneurship,* ed. D. L. Sexton and R. W. Smilor (Cambridge, Mass.: Ballinger, 1986), 85–108, and "Angels and Risk Capital," *Sloan Management Review* 24 (1983): 23–34; and A. S. Bean, D. D. Schiffel, and M. E. Mogee, "The Venture Capital Market and Technological Innovation," *Research Policy* 4 (1975): 380–408.

14. See also Edward J. Malecki, *Technology and Economic Development: The Dynamics of Local, Regional, and National Change,* 2d ed. (New York: Longman Scientific & Technical and John Wiley & Sons, 1997), 175; C. Hoffman, "The Role of the Commercial Loan Officer in the Formation and Growth of New and Young Technical Companies," in *Technical Entrepreneurship: A Symposium,* ed. A. C. Cooper and J. L. Komives (Milwaukee, Wis.: Center for Venture Management, 1972), 165–188; and A. Shapero et al., *The Role of the Financial Community in the Formation, Growth, and Effectiveness of Technical Companies: The Attitude of Commercial Loan Officers* (Austin: Multi-Disciplinary Research, Inc., 1969).

15. Martin Kenney and Richard Florida, "Venture Capital in Silicon Valley: Fueling New Firm Formation," in *Understanding Silicon Valley: The Anatomy of an Entrepreneurial Region,* ed. M. Kenney (Stanford, Calif.: Stanford University Press, 2000), 98–123.

16. Daniel Sullivan, "Local Economic Development Organizations in Small- and Middle-Sized Communities: The Case of Wisconsin," *Research in Community Sociology* 8 (1998): 143–157; S. Clarke, "Institutional Logics and Local Economic Development," *International Journal of Urban and Regional Research* 19 (1995): 513–533; and C. R. Humphrey, R. A. Erickson, and E. J. Ottensmeyer, "Industrial Development Groups, Organizational Resources, and the Prospects for Effecting Growth in Local Economies," *Growth and Change* 19 (1988), 1–21.

17. Kenney and Florida, op. cit.

18. Quoted in "Lori Fisher Speaks at EVC November Meeting," *Softalk, the Softec E-mail Newsletter,* November 1997.

19. But see Olav Sorenson and Toby E. Stuart, "Syndication Networks and the Spatial Distribution of Venture Capital Investments," *American Journal of Sociology* 106 (2001): 1546–1589. For Los Angeles metropolitan data, see Debora Vrana, "Venture Capital Funding Rises 92% in Los Angeles Area in '98," *Los Angeles Times,* February 15, 1999.

20. Richard E. Caves, *Creative Industries: Contracts between Art and Commerce* (Cambridge, Mass.: Harvard University Press, 2000), 102; and Susan Christopherson, "Flexibility and Adaptation in Industrial Relations: The Exceptional Case of the U.S. Media Entertainment Industries," in *Under the Stars: Essays on Labor Relations in Arts and Entertainment,* ed. L. S. Gray and R. L. Seeber (Ithaca, N.Y.: ILR Press/Cornell, 1996), 86–112.

21. Douglas Henton, "Lessons from Silicon Valley," in *Global City-Regions: Trends, Theory, Policy,* ed. A. J. Scott (Oxford: Oxford University Press, 2001), 391–400.

22. Fixer-type goals are not carried out by business associations only. As I elaborate in Chapter 7, San Luis Obispo's university took the lead in a research park proposal that would likely have included a business incubator component. During the period of my research, the city of Santa Monica was in the process of establishing a high-speed Internet infrastructure that local businesses acknowledged they would use, according to city surveys.

23. Troustine and Christensen, op. cit.

24. That the Economic Community Project in large part follows the traditional urban business community's lead is also borne out through its "leadership group," a forty-person advisory body (including the board of directors) whose duties entail local vision more than detail work. Technology representatives comprise only 20 percent of this body, whereas representatives from business services (40 percent), education (12.5 percent), other industries (15 percent), government (10 percent), and the media (2.5 percent) account for the rest.

25. Paul-Brian McInerney, "Thinking Globally, Acting Locally: The Global Economy and the Case of Silicon Alley" (paper presented at the annual meeting of the American Sociological Association, Chicago, Ill., August 1999, 18–19).

26. E.g., Philip Evans and Thomas S. Wurster, *Blown to Bits: How the New Economics of Information Transforms Strategy* (Boston: Harvard Business School Press, 2000).

27. Allen J. Scott, *The Cultural Economy of Cities* (London: Sage, 2000), 8; see also Michael Storper and Susan Christopherson, *The Changing Location and Organization of the Motion Picture Industry: Interregional Shifts in the United States* (Los Angeles: School of Architecture and Urban Planning, University of California, Los Angeles, 1985).

28. Caves, op. cit., pp. 196–197.

29. John Amman, "The Transformation of Industrial Relations in the Motion Picture and Television Industries: Craft and Production," in *Under the Stars: Essays on Labor Relations in Arts and Entertainment,* ed. L. S. Gray and R. L. Seeber (Ithaca, N.Y.: ILR Press/Cornell, 1996), 113–155; and Alan Paul and Archie Kleingartner, "Flexible Production and the Transformation of Industrial Relations in the Motion Picture and Television Industry," *Industrial and Labor Relations Review* 47 (1994): 663–678.

30. Storper and Christopherson, op. cit., p. 113.

31. One software executive whom I interviewed was also a former executive at the parent corporation for the *Los Angeles Times,* and he told me that the newspaper's leadership has struggled to sustain an informal business leadership network since the decline of the region's old and predominantly downtown-based corporations. As the increasingly dominant sector in Los Angeles, entertainment provides a logical contemporary successor to the "grandees" of old. The corporate consolidation of film studios and TV networks into media conglomerates aids the reconstruction of "this notion of big entities with the *Los Angeles Times* at the center," as do the lucrative advertising revenues generated by film advertisements. However, production companies, postproduction facilities, and other small entertainment firms largely "fall off the radar" of the newspaper's leadership by virtue of their size. The same is true, this executive noted, for most firms in the local software sector.

32. For 1994 bed tax revenues, the city of Santa Monica took in $9,310,219; the city of Santa Barbara took in $6,445,357; and the city of San Luis Obispo took in $2,462,000. The last figure dramatically understates regional bed tax revenues, since Pismo Beach and Morro Bay have comparable hotel markets. Dean Runyan Associates, *California Travel Impacts by County, 1992–1995* (Portland, OR: Dean Runyan Associates, 1997).

33. Roger Friedland, *Power and Crisis in the City: Corporations, Unions, and Urban Policy* (New York: Schocken Books, 1983).

CHAPTER SIX

1. Val Burris, "The Two Faces of Capital: Corporations and Individual Capitalists as Political Actors," *American Sociological Review* 66 (2001): 361–381; and Michael Useem, *The Inner Circle: Large Corporations and the Rise of Business Political Activity in the U.S. and U.K.* (New York: Oxford University Press, 1984).

2. John R. Logan and Harvey L. Molotch, *Urban Fortunes: The Political Economy of Place* (Berkeley: University of California Press, 1987); and Mark Gottdiener, *Planned Sprawl: Private and Public Interests in Suburbia* (Beverly Hills, Calif.: Sage Publications, 1977).

3. William H. Flanigan and Nancy H. Zingale, *Political Behavior of the American Electorate,* 8th ed. (Washington, DC: CQ Press, 1994), 33.

4. Jerome Himmelstein, *Looking Good and Doing Good: Corporate Philanthropy and Corporate Power* (Bloomington, Ind.: Indiana University Press, 1997); and Edward Handler and John R. Mulkern, *Business in Politics: Campaign Strategies of Political Action Committees* (Lexington, Mass.: Heath, 1982).

5. G. W. Domhoff, *Who Rules America? Power and Politics in the Year 2000,* 3d ed. (Mountain View, Calif.: Mayfield Publishing Company, 1998), 180; Clarence N. Stone, *Regime Politics: Governing Atlanta, 1946–1988* (Lawrence, Kans.: University of Kansas Press, 1989), 170; Steven L. Elkin, *City and Regime in the American Republic* (Chicago: University of Chicago Press, 1987), 72–73; and Joseph Galaskiewicz, *Social Organization of an Urban Grants Economy: A Study of Business Philanthropy and Nonprofit Organizations* (Orlando, Fla.: Academic Press, 1985).

6. See, e.g., John Mollenkopf, *The Contested City* (Princeton, N.J.: Princeton University Press, 1983), 164.

7. Kee Warner, Harvey Molotch, and Amy Lategola, *Growth Control: Inner Workings and External Effects* (Berkeley: California Policy Seminar, University of California, 1992), 96; Amy Rose Lategola, "Who's Giving to Whom?: An Analysis of Local Campaign Contributions and Competing Development Interests in Santa Barbara, California" (master's thesis, Department of Sociology, University of California, Santa Barbara, Calif., 1992); see also Logan and Molotch, op. cit., pp. 231–232.

8. Warner, Molotch, and Lategola, op. cit., p. 96.

9. Clarence N. Stone, "Systemic Power in Community Decision Making: A Restatement of Stratification Theory," *American Political Science Review* 74 (1980): 978–990.

10. Warner, Molotch, and Lategola, op. cit., p. 91.

11. Reported in Jean Merl, "The High—and Low—Cost of Doing Business," *Los Angeles Times,* January 25, 1998.

12. Ibid.

13. Additionally, many businesses find California's property tax codes attractive compared to other states that reassess property taxes each year according to their market value (a practice halted by California's 1978 property tax referendum, Proposition 13).

14. Firms with coastal locations also have to deal with another level of government, the California Coastal Commission, in order to comply with the state's coastal land-use plans. Given its geographical and political distance from local jurisdictions, the Coastal Commission has often been viewed as a difficult obstacle for firms without lobbyists. A restaurateur with businesses in Santa Monica and neighboring Marina Del Rey (in unincorporated Los Angeles County) acknowledged that his frustration with Santa Monica's licensing and permitting requirements pales in comparison to the bureaucratic maze he negotiates with the other restaurant, for which he had to obtain additional permits from the Coastal Commission and Los Angeles County: "It's outrageous. It's bureaucracy at its finest, without a doubt."

15. See Domhoff, op. cit.; and Mark S. Mizruchi, *The Structure of Corporate Political Action: Interfirm Relations and their Consequences* (Cambridge, Mass.: Harvard University Press, 1992).

16. Some general observations about these elections: Santa Monica candidates raised the most campaign cash in a single election year: $230,945 (or $2.66 per resident), which is about 70 percent more than Santa Barbara candidates (who raised $135,299, or $1.58 per resident) and 12 times more than San Luis Obispo candidates (who raised $19,193, or $0.45 per resident). Among those who accepted campaign contributions (Table A.3 in the Methodology Appendix lists the candidates who did not), each Santa Monica candidate raised an average of $28,868; each Santa Barbara candidate raised an average of $19,328; and each San Luis Obispo candidate raised an average of $3,838. While conservative candidates raised more than their progressive or centrist rivals in all three places, the difference was not that great; progressive and centrist combined candidates took in one-fourth to one-third more contributions than conservatives.

17. In Santa Monica, five software contributors gave to progressives, four to centrists, and two (also centrist contributors) gave to conservatives. In Santa Barbara, three software contributors gave to progressives, three (including one progressive contributor) to centrists, and three (including one centrist contributor) to conservatives. In San Luis Obispo, the software sector yielded only one contributor, who gave to a centrist candidate.

18. In Santa Monica, twenty-five entertainment contributors gave to progressives; nine gave to centrists; and six gave to conservatives. In Santa Barbara, six entertainment contributors gave to progressives, and one gave to conservatives. In San Luis Obispo, one entertainment contributor gave to centrists.

19. Entertainment's progressive support in local politics is also revealed in a second indicator specific to Santa Monica: contributions to the SMRR party alone. Of the three sectors and banks, entertainment gives the most to SMRR both on average and in absolute dollars. Eighteen entertainment contributors gave over one-tenth of *all* reported monetary contributions (or $9.07 per firm) to SMRR, making their sector the party's second-highest contributing sector (after health care). SMRR records also show a strong party consciousness among entertainment contributors; about three-fourths of progressive entertainment contributors in Santa Monica gave to SMRR directly, not to candidates' individual campaigns (which the SMRR fund supplements).

20. In Santa Monica, 11 tourism contributors gave to progressives, 34 gave to centrists, and 24 gave to conservative candidates. In Santa Barbara, nine tourism contributors gave to progressives, 16 gave to centrists, and eight gave to conservatives. In San Luis Obispo, one tourism contributor gave to progressives, five gave to centrists, and seven gave to conservative candidates.

21. Leonard Nevarez, "Just Wait Until There's a Drought: Mediating Environmental Crises for Urban Growth," *Antipode* 28 (1996): 246–272; and Roger Friedland, Frances Fox Piven, and Robert R. Alford, "Political Conflict, Urban Structure, and the Fiscal Crisis," *International Journal of Urban and Regional Research* 1 (1977): 447–461.

22. Jim Newton, "Goodwill Hunting for the Democratic Convention," *Los Angeles Times*, July 27, 1998.

23. "Sony's Boonshaft named to county commission," *Argonaut* (West Los Angeles), April 16, 1998.

24. Patrick McGreevy, "Council's Plan to Take Over CRA Highlights its Problems," *Los Angeles Times*, January 17, 1999. In 1996, the Los Angeles Community Redevelopment Agency subsidized developer TrizecHahn's "Hollywood and Highland" project, a themed entertainment-retail complex that advocates believe will revive the historic Hollywood Boulevard district in the manner of New York's Times Square (another TrizecHahn redevelopment). Proclaimed music producer and entrepreneur Quincy Jones, "Hollywood and Highland will serve as our Empire State Building and Eiffel Tower." Quoted in Greg Goldin, "Mall-Ywood," *LA Weekly*, December 18, 1998.

25. This does not preclude software and entertainment leader participation in higher and more visible levels of government. In March 1999, California's newly elected Democratic governor, Gray Davis, appointed two entertainment industry representatives to state positions. Rob Reiner, organizer of the successful cigarette tax initiative campaign, was appointed chair of the Children and Families First Commission (a new state entity). Paramount Studios chief executive Sherry Lansing was appointed to a 12-year term on the University of California Board of Regents.

26. John Heilemann, "Outsiders Inside: How Silicon Valley's Peter Pans Finally Grew Up," *The New Yorker,* June 1, 1998.

27. Quoted in Bloomberg News, "Net Companies Join Forces to Influence Lawmakers," *CNET News.com* [database online] (n.p., 1999 [cited October 6, 1999]); available from http://news.cnet.com/news/0-1005-200-808878.html; INTERNET.

28. Charles Piller, "GOP Targets Clinton Turf in Silicon Valley," *Los Angeles Times,* September 23, 1998.

29. Quoted in Maria Ganga, "Bush Has Right Message in Silicon Valley," *Los Angeles Times,* July 2, 1999.

30. Ibid.

31. Quoted in Heidi Kriz, "Silicon Valley's Overtime Mandate," *Wired News* [database online] (n.p., 1999 [cited July 13, 1999]); available from http://www.wired.com/news/news/politics/story/20692.html; INTERNET.

32. Dan Morain, "Wealth Buys Access to State Politics," *Los Angeles Times,* April 18, 1999.

33. Quoted in Dan Morain, "California is Top Source of Federal Political Funds," *Los Angeles Times,* January 19, 1999.

34. Paulina Borsook, *Cyberselfish: A Critical Romp Through the Terribly Libertarian Culture of High-Tech* (New York: Public Affairs, 2000).

35. Beth Mintz and Michael Schwartz, *The Power Structure of American Business* (Chicago: University of Chicago Press, 1985); and Useem, op. cit.

36. Dan Morain, "Wealth Buys Access to State Politics," *Los Angeles Times,* April 18, 1999. Reiner expressed his intent to organize similar campaigns in other states: "My agenda is a national agenda. Even though it's only a ballot initiative, California's a bellwether state. And if we pass it here, it will have a tremendous ripple effect, I hope, on the rest of the country." Quoted in Irene Lacher, "Kids Learn the Darndest Things," *Los Angeles Times,* September 20, 1998.

37. Quoted in Sean Mitchell, "A Charitable Role?" *Los Angeles Times,* May 25, 1999.

38. Ibid.

39. Data provided by the Center for Responsive Politics, quoted in Brad King, "DC Awash in Entertainment Cash," *Wired News* [database online] (2000 [cited September 6, 2000]); available from http://www.wired.com/news/politics/0,1283,38407,00.html; INTERNET.

40. Reported in Alexander Cockburn, "Ballona and the Folly of Wealthy Men," *Los Angeles Times,* January 9, 1997.

41. City of Los Angeles Ethics Commission, *Campaign Contributions in City Campaigns* (Los Angeles: City Ethics Commission, 1998). Contributions from this group to the 1993 and 1997 city elections totaled $285,021. Employee contributions comprised 78.2 percent of this sum, while firm contributions made up the remaining 21.8 percent. Unfortunately, the City Ethics Commission report from which these data come does not break down contributions to progressive, centrist, and conservative candidates, as I have in this chapter.

42. See Neil M. Coe, "On Location: American Capital and the Local Labour Market in the Vancouver Film Industry," *International Journal of Urban and Regional Research* 24 (2000): 79–94; and James Bates, "Hollywood Jobs Take Spotlight as Legislators Propose Tax Breaks," *Los Angeles Times,* March 27, 1999.

43. See Burris, op. cit.

CHAPTER SEVEN

1. Retired software CEO Peter Norton, quoted in Peter Y. Hong, "Foundations Must Change to Meet Future Needs," *Los Angeles Times,* April 26, 1998.

2. See James S. Post et al., "Managing Public Affairs: The Public Affairs Function," *California Management Review* 26 (1983) 135–150; and Michael J. Merenda, "The Process of Corporate Social Involvement: Five Case Studies," in *Research in Corporate Social Performance and Policy,* vol. 3, ed. L. E. Preston (Greenwich, Conn.: JAI Press, 1981), 17–41.

3. Cf. Joseph Galaskiewicz, *Social Organization of an Urban Grants Economy: A Study of Business Philanthropy and Nonprofit Organizations* (Orlando, Fla.: Academic Press, 1985).

4. Jerome Himmelstein, *Looking Good and Doing Good: Corporate Philanthropy and Corporate Power* (Bloomington, Ind.: Indiana University Press, 1997); and Michael Useem, *The Inner Circle: Large Corporations and the Rise of Business Political Activity in the U.S. and U.K.* (New York: Oxford University Press, 1984); see also Lee E. Preston, "Corporate Power and Social Performance: Approaches to Positive Analysis," in *Research in Corporate Social Performance and Policy,* vol. 3, ed. L. E. Preston (Greenwich, Conn.: JAI Press, 1981), 1–16.

5. Andrew Scott Ziner, "Evaluating the 'Good Works' of Utility Companies: Multiple Motivations, Methods, and Audiences" (paper presented at the annual meeting of the American Sociological Association, Toronto, Canada, August 1997); and Galaskiewicz, op. cit.

6. G. William Domhoff, *Who Rules America? Power and Politics in the Year 2000,* 3d ed. (Mountain View, Calif.: Mayfield Publishing Company, 1998); Steven R. Neiheisel, *Corporate Strategy and the Politics of Goodwill: A Political Analysis of Corporate Philanthropy in America* (New York: Peter Lang Publishing, 1994); Galaskiewicz, op. cit.; and Useem, op. cit.

7. Ira Silver, "Buying an Activist Identity: Reproducing Class Through Social Movement Philanthropy," *Sociological Perspectives* 41 (1998): 303–321; J. Craig Jenkins, "Channeling Social Protest: Foundation Patronage of Contemporary Social Movements," in *Private Action and the Public Good,* ed. W. Powell and E. Clemens (New Haven, Conn.: Yale University Press, 1998), 206–216; H. H. Haines, "Black Radicalization and the Funding of Civil Rights: 1957–1970," *Social Problems* 32 (1984): 31–43; and Paul DiMaggio, "Can Culture Survive the Marketplace?" *Journal of Arts Management and Law* 13 (1983): 61–87.

8. Talmadge Wright, "Corporate Interests, Philanthropies, and the Peace Movement," *Monthly Review* 36 (1985): 19–31; Walter W. Powell and Rebecca Friedkin, "Political and Organizational Influences on Public Television Programming," in *Mass Communication Review Yearbook,* vol. 4, ed. E. Wartella and D. C. Whitney (Beverly Hills, Calif.: Sage, 1983), 413–438; and Michael Pertschuk, *Revolt Against Regulation* (Berkeley: University of California Press, 1982).

9. William S. Hendon and Douglas V. Shaw, "The Arts and Urban Development," in *The Future of Winter Cities,* ed. G. Gappert (Newbury Park, Calif.: Sage, 1987), 209–217; and Sylvia Tesh, "In Support of 'Single-Issue' Politics," *Political Science Quarterly* 99 (1984): 27–44.

10. Alberta M. Sbragia, "Pittsburgh's 'Third Way': The Nonprofit Sector as a Key to Urban Regeneration," in *Leadership and Urban Regeneration,* ed. D. Judd and M. Parkinson (Newbury Park, Calif.: Sage, 1990), 51–68; and J. Allen Whitt, "Mozart in the Metropolis: The Arts Coalition and the Urban Growth Machine," *Urban Affairs Quarterly* 23 (1987): 15–36.

11. Paulina Borsook, *Cyberselfish: A Critical Romp Through the Terribly Libertarian Culture of High-Tech* (New York: Public Affairs, 2000), 178.

12. Quoted in Peter H. Lewis, "Cashed Out and Tuned In To Contemporary Art," *New York Times,* April 11, 1993.

13. Quoted in Matthew Mirapaul, "High-Tech Companies Slow to Support High-Tech Art," *New York Times,* November 12, 1998. Many Silicon Valley observers believe that Hewlett-Packard remains the prominent exception to the rule of philanthropic stinginess among the region's companies. However, at least a few of the philanthropic software executives I interviewed in Southern California had worked at Hewlett Packard earlier in their careers and could recall having an ethic of community charity "drilled into us" during those years.

14. E.g., Waldemar A. Nielsen, *Inside American Philanthropy: The Dramas of Donorship* (Norman, Okla.: University of Oklahoma Press, 1996).

15. Ann Castle, "The 1996 SLATE 60: The 60 largest American charitable contributions of 1996," in *Slate* [electronic bulletin] (February 1–8, 1997); available from http://www.slate.com/Features/Slate60/Sidebar1Slate60.asp; INTERNET.

16. Karl T. Greenfeld, "Bill and Melinda Gates: Giving Billions Isn't Easy," *Time* 156 (2000).

17. Quoted in Paul Bennett, "Giving (Some of) it Away," *Silicon Alley Reporter* 4(6) (2000): 108.

18. For a discussion of how traditional industry leaders set the norms for civic behavior among other firms, see Galaskiewicz, op. cit.; and Useem, op. cit.

19. See Stanley E. Hyland, Alicia Russell, and Fontaine Hebb, "Realigning Corporate Giving: Problems in the Nonprofit Sector for Community Development Corporations," *Nonprofit and Voluntary Sector Quarterly* 19 (1990): 111–119; Susan Rose-Ackerman, "United Charities: An Economic Analysis," *Public Policy* 28 (1980): 323–350; and Frances Fox Piven and Richard A. Cloward, *Poor People's Movements* (New York: Pantheon, 1977).

20. See Pertschuk, op. cit.

21. Kathryn Troy, *Annual Survey of Corporate Contributions, 1984 Edition* (New York: Conference Board, 1984).

22. Ronald S. Burt, "Corporate Philanthropy as a Cooptive Relation," *Social Forces* 62 (1983): 419–449.

23. Quoted in Paul Didier, "The Future of Nonprofit Organizations," *Santa Barbara News-Press,* January 9, 2000.

24. Quoted in David Cay Johnston, "In the Wealthy Silicon Valley, a United Way Runs Dry," *New York Times,* May 16, 1999.

25. Ibid. There may be a special factor to explain Seattle's high-tech generosity to the United Way: Bill Gates's mother was once chair of United Way International. Ken Auletta, "Hard Core," in *The New Gilded Age: The New Yorker Looks at the Culture of Affluence,* ed. David Remnick (New York: Random House, 2000), 89.

26. Scott Kirsner, "Nonprofit Motive," *Wired Magazine* 7 (1999): 110–118.

27. Quoted in ibid.

28. See Richard C. Hula, Cynthia Y. Jackson, and Marion Orr, "Urban Politics, Governing Nonprofits, and Community Revitalization," *Urban Affairs Review* 32 (1997): 348–377.

29. But see Jill Stewart, "DreamJerks," *New Times Los Angeles,* June 3, 1999.

30. Terry Nichols Clark and Edward Goetz, "The Antigrowth Machine: Can City Governments Control, Limit or Manage Growth?" in *Urban Innovations: Creative Strategies for Turbulent Times,* ed. T. N. Clark (Thousand Oaks, Calif.: Sage, 1994), 104–145; and Mark Baldasarre and William Protash, "Growth Controls, Population Growth and Community Satisfaction," *American Sociological Review* 47 (1982): 339–346.

31. Mitchel Benson, "Look Who's Talking: Foes Come Together on Growth," *Wall Street Journal,* April 29, 1998.

32. Himmelstein, op. cit. p. 149.

33. University of California Santa Barbara College of Engineering, *1996–1997 Annual Report of Private Giving* (Santa Barbara, Calif.: University of California Santa Barbara College of Engineering, 1997), 14.

34. Walter W. Powell and Jason Owen-Smith, "Universities as Creators and Retailers of Intellectual Property: Life Sciences Research and Commercial Development," in *To Profit or Not: The Commercialization of the Nonprofit Sector,* ed. V. Weisbrod (Cambridge, UK: Cambridge University Press, 1998), 169–193; and Doreen Massey, Paul Quintas, and David Wield, *High-Tech Fantasies: Science Parks in Society, Science and Space* (London: Routledge, 1992).

35. Additionally, higher education institutions can obtain money through efforts other than direct corporate solicitations, such as alumni donations. UCSB solicited money through a second philanthropic campaign, the "honor roll" of individual donors, in which local software CEOs and many employees participated, although the scale of these donations was far smaller than the corporate gifts shown in Table 7.3. Since the "honor roll" campaign involved matching corporate gifts of undisclosed ranges, I did not incorporate it into Table 7.3.

36. Cal Poly's president recently closed a university-backed marketing firm only three months after it formed, when the chamber of commerce and other San Luis Obispo businesses (including Cal Poly contributors) complained of "inappropriate" public-sector competition. Silas Lyons, "Poly Pulls Plug on PowerHouse," *San Luis Obispo Telegram-Tribune,* January 16, 1998. For reasons such as this, only 15 percent of San Luis Obispo chamber members agreed with a survey statement, "I believe we can trust Cal Poly to do what's in the best interest of our community." Reported in Steven T. Jones, "Big Money on Campus," *San Luis Obispo New Times,* December 11, 1997.

37. A city study estimated that the performing arts center generated $8.3 million and 146 jobs in its first year. The last estimates for the sports complex (which the city will not jointly fund) cited an estimated $9 million construction cost. Reported in Jamie Hurly, "PAC's Been Music to Businesses' Ears," *San Luis Obispo Telegram-Tribune,* March 26, 1998.

38. Quoted in *Softalk: The Softec E-mail Newsletter* [electronic bulletin], October 1997.

39. Bechtel Infrastructure Corporation, *California Central Coast Research Park: Pre-Feasibility Study,* executive summary, (San Luis Obispo, Calif.: Bechtel Infrastructure Corporation, 1998).

40. See also Massey, Quintas, and Wield, op. cit.; and David C. Perry, "Recasting Urban Leadership in Buffalo," in *Leadership and Urban Regeneration,* ed. D. Judd and M. Parkinson (Newbury Park, Calif.: Sage, 1990), 258–276.

41. Cf. Deirdre Boden and Harvey L. Molotch, "The Compulsion of Proximity," in *NowHere: Space, Time and Modernity,* ed. R. Friedland and D. Boden (Berkeley, Los Angeles and London: University of California Press, 1994), 257–286.

42. John R. Logan and Harvey L. Molotch, *Urban Fortunes: The Political Economy of Place* (Berkeley: University of California Press, 1987).

43. See Domhoff, op. cit.

CHAPTER EIGHT

1. Marc Cooper, "Lights! Camera! Attack! Hollywood Enlists," *The Nation,* December 10, 2001, p. 14.

2. For a discussion of the music industry's battle against Internet firms that enable peer-to-peer music distribution, see John Alderman, *Sonic Boom: Napster, P2P and the Battle for the Future of Music* (New York: Perseus Press, 2001).

3. See also Saskia Sassen and Frank Roost, "The City: Strategic Sites for the Global Entertainment Industry," in *The Tourist City,* ed. D. R. Judd and S. S. Fainstein (New Haven, Conn.: Yale University Press, 1999), 143–154; John Hannigan, *Fantasy City: Pleasure and Profit in the Postmodern Metropolis* (New York: Routledge, 1998); and Janet Wasko, *Hollywood in the Information Age: Beyond the Silver Screen* (Austin: University of Texas Press, 1994).

4. Hannigan, op. cit.; and Richard Foglesong, "Walt Disney World and Orlando: Deregulation as a Strategy for Tourism," in *The Tourist City*, ed. D. R. Judd and S. S. Fainstein (New Haven, Conn.: Yale University Press, 1999), 89–106.

5. Sharon Zukin, *Landscapes of Power: From Detroit to Disney World* (Berkeley, Calif.: University of California Press, 1991); John Urry, *Consuming Places* (London: Routledge, 1995); and Mark Gottdiener, *The Theming of America: Dreams, Visions, and Commercial Spaces* (Boulder, CO: Westview, 1997).

6. Richard P. Appelbaum and William J. Chambliss, *Sociology*, 2d ed. (New York: Longman, 1997), 89.

7. Norton E. Long, "The Local Community as an Ecology of Games," *American Journal of Sociology* 64 (1958): 251–261.

8. Clarence N. Stone, "Urban Regimes and the Capacity to Govern: A Political Economy Approach," *Journal of Urban Affairs* 15 (1993): 1–28; and Richard E. DeLeon, *Left Coast City: Progressive Politics in San Francisco, 1975–1991* (Lawrence, Kans.: University Press of Kansas: 1992).

9. DeLeon, op. cit., p. 8.

10. David Brooks, *Bobos in Paradise: The New Upper Class and How They Got There* (New York: Simon and Schuster, 2000); and Joel Kotkin, *The New Geography* (New York: Random House, 2000).

METHODOLOGY APPENDIX

1. Cliff Kono et al., "Lost In Space: The Geography of Corporate Interlocking Directorates," *American Journal of Sociology* 103(1998): 863–911; Beth Mintz and Michael Schwartz, *The Power Structure of American Business* (Chicago: University of Chicago Press, 1985); and Robert Perrucci and Marc Pilisuk, "Leaders and Ruling Elites: the Interorganizational Basis of Community Power," *American Sociological Review* 35 (1970): 1040–1057.

2. See, e.g., Kee Warner, Harvey Molotch, and Amy Lategola, *Growth Control: Inner Workings and External Effects* (Berkeley: California Policy Seminar, University of California, 1992), 96–98.

3. See, e.g., Allen J. Scott, "Regional Motors of the Global Economy" *Futures* 28 (1996): 391–411; Gary Gereffi and Miguel Korzeniewicz (ed.), *Commodity Chains and Global Capitalism* (Westport, Conn.: Praeger, 1994); Peter Dicken, *Global Shift: The Internationalization of Economic Activity,* 2nd ed. (New York: Guilford Press, 1992); and Saskia Sassen, *The Global City: New York, London, Tokyo* (Princeton, N.J.: Princeton University Press, 1991).

4. Leonard Nevarez, Harvey Molotch, Randolph Bergstrom, and Perry Shapiro, *Petroleum Extraction in Santa Barbara County: An Industrial History,* OCS Study MMS 98-0048, under Contract No. 14-35-0001-30796 (Camarillo, Calif.: U.S. Department of Interior, Minerals Management Service, Pacific Outer Continental Shelf Region, 1998); and Leonard Nevarez, Harvey Molotch, and William Freudenburg, *San Luis Obispo County: A Major Switching,* OCS Study MMS 96-96-0037, under Contract No. 14-35-001-30663 (Camarillo, Calif.: U.S. Department of Interior, Minerals Management Service, Pacific Outer Continental Shelf Region, 1996).

5. For a discussion of how most social processes have an organized structure that makes likely that certain situations (such as the business of a trade association meeting) will proceed as planned, see Mitch Duneier, *Sidewalk* (New York: Farrar, Straus and Giroux, 1999), 338.

6. Select Phone, 1999 version, InfoUSA Inc., Omaha, Neb.

7. Select Phone 99 introduced at least two kinds of error in my industry counts. First, there was a modest number of miscoded and missing businesses in the industry totals. After reviewing which companies *were* listed under the sector categories, I estimated that the errors of inclusion and exclusion were random and therefore canceled each other out. Second, as many economic analysts have noted, the pre-1997 federal SIC classification system underlying this method frequently fails to include dynamic new industries, such as multimedia, under what should be the most appropriate SIC; this underestimated the numbers of firms in a particular sector. In the other direction of overestimation, I used a few industry categories that listed some irrelevant firms (for instance, "Records, tapes, & compact discs—wholesale" [SIC 509909] includes important record companies but also some music retail stores). Again, I estimated that the errors of inclusion and exclusion were random across places and sectors and therefore canceled each other out.

8. In Santa Monica, citizens vote only for city council candidates, and the mayor is appointed from city council incumbents by the council. By contrast, in Santa Barbara and San Luis Obispo, citizens vote for both mayoral and city council candidates.

9. The $100 contribution threshold for contributor identification is set by the municipal codes of Santa Monica, Santa Barbara, and San Luis Obispo. Other municipalities set different thresholds; for example, the city of Los Angeles requires contributor identification for contributions of $500 or more to mayoral candidates and $250 or more to city council candidates. Unfortunately, any threshold for contributor identification introduces analytical error in localities where campaign contributions often fall under the threshold amount. This source of error most likely affected my analy-

sis of San Luis Obispo candidates. For example, conservative candidates there raised $14,835.50 in gross reported monetary contributions; from that amount, I threw out $6,592.50 (or 44.6 percent) because they came from 119 contributors who gave less than $100 and therefore were not required to report their occupation.

10. Contributions to SMRR also help fund several progressive Santa Monica candidates running for the rent control, school, and community college district boards. In 1996, SMRR collected $125,777 in donations; of this amount, $23,705 came from 172 supporters whose contributions were large enough to be reported on SMRR's recipient committee campaign statement.

11. Amy Rose Lategola, "Who's Giving to Whom?: An Analysis of Local Campaign Contributions and Competing Development Interests in Santa Barbara, California" (master's thesis, Department of Sociology, University of California, Santa Barbara, Calif., 1992).

Index

Los Angeles, viii, 14, 23, 70, 89, 93, 206nn. 9,
209n. 25, 210n. 41; business community, 42,
65, 92, 98, 148; Digital Coast Roundtable,
117; entertainment firms in, 25, 29, 121,
123, 208n. 31; Internet, 116; music industry
in, 43; philanthropy in, 155; software firms
in, 24, 25, 119; tourism in, 25, 28, 29; urban
problems of, 75, 155; west, 128, 206n. 9;
wetlands of, 23, 98–99, 206nn. 22

M

Maguire Thomas Partners, 98–99, 206n. 22
manufacturing, 18, 33, 82, 180; firms, 36; hardware, 172; light, 21; traditional, 1, 24
marketing, 16, 33, 120
markets: consumer, 6, 72; demands of, 15; global,
26, 38, 107; labor, 6, 7, 62, 63, 65, 72, 78,
170; local, 3, 29, 107, 108, 166; mass, 33,
38; tourist, 177, 178
Marshall, Alfred, 39
Marx, Karl, 3, 15
Massachusetts Route 128: defense contractors of,
38
MCA/Universal, 89, 100, 133, 142, 205n. 13
McCain, John, 135
media: new, 26, 45, 87, 116, 170; the, 16, 17
Microsoft Corporation, 67, 135, 149
migrants: pioneer, 64–65, 82–83; quality-of-life,
65, 66–67, 75, 84, 85, 204n. 48; residential
theory of, 56; Silicon Valley, 66, 204n. 37
Molotch, Harvey, 6
Morain, Dan, 210n. 36
Morro Bay, 102
Motion Picture Association of America, 121
Motorola, 35
music industry, 107, 122; centers of, 43; consoli-
dation of, 170; elites, 48; labor for, 45; organizations, 134; popular, 121

N

National Academy of Recording Arts and Sciences, 122, 154
Nature Conservancy, 103
networking, 18, 115, 116–17, 181; business (see
business networking); forums, 105, 115,
116–17, 119; informal, 48–49, 117, 148;
local, 119, 166; software industry, 116, 119
new industrial space, 37–43, 166, 178, 180–81,
198n. 72; aspects of, 69, 72; centers of the,
31–54, 57; contradictions of, 59; elite workers in, 66; environmental strains on, 78; for
tourism, entertainment, and software firms,
18, 19; growth coalitions and, 19, 54; higher

education and, 167; labor and, 43–53; locations of, 29–30; of production and labor, 18;
philanthropic division of labor and, 163;
quality-of-life districts and, 73, 78
new urban economy, vii, xi, 14, 35, 77, 171,
177–78, 184; building a site in the, 80–104;
capital in the, 147, 180; corporate power in,
1–30; development politics of firms in the,
80; environmental groups and the, 156; existence of, 14–19; financing the, 112–15;
firms, 2, 124–25, 146, 148, 162, 171, 176;
globalization and, 31; growth, 177; higher
education and, 161; leaders, 134; lessons
from, 171–79; local governance and, 18; local
growth and the, 167; philanthropy and the,
148, 151, 162, 166–68; politics and, 1, 19,
143, 146, 175; problems of the, 15–17; sectors of, x, 24–29, 37, 52, 94, 104, 128, 143,
156, 168, 170, 174–75, 179, 183; stratification of place and, 178–79; systemic relationships and the, 125; workspaces in the, 81–91
New York City, 2, 84; entertainment sector in,
121; music industry in, 43; Silicon Alley of,
40, 47, 67, 85
New Zealand, 42
nonprofit and business alignments, 166–68
nonprofits, 2, 13, 147–48; community, 150–51;
corporate support for, 30, 147–48, 164;
grassroots (see grassroots organizations); local,
13, 88–89, 136; philanthropy to, 13, 141,
147, 156–61
North Carolina's Research Triangle, 153
Norton, Peter, 148–49

O

offshore drilling, vii, ix, 124; San Luis Obispo and,
24, 77, 159; Santa Barbara and, 23, 159;
Santa Monica and, 77

P

Painter, Joe, 8
Paramount Pictures, 133, 142, 209n. 25
Pebble Beach, 102
philanthropy, 2, 9, 154; corporate (see corporate
philanthropy); corporate elites and, 30, 139;
entertainment industry and, 140, 149,
152–58, 162, 166, 174; environmental,
156–61; higher education and, 151, 161–66;
in-kind donations, 152–53; local, 110,
147–68; Silicon Valley and, 148–49, 153,
154, 163; software industry and, 149–50,
151–54, 156, 162–63, 166, 174, 211n. 13;
targets of, 150–51; to community nonprofits,